The *Miracle* Case

LANDMARK LAW CASES

&

AMERICAN SOCIETY

Peter Charles Hoffer

N. E. H. Hull

Series Editors

For a complete list of titles in the series go to www.kansaspress.ku.edu

LAURA WITTERN-KELLER AND
RAYMOND J. HABERSKI JR.

The *Miracle* Case

Film Censorship and the Supreme Court

UNIVERSITY PRESS OF KANSAS

Published by the University Press of Kansas (Lawrence, Kansas 66045), which was organized by the Kansas Board of Regents and is operated and funded by Emporia State University, Fort Hays State University, Kansas State University, Pittsburg State University, the University of Kansas, and Wichita State University

Library of Congress Cataloging-in-Publication Data

Wittern-Keller, Laura, 1951–

The Miracle case : film censorship and the Supreme Court / Laura Wittern-Keller and Raymond J. Haberski Jr.

p. cm. — (Landmark law cases & American society)

Includes bibliographical references and index.

ISBN 978-0-7006-1618-3 (cloth : alk. paper)

ISBN 978-0-7006-1619-0 (pbk. : alk. paper)

1. Motion pictures—Censorship—United States—History—20th century—Cases. 2. Miracolo (Motion picture) 3. Joseph Burstyn, Inc.—Trials, litigation, etc. I. Haberski, Raymond J., 1968– II. Title. III. Series.

KF4300.W75 2008

344.7305'31—dc22

2008024005

British Library Cataloguing-in-Publication Data is available.

Printed in the United States of America

10 9 8 7 6 5 4 3 2 1

The paper used in this publication is recycled and contains 30 percent postconsumer waste. It is acid free and meets the minimum requirements of the American National Standard for Permanence of Paper for Printed Library Materials Z39.48-1992.

For our daughters,

Amanda Katherine Pavlick

and

Devon Kathryn Kroupa-Haberski

CONTENTS

EDITORS' PREFACE

Could a lone New York City movie distributor named Joseph Burstyn bring the state's censorship machinery to a halt? Could he outlast and outduel New York City Cardinal Francis Spellman, the most powerful Roman Catholic cleric in the United States? It would take a miracle.

Going to the movies was the number one public entertainment activity for Americans for much of the twentieth century. But most moviegoers did not realize that what they saw on the screen had been prescreened and pruned to pass through censors. States, cities, and localities censored movies, as did the industry itself to anticipate what the censors would decide. The morality of the movies might or might not reflect the mores of the times, for the censors had their own codes of decency, and those codes were drafted by individuals representing special interest groups. No movie could offend, portray immorality, or show the triumph of crime or evil, though these were all part of life and often the heart of fine works of cinema art.

One case challenged this entire system, and it is the centerpiece of Laura Wittern-Keller and Ray Haberski Jr.'s entertaining and admonitory book. Far more than the inside story of *Burstyn v. Wilson* (1952), the work explores the unique place the movies occupied in U.S. culture, and how that culture was shaped by the pressures of religious anxiety. For the era of the rise of the movies was also the era of the rise both of religious fundamentalism in the countryside and a far more assertive Roman Catholic hierarchy in the cities. The cold war was in its full fury, and anyone suspected of radical sympathies faced the House Un-American Activities Committee's search for communists in the movie industry. Much more was at stake than meets the eye in the censoring of Roberto Rossellini's little allegorical film on Italian villagers and their faith.

Although the case had national significance, the authors demonstrate that the case would not have come about as it did were it not for its introduction in New York City. The center of avant-garde culture and the print media, including movie critics like Bosley Crowther of the *New York Times*, New York City was as liberal in its culture as anywhere in the country. But its Roman Catholic establishment, headed by the redoubtable Francis Cardinal Spellman, had proven itself a formidable opponent of cultural modernity. From his elevation to head New York City's archdiocese in 1939, Spellman kept a close eye on books, plays, and movies that posed a threat to Catholic teachings. He never hesitated to speak his views strongly in public, sometimes from the altar, and New York City and state politicians had learned to listen.

At first, the film had passed the state's censors, but Spellman found in its message of simple piety hints that the virgin birth might not be as depicted in Catholic teachings. This was sacrilege, and though the film had already screened for a number of weeks, it must be denied further showings. Only a "spoiler" would reveal the rest of the story Wittern-Keller and Haberski tell in the following pages, but suffice to say it is compelling reading for anyone interested in film or in freedom.

PREFACE

The collaboration that resulted in this book came from the academic version of Internet dating: Laura posted a query on the H-Film listserv and Ray generously answered. From that first happy encounter (about Joseph Burstyn and the *Miracle* case), we realized that although we had different interests — Ray was researching film critics and Laura was looking at film censorship — we were working on the same thing. It was movie freedom.

Like other Internet meeting scenarios, after some e-mail exchanges we decided to meet in person. The opportunity came at the Researching New York Conference at the State University of New York–Albany in November 2001. That meeting led to three joint conference presentations — what Ray likes to call "our road show." The more we worked together, the more we came to respect each other's scholarship and value each other's friendship.

Our partnership was based on our shared respect for a long-forgotten foreign film importer named Joseph Burstyn, the man who fought for the right of *The Miracle* to be seen. The more we talked about Burstyn's case seeking freedom of the screen, the more we wanted to write a joint book — one that would explain not only the legal ramifications of the Burstyn case but also the considerable consequences for film culture and the broader popular culture. And so, we set to work. Happily, we found the University Press of Kansas and its Landmark Law Cases and American Society series. Editor in Chief Michael Briggs and the series editors, Peter Hoffer and N. E. H. Hull, believed in this project from the start despite the inescapable fact that *Burstyn v. Wilson* does not usually rush to mind when legal historians list landmarks of American law. Yet, we — and the editors — believe that it should. UPK has allowed us to bring this dramatic story of a Polish immigrant film importer, a forty-minute Italian film, the American Catholic Church, and the Supreme Court to a wider audience. For that, we will always be grateful. Hoffer and Hull's generous comments undoubtedly made this a better book (although any flaws in the book are entirely our own). The revision process, normally quite agonizing, was pleasant and constructive, thanks to the staff at UPK, especially Susan Schott and Jennifer Dropkin.

Aside from our interest in Burstyn's case, we share another similarity. Whenever we told colleagues that we were coauthoring a book, we met the same concerned response. "Oh, really? That must be frustrating. How is that going?" To which each of us has had the unmitigated pleasure of saying, "It's great"! With different specialties (Laura is a policy historian and Ray is a cultural historian) our contributions have complemented each other, and the questions we've asked of each other over the years have helped to refine and clarify our arguments. Coauthoring this book has been a nonstop learning experience of the best kind.

And there's no way it could have been completed without lots of professional assistance. Our thanks first goes to David Steigerwald of Ohio State University for his willingness to chair two panels on which we presented different aspects of this project on film censorship and U.S. culture. Dave's comments and consistent interest in this topic have made our road show better and increasingly more popular. We must also thank Richard Hamm of the University at Albany who started teaching Laura "to think like a lawyer" in 1998 and is still patiently working on her.

We also owe debts of gratitude to the New York Archives Partnership Trust and Dr. James Folts of the New York State Archives; Adrienne Sonder, former assistant archivist of the Tom Clark papers at Tarlton Law Library at the University of Texas at Austin; and the archivists and librarians at the Maryland Archives, Pennsylvania Archives, Virginia State Library, Ohio Historical Society, L. Tom Perry Special Collections Library at Brigham Young University, Oral History Project at Columbia University, and Seeley G. Mudd Manuscript Library at Princeton University.

Because we are both teaching historians, we also want to acknowledge our academic support systems. Ray thanks his students and colleagues at Marian College, who, with good humor and genuine enthusiasm, have given him an environment in which to wrestle with controversial culture. And Laura, with one foot at the University of North Carolina–Wilmington and another at the University at Albany, gratefully thanks both history departments and both overworked interlibrary loan staffs.

Of course, this project could not have been as happy as it has been without the love and support of our respective families. Historians may often work alone, but they never work unaided. Ray thanks his parents, sisters, their spouses, and his large extended family for once again supporting him with open minds and open houses (for his many research trips). He thanks especially his wife, Shenan, for her support — both in the writing of this book and for the help that was crucial in the pursuit of a Fulbright, even though the latter will turn their lives a bit upside down in 2008 and 2009. Laura thanks her long-suffering husband, Jim Keller (who secretly wishes she'd just retire and play golf, yet always manages to crank up supportive enthusiasm when there is another archive to visit or another round of revisions to make).

And, finally, our daughters (one in grad school, one in preschool) to whom we lovingly dedicate this book: Laura's daughter, Amanda Pavlick, is just embarking on a doctorate in classical archaeology and Ray's daughter, Devon, is just starting out on her educational journey. Their curiosity and love of learning have been our constant source of inspiration.

Introduction

Every motion picture has certain basic elements — characters, settings, story lines, plot twists, conflicts. And all movies go through similar life cycles — they are written, produced, distributed, viewed, reviewed, and archived. But occasionally, a movie comes along that sparks a drama of its own. The movie itself then becomes a character caught up in story lines and plot twists. *The Birth of a Nation* (1915) was the first such movie. *The Miracle* (1948) was another.

The story of *The Birth of a Nation*'s postproduction life has been recounted often and is well known, but the story of an equally significant movie, *The Miracle*, discussed by legal scholars at the time and by a few historians since — notably Gregory Black, Frank Walsh, and most recently William Bruce Johnson — is still largely unknown even to film aficionados. The legal case *The Miracle* generated, *Burstyn v. Wilson*, is usually mentioned only as the case that attached the First Amendment to movies.

Little attention is paid to the people involved — the individual who brought the suit, the lawyers who argued the case, the justices who made the decision — and what the case meant, both in the legal culture and in its broad implications for U.S. culture.

In this book, we seek to add dimensions to this story of movies, censorship, and the expanding interpretation of the First Amendment. A small band of legal scholars and social philosophers had been working to expand free speech rights since the onset of the Comstock antiobscenity laws in the 1870s. They have been well studied, particularly by David Rabban, Paul L. Murphy, and Mark Graber. But there are three other groups whose contributions have been less noted. First came a handful of independent distributors who brought suits against statutory film censorship despite dismal chances of winning in a judicial environment that showed little sympathy for their claims. The second group was the justices of the Supreme Court, who moved ahead of public opinion on movie freedom in 1952 despite the decidedly speech-restrictive political environment of the time. And the third group was the cultural critics who viewed film censorship, and in particular the controversy generated by *The Miracle*, as part of a larger intellectual battle over who controlled access to cultural expression.

Between 1948 and 1952, the United States was going through what contemporary legal commentator John P. Frank likened to a spasm of impassioned repression. This was the era of loyalty oaths, government subversives lists, alien deportations, and congressional investigations into internal communism. When these issues came before the Supreme Court, its general trend was to uphold governmental action. The justices were divided, according to Court historian William Wiecek; "the results, however, were clear": when the Court had to weigh First Amendment freedoms versus regulatory action, it usually came down on the side of governmental power. The fact that the *Miracle* case made it to the nation's highest court in such an environment is remarkable. Its journey and its effect on the First Amendment are the focus of the first part of this book.

Two of the central players involved in midcentury movie culture, the American Catholic Church and Hollywood, were profoundly affected by the *Miracle* case. Years before, in the early 1930s, the movie industry had made peace with the idea of repression by allying itself with the Catholic Church in order to secure safe, and therefore profitable, films. But the rather dubious relationship between the two was never the same after the Supreme Court's ruling in *Burstyn v. Wilson*. The second part of this book looks at how this case invigorated a debate among critics, Catholics, and moviegoers over the role movies played in the broader social revolution that was beginning to grow during the mid-1950s and into the 1960s. The final chapters ponder the implications of a cinema freed from Catholics, censors, courts, and codes — one that is under the protection of the First Amendment but beholden to a rating system.

A Roberto Rossellini–Federico Fellini collaboration, *The Miracle* is a small film, running just forty minutes. *Il Miracolo*, as it was known in its native Italy, tells the story of an unbalanced, religiously zealous homeless woman. To support herself, she takes on odd jobs, one of which is herding goats. One day she is tending a herd up in the hills of the Amalfi Coast when a bearded stranger passes by on the trail. She becomes infatuated with this man, and convinces herself that he is her favorite saint, Joseph. When she insists that he stay with her, he recognizes an easy mark, and plies her with wine. She becomes rapturous, and just as her inhibitions loosen, the camera cuts away. She awakes later, alone, confused and dazed, and wanders back down the mountainside where she encounters two priests — one who tells her that saints can indeed appear to humans and another who scoffs at such a notion. In the next scene, the woman is playing with some village children (she is as childlike and as innocent as they). She faints, and when some village women rush to her aid, they realize that she is pregnant. Dumbfounded, she mutters that it must be "the grace of God." Her belief that she is carrying Saint Joseph's child is too much for the villagers, who ridicule and taunt her. She flees to the mountains, wandering alone and hungry with only a goat for company. When the baby is due, she returns to the outskirts of the village but realizes that she cannot go back. She returns to the mountains, making her way to a deserted mountain church, where she gives birth to a son, and, according to Rossellini, is transformed by love for the child she has just delivered. *The Miracle*'s reception within Italy, a place teeming with movie creativity after World War II, was little more than a collective yawn, and it failed to earn back even half its modest production cost.

Hoping to recoup his costs, Rossellini had the film shown at the Venice Film Festival, where Joseph Burstyn saw it, fell in love with it, and bought the rights for U.S. distribution. At that moment this otherwise forgettable film was destined for something much bigger. *The Miracle* was to become, constitutionally speaking, one of the most important movies ever made, the central character in a dramatic conflict played out in New York State between the American Catholic Church, Catholic laypeople, Protestant leaders, New York City officials, motion picture censors, the American Civil Liberties Union, moviegoers, and film critics.

But this cast of characters has one major player missing. It seems obvious that any fight over control of a movie would necessarily include the movie industry itself. In the scenario that played out over

The Miracle, however, Hollywood had no part. Its trade industry organization, the Motion Picture Association of America (MPAA), was not interested.

Joseph Burstyn had little choice but to be interested when both the Catholic Church and the State of New York told him that his movie, although neither obscene nor immoral nor indecent, was unfit to be shown on theater screens. Burstyn, who adored the movie, was not going to stand for this kind of legal and cultural interference. He was determined to bring *The Miracle* to the American people.

A fifty-year-old Polish-Jewish immigrant, Burstyn was a highly respected but small-time film importer when he acquired *The Miracle*. He had been a pioneer of foreign film appreciation in the United States since 1936 when he joined forces with the publicity director for Paramount Pictures, Arthur Mayer. Together, they were determined to offer U.S. moviegoers an alternative to the typical Hollywood formulaic movies. The two spent years building a superb reputation by importing only what Burstyn considered exceptional European films. While Burstyn was doing the buying, Mayer was managing the Rialto Theater in New York City, a source of cash for the often strapped partnership. By 1950, Burstyn had become the "kingpin" in the expansion of the audience for foreign films. Thomas Pryor of the *New York Times* gave Burstyn credit for significant improvement in film artistry and freedom, noting that he had "come to be regarded in his field as a conquering hero."

As well respected as they were in New York, Burstyn and Mayer were just bit players in the U.S. film market, heavily dominated as it was by Hollywood studio products before and during World War II. But after the war, some Americans were becoming more interested in the new creative style of realistic filmmaking coming from Italy. Burstyn and Mayer's groundwork finally started to pay off, and they began making inroads into the market. Within a few years after the war, they had had many successes with critically acclaimed and prizewinning films like *Paisan*, *Open City*, and *The Bicycle Thief*. No importer did more to advance appreciation of European films than did the happy partnership of Arthur Mayer and Joseph Burstyn. In 1950, though, Burstyn decided to take on the business as a solo act, and he bought Mayer out of his share. No longer partners, the two remained fast friends.

The business was based in Manhattan, the best market for foreign films in those early postwar years. A good run in New York City was a necessary prelude to a profitable U.S. run for any foreign film. This made the censor board of New York State, which had had the legal authority to ban and censor all films shown commercially in the state since 1922, extremely influential. But Burstyn had no censorship worries. *The Miracle* had already been cleared both by customs inspectors, who screened all imported films for obscenity, and by New York State's censors, who also checked to see if it was "immoral," "indecent," "inhuman," "likely to incite to crime," or "sacrilegious."

With a New York State censor seal of approval, Burstyn was ready to show his new film, but he was totally unprepared for what would happen after its premiere. Waiting for critics' reviews, he would learn that some Catholics interpreted the film not as the story of man's inhumanity to man, as Burstyn had seen it and as Rossellini said he had made it, but as a mockery of the virgin birth. Burstyn was headed for a showdown with outraged lay Catholics and officials of the American Catholic Church.

In late 1950, as *The Miracle* opened at the Paris Theatre in midtown Manhattan, movie censorship was not a hot-button issue for most New Yorkers. They were far more likely to be concerned about the frightening events defining the early cold war, especially the Korean War, which had broken out six months earlier and was going badly. Then there was the disturbing news that the Soviets had the atomic bomb, the equally frightening victory of communist forces in China, J. Edgar Hoover's alarming report that there were 55,000 Communist Party members in the United States, and Senator Joseph McCarthy's recent allegations that communists had infiltrated the U.S. State Department.

Unwittingly, Burstyn was about to bring a new issue to the front pages of newspapers. His movie was poised to set off a firestorm of religious controversy that pitted Protestants against Catholic officials and the American Civil Liberties Union (ACLU) against the Legion of Decency, New York City officials, and the state censors. Even though 1951 and 1952 were the height of anticommunist hysteria, a time characterized more by consensus than controversy in culture, the two-year fight that Burstyn waged through the courts of New York and the Supreme Court of the United States against the authority of the state and the state's relationship to the Catholic Church led not to new repression but to a new era of movie freedom.

Beyond the significant legal implications of *Burstyn v. Wilson*, the case also forced a debate over cultural assumptions that had supported censorship since the early years of filmmaking. Although the Supreme Court had defined movies as a business "pure and simple" in 1915, the rest of the moving picture world had never come to consensus over whether movies were art or commerce or some combination of both. *Burstyn v. Wilson* gave the question a sense of urgency. If movies were an art, then filmmakers had the right to explore the full potential of the medium without prior restraint by government censors, and, more problematic for the censors, moviegoers had the right to decide what they would and would not tolerate on the screen through their patronage of films. If movies were art, like books and paintings and theater, what justification could exist for governmental censorship of films, something that had been going on in five other states besides New York and dozens of cities? In short, this case raised many questions, and ultimately had a profound effect on both the legal culture and the public culture in which movies existed.

Since 1907, with the introduction of the first governmental censorship ordinance in Chicago, censorship and scrutiny of movies had existed on multiple levels, from state governments to the industry's own trade group to civic and religious groups. These regimes of censorship, each operating differently, shared the assumption that because movies were popular they had the potential to cause broad social harm. For example, in the summer of 1951, at the same time that Burstyn was fighting Catholic influence in his case against New York State's censors, Elia Kazan was battling Hollywood's self-censorship office, the Production Code Administration (PCA) over cuts to *A Streetcar Named Desire*. Warner Brothers, the studio distributing the film, had been told that if Kazan refused to soften the "carnal" nature of *Streetcar*, the Catholic Church's Legion of Decency would slap it with a condemned rating and the PCA would refuse to give it an official "seal." Frightened by the prospect of bad publicity and poor ticket sales, Warner Brothers leaned on Kazan. He later said, "The plain fact was — and I had to recognize it — the picture had been taken away from me, secretly, skillfully, without a raised voice." Hollywood and the Catholic Church influenced scores of films in this way, doing their most effective and destructive work behind the scenes. When Burstyn squarely challenged statutory censorship, he exposed cracks in what had been a monolithic wall of control surrounding the production, distribution, and exhibition of motion pictures.

The *Burstyn* case was not merely about a single controversial film. It was an illustration of the postwar struggle between two states of the American mind. Conservatives, in this case represented most forcefully by the Catholic Church, wanted to affirm a romantic (or, one might also say, reactionary) notion of traditional values that placed limits on individual behavior in service of a greater common good. Most liberals, though, considered this approach repressive, and hoped to offer a more democratic understanding of culture, one that existed outside the moral precepts of institutions such as the Catholic Church. Moreover, this case fit neatly into another liberal project: the elevation of civil liberties such as free speech to the level of a heroic cause. Although such a cause might be less than heroic, *Burstyn* at least forced a nation that has long claimed to favor free speech to consider whether open expression was to be reserved only for political speech or whether it extended to cultural and artistic expression as well.

The case generated a surprisingly high level of intellectual discourse. In magazines and newspapers both secular and religious, critics and readers engaged the issues raised by *Burstyn* in a way that revealed a postwar cultural shift. Film critics took the opportunity to strike against censorship and champion a freer screen. Among the most ardent advocates of this position was the most powerful film critic in the country, Bosley Crowther of the *New York Times*. Crowther became an ally of Burstyn's, and with critics at other New York papers and magazines, kept the issue of a free screen in the press and on the minds of many readers. These critics were joined by a few somewhat lonely lay Catholics who, writing mostly in *Commonweal*, revealed their frustration with the Church's somewhat unsavory tactics. Taken as a whole, the literature surrounding this case reads like a brief for the cultural equivalent of the Supreme Court's ensuing ruling. Movies had always been more than merely commercial entertainment, and many argued it was time to realize that potential in an atmosphere both freed from fear and mindful of that freedom's worth.

Thus *Burstyn* has a dual legacy: when it raised substantial questions about the amount of control the state could exercise over movies, it also created a new threshold for cultural tolerance. The case encouraged movie critics to challenge censorship, champion pluralism, and argue that there was worth in many different and even offensive cultural expressions. By the late 1960s, a decade of pluralism had hastened the demise of the Production Code, the diminution of the Legion of Decency's power, and the end of most state censorship. For Catholic pressure groups such as the Legion, the Catholic Welfare Conference, and the National Office for Decent Literature, *Burstyn* was a major blow. The Legion of Decency continued to work against what it considered indecent movies, but it never again asked the state for assistance in its work (as it had in *The Miracle* situation). Many liberal Catholics saw the *Burstyn* decision as the opportunity to encourage more traditional Catholics to give up their overwrought denunciations of modernism and accept secularism in state affairs. The church's attempt to engage the state government to suppress heresy had failed, slapped down by the U.S. Supreme Court.

Hollywood rebounded much better. Although the PCA lost its credibility among studios in the years following *Burstyn*, the movie industry never abandoned the idea that it needed to protect its product from scrutiny that could harm ticket sales. Thus, as the old censorship regimes faded, and movie culture expanded to include everything from Disney cartoons to hard-core pornography, Hollywood embraced a rating system built to take advantage of a freer screen while keeping moralists at bay. The rating system administered by a new organization called the Classification and Rating Administration (CARA) is what moviegoers presently experience. However, as much as CARA has attempted to distinguish itself from the old PCA, familiar questions persist. The most serious among them is this: are movies still a product of compromises made with censors? *Burstyn* inspired the dawning of a new movie culture, but it did not put to rest the ability to coerce filmmakers into cutting their work.

This book looks at the single most important case in the jurisprudence surrounding motion picture expression, the case upon which all later cases were layered, the case that showed a Supreme Court acting upon a gradually expanding view of free speech and realizing that movies deserved to be included with works of art like books and plays. Chapter 1 starts with the origins of governmental motion picture censorship in the Progressive Era, the movie industry's self-censorship in response to governmental censorship, and some early, mostly fruitless litigation. Considering the issue of film freedom in 1915, the Supreme Court decided that movies were not worthy of free speech protection. Even so, some intrepid independent distributors continued to challenge government censors in state courts, but through World War II, they met with no real success. Chapter 2 looks at how an emerging recognition of movies as art created a compelling cultural rationale to reject prior censorship. Chapter 3 brings *The Miracle* to its debut with the censors and the moviegoing public of New York City. Although the censors had no problem with the film, many prominent Catholics considered it sacrilegious and blasphemous. After frenzied denunciation, they turned to the state and demanded the movie's suppression, a situation that neither Burstyn nor the New York Civil Liberties Union could accept. Chapter 4 moves with *The Miracle* to the U.S. Supreme Court after two losses in the New York State courts, detailing the arguments on both sides of movie freedom and the decision that established the case as a landmark in the history of motion pictures. Chapter 5 deals with five post-*Burstyn* cases as film distributors sensed a change in the legal culture and sought definitive pronouncement that motion picture censorship was unconstitutional. Chapter 6 looks at the variety of responses to the Supreme Court's decision and what this diversity of opinion revealed about the declining power of the Legion of Decency. Chapter 7 examines the *Burstyn* legacy in light of both the emergence of the rating system and the rise of movies with more explicit sexual content. Chapter 8 considers how, in the absence of governmental censorship, Hollywood's rating system has dealt with controversial movies, especially those that contain violence.

Joseph Burstyn and his attorney, Ephraim London, deserve credit for bringing the Court's attention to movie freedom and to the misuse of the state for the suppression of heresy. They deserve credit also for bringing public attention to censor interference with everyone's entertainment. Together Burstyn and London stood up to the City of New York, the State of New York, the Legion of Decency, and the Catholic archdiocese. They carried their fight to the Supreme Court with the assistance only of the New York Civil Liberties Union and later the ACLU. The case they championed caused both the Legion of Decency and the PCA to change their methods and started the legal ball rolling that would eventually cause the destruction of all statutory censorship.

Joseph Burstyn probably never could have imagined the levels of sex and violence available on screens today. Whether that is good or bad depends on the individual's point of view. The important thing is that it is no longer up to a legislatively empowered bureaucrat or the legal system to decide whether it is good or bad. Thus *Burstyn v. Wilson* signaled a cultural as well as legal shift away from codes, courts, and censors. In the long view, this case helped create a world that for better and worse is at once more profound as well as more profane.

Movie Censorship

Origins and Early Challengers

In late 1950, when the story of *The Miracle* in the United States begins, New York State had been prescreening every commercially exhibited film for three decades. Five other states were also exercising prior restraint against all movies. Pennsylvania, Ohio, Kansas, Maryland, and Virginia insisted on reviewing all movies before they could be shown to the public, banning some and ordering cuts in others. Two more, Massachusetts and Rhode Island, empowered local officials to prescreen movies. Dozens of large cities, including Chicago, Atlanta, Dallas, Milwaukee, Seattle, and Memphis, as well as uncounted small ones like Highland Park, Illinois; Greeley, Colorado; and Greensboro, North Carolina, also restricted movie exhibition.

This censoring was left over from the Progressive Era, when moral panic over the unrestrained content of early movies led to calls for governmental censorship of the wildly popular new medium. Motion pictures had appeared at the turn of the twentieth century, a time of great cultural flux, when previously distinct lines between private matters and public discourse were blurring. Victorian norms of privacy, modesty, self-control, and reserve were directly challenged by new amusements like vaudeville, dance halls, night clubs, and amusement parks. As motion pictures burst onto the cultural scene, they were seen by many people as vehicles bringing dangerous new ideas to society's most impressionable members—children, immigrants, the uneducated, and the unchaperoned.

That those who considered themselves the moral guardians of society should turn to censorship is not surprising. Americans had long accepted censorship of the theater. Moreover, since movies were able to bypass traditional communal filters—family and clergy—without any oversight, some saw the need to restrain them for the good of society. Many of the leading social critics of the Progressive Era were wary of the power of movies. Jane Addams, the founder of Chicago's Hull House, for example, viewed movies as a force that could wreak havoc on the delicate nature of society's most vulnerable members, its children. In 1909, Addams included a chapter on movies—"House of Dreams"—in her account of urban life, *The Spirit of Youth and the City Streets*. Her observations echoed the views of most social reformers of the time.

"Going to the show" for thousands of young people in every industrial city is the only possible road to the realms of mystery and romance; the theater is the only place where they can satisfy that craving for a conception of life higher than that which the actual world offers them. In a very real sense the drama and the drama alone performs for them the office of art as is clearly revealed in their blundering demand stated in many forms for "a play unlike life." The theater becomes to them a "veritable house of dreams" infinitely more real than the noisy streets and the crowded factories.

Addams found movies a poor substitute for more traditional forms of dramatic art, and felt a genuine concern for the harm this "debased art" might do to children. Her alarm was by no means rare, and many civic authorities heeded her warnings.

In 1907, her home city of Chicago had been the first of many localities to create and enact official censorship of movies. By 1918, though, the city's efforts to curb salacious cinema had faltered, mostly because the police department only issued permits to indicate movies suitable for patrons over the age of twenty. This well-intentioned policy turned out to provide free advertising for the most sensational movies. To strengthen enforcement of the city's censorship code, Chicago created a commission to determine the best ways to contain the influence of movies. Composed of representatives who viewed themselves as the social conscience of the city, Chicago's Motion Picture Commission began hearings in 1919 to determine how best to contain the harmful influence of the movies. Testimony came from a surprisingly broad cross-section of the public, including representatives from the movie industry itself who were less than happy about the prospect of censorship. The vice president of Famous Players-Lasky and chair of the executive committee of the industry's trade group, the National Association of the Motion Picture Industry (NAMPI), Walter W. Irwin, snarled: "why don't you submit this question [of censorship] to the people and if the people say 'Censor the pictures,' then I want the pictures censored too." FitzGeorge Dinneen, a Jesuit priest representing the Knights of Columbus (consistently among the most active advocates of movie censorship), shot back: "This commission has sent out 1,200 letters to the clergy of Chicago, to the judges, the professional people, principals of schools, social workers, and to every class who could most intelligently express the sentiment of the community on the subject. Every answer to that communication insisted in as strong words as it could make it that this commission should set up in Chicago a board of high-class people to censor the pictures." The public, so conceived by civic leaders like Dinneen, had spoken, and the upstart film industry had to listen.

Thus, even though Chicago's commission seemed to consider a varied range of opinions, its central logic remained hard-line and its conclusion foregone. Its final report, published in 1920, concluded: "It cannot be that in this progressive age we should silently consent or concur in having our wives and children, our homes, our schools, and our churches turned over to the entertainer in order that he may make a profit regardless of the consequence to the individual." Having decided on control, all that was left was to figure out how best to protect society from an industry assumed to prey upon the worst impulses of human nature.

Much of the hostility toward movies in the early part of the twentieth century also stemmed from religious antagonism. Protestant reformers were starting to feel their influence slip away in the rapidly urbanizing and nationalizing culture, and they feared the new movies and their appeal to the lower elements of society. Movies began as distinctly "lowbrow" entertainment, a situation that constantly left them vulnerable to attack from purity reformers. That they were made mostly by Jewish immigrants made the situation even more volatile.

But the movie that created the most ruckus in the Progressive Era was made by a man who was neither immigrant nor Jewish: *The Birth of a Nation* (1915) was produced and directed by Kentucky-born D. W. Griffith. With this movie, Griffith not only established modern movie culture by introducing the feature-length film but also managed to instigate a censorship furor that still has not died out today. *The Birth of a Nation* shocked, appalled, and inspired audiences and critics. It was much longer than other films; it was more elaborately produced, shot, and edited; and it focused on the most wrenching period in U.S. history—the Civil War and Reconstruction. The film continues to occupy a special place in the history of motion pictures, both reviled for its overt racism and championed for its technical virtuosity.

The public response to Griffith's movie also revealed the basic conflict between competing understandings of movie power. On one side were those who argued that Griffith had made a major contribution to film as art. *The Birth of a Nation* introduced Americans to close-ups, dissolves, panning, and flashbacks. On the other side were those who believed his film proved the absolute need to control cinema content. The controversy ignited by *The Birth of a Nation* was so profound that it established a precedent for public outcry against movies. In Boston, audiences threw rotten food at the screen and amassed in such numbers outside the theater that state political leaders held special public and private discussions to deal with popular protest. At the same time, audiences in the South responded by attacking African Americans. Bosley Crowther, film critic for the *New York Times* from 1940 to 1967, recalled being unnerved by popular reaction to the film in his boyhood hometown of Winston-Salem, North Carolina. "There were very, very few Negroes that could be seen within blocks of the theater. If the people coming out did no more than abuse the Negroes they saw in the street it was fortunate. Actually, a lot of people would throw rocks at them and do things of that sort. It was an unpleasant, a mischievous sort of thing."

The National Association for the Advancement of Colored People (NAACP) attacked the film, its director, and Thomas Dixon, the author of the book on which it was based. In a forty-seven-page pamphlet, the group declared its hope that a censorship law would ban *The Birth of a Nation* and any other film to "save every group of our varied citizenship from insult and indignity." Griffith fired back with a pamphlet entitled "The Rise and Fall of Free Speech in America," which likened movies to "the laboring man's university," and the "pictorial press." Griffith spoke directly to the predicament that constantly plagued the movies: "It is said the motion picture tells its story more vividly than any other art. In other words, we are to be blamed for efficiency, for completeness. . . . We have no wish to offend with indecencies or obscenities, but we do demand, as a right, the liberty to show the dark side of wrong that we may illuminate the bright side of virtue – the same liberty that is conceded to the written work – that art to which we owe the Bible and the works of Shakespeare."

Griffith had stated the case plainly – movies were highly effective at connecting with audiences because they made ideas accessible through images. Movies had power and, he believed, that power gave movies respectability. On what was that power based, though – on attendance or on intrinsic cultural worth? The answer in the early part of the century came from the size of the audiences. Because movies were popular, they were powerful. It was their popularity with the masses, rather than their intellectual merit, as Griffith argued, that made movies forces to be reckoned with. Those who wanted to control movie content would return again and again to this argument: movies were appealing and therefore potentially dangerous. That they also carried significant messages that deserved to be heard was an argument that would have to wait. Those who demanded control of this purportedly dangerous, wildly popular new medium fit well into the political environment of the Progressive Era. A rapidly expanding belief that government could and should be used to ameliorate social problems was merging with a modernist philosophy that agencies managed by presumed experts could improve conditions for all. Such a climate proved fertile ground for the creation of agencies of control.

Like the political environment, the legal culture aided those who would control movie content. Free expression was not a hot topic in the Progressive Era. Even free speech activists were more concerned with political speech. Separating commercial and entertainment speech from political discourse, these activists viewed restrictions on movie expression as something properly within the realm of the state's police powers – that is, the government's legitimate role to protect the public welfare. Moreover, the judiciary was downright hostile to claims that free speech rights had been violated. A few dedicated legal scholars had been speaking out in favor of free speech since 1878, as historian David Rabban has shown. But they had been largely unsuccessful in influencing the legal community. Within such an atmosphere, calls for governmental control of salacious and violent movie content were debated widely and often — and almost always — answered positively throughout the country.

Movie Censorship Begins

Chicago had been the first in 1907 when it authorized its chief of police to pass judgment on all movies. Pennsylvania followed in 1911, Ohio and Kansas in 1914, Maryland in 1916, New York in 1921, and Virginia in 1922. Massachusetts tried to adopt a censorship law by public referendum in 1922 but failed after a well-orchestrated opposition campaign from the movie industry's new trade organization, the Motion Picture Producers and Distributors Association (MPPDA). A few years later, Massachusetts found a way around this setback by using an old "Lord's Day Observance" statute to authorize local officials to restrain movies they considered unfit for showing on Sunday (effectively keeping most from being seen on any other day of the week).

Many of these censoring statutes were remarkably similar, calling for censors to prohibit movies that fit certain categories such as "indecent," "inhuman," "obscene," "immoral," "sacrilegious," or "likely to incite to crime." Ohio also used a catchall phrase, authorizing its censors to keep out movies unless they were deemed "moral, educational, or amusing and harmless." In none of the statutes was the terminology explained. The censors were free to label a movie as inhuman or immoral without any guidelines from the legislators as to what they had intended those words to mean.

In most states and cities, the men and women appointed to serve as censors were hardly the well-qualified "experts" that many of the moral reformers had envisioned. Before 1927, the censors were all political appointees — patronage or spoils positions. Often, governors appointed their political cronies to the censor posts or used the positions to pay off political debts. After 1927, two states, New York and Ohio, reorganized their censor boards under their education departments and required civil servants to review films. In Virginia, the censors were organized under the state's legal division, but the censor jobs there, as in Pennsylvania, Kansas, and Maryland, remained patronage plums at the governor's disposal. Most censors were poorly paid (some were even volunteers) and were rarely qualified to pass judgment on the artistic merits of movies. Even in New York, where the censor board (known as the Motion Picture Division) was certainly the most influential because of the large and important New York City market, the civil service requirements for a censor job demanded no special knowledge of film or the movie business.

The censoring statutes had more in common than their vague language and dubiously qualified censors. They all set up systems of prior restraint despite the states having free speech protection written into their constitutions. Prior restraint refers to governmental control of speech before it reaches the public. Current courts do not uphold prior restraint except in extraordinary circumstances such as matters of national security, and then the national security need must be compelling. In the Pentagon Papers case of 1971, for example, the executive branch tried to restrain publication of documents relating to the history of U.S. involvement in the Vietnam War, but the Supreme Court refused to allow the restriction precisely because it was prior restraint of publication. Indeed, U.S. and British legal history have shared a traditional aversion to prior restraint of news media and political opinion, with many legal commentators of the eighteenth century considering it inimical to the operation of a free society and a representative government. These ideas were immensely influential during the Constitutional Era of the late eighteenth century. But mid-twentieth-century courts routinely accepted prior restraint for movies even though it had been stripped as an unconstitutional abridgment of the right to free speech and free press for newspapers, books, and magazines. Movies, because of their mass appeal, their attractiveness, and their influence, were believed to hold a "special capacity for evil," an ability to sway people in ways unimaginable in older media. Because of the potential for harm, both the public and the legal culture had no problem accepting that movies needed and deserved prior restraint. In 1950, when Burstyn brought *The Miracle* to New York, films remained legally subject to governmental standards of appropriateness before ever being seen by the public.

Prior restraint did more than keep potentially or allegedly harmful content from movie screens. It also served to keep nonmainstream ideas from the public discourse. A publisher did not have to submit book or magazine content to a review board before publication. However, after the book was sold, local authorities could, if they believed it to be dangerous to society, prosecute the seller for violation of penal laws restricting obscene or otherwise dangerous material. Then the case would go to a jury, which would decide whether the prosecution had been appropriate. Although the sale would have been halted, the material in the book would have made it into what Supreme Court Justice Oliver Wendell Holmes called "the marketplace of ideas" for public airing, legal debate, and a jury decision – an open process.

This was not the case for movies. Their content was legally filtered by governmentally appointed censors, some qualified to make such decisions, most not. Distributors submitted a copy of the film and a script, paid a fee, and waited to learn whether the movie would be licensed for exhibition. Some censors worked rapidly, letting the distributor know their determination within days; others took longer. In the business of film distribution, where release dates are key, this interference was problematic. The first major challenge to governmental film censorship in 1915 concerned in part this very issue: knowing when a movie could be premiered. Under any system of prior restraint, a film distributor could not be sure if or when his film would be released for viewing.

When a distributor was denied an exhibition license or if he was required to make cuts and resubmit the film before a license would be issued, he was rarely told why beyond a recitation of the category into which his offensive film had been placed. The distributor could bring suit against the censors, but the cases came through appellate review and there was no jury. So, although the censors could claim that the process was fair because it allowed for judicial review, a legal challenge left the distributor without recourse to a jury and with a product he could not sell, held up as long as the legal system took to grind his case through the system. Throughout the 1930s and 1940s, court cases against censors usually took at least a year and often longer. One infamous case, the foreign film *Ecstasy*, was tied up in court challenges for six years in ten different courts before finally being released for viewing in hacked-up form. By the time Burstyn's film *The Miracle* was ordered released, it had been legally shackled for a year and a half.

Between the six censoring states and other areas covered by municipal censorship by the early 1920s, much of the United States was covered, either directly or indirectly, by governmental censorship. For example, the states of Illinois, Tennessee, and Georgia had no real incentive to create film review boards since their major cities actively censored all films. A distributor cutting scenes to get an exhibition license for Chicago was not likely to restore those scenes for showing in Kankakee.

Hollywood and Its Production Code

While city councils and state legislators were busy considering censorship bills, the movie industry was actively engaged in efforts to stave off an even bigger potential threat: federal censorship. Many Protestants, including the Women's Christian Temperance Union, worked for governmental censorship, believing that enlightened expert censors would provide the best control. Although they were happy to get state censorship bills passed, many of these groups still hoped for a federal censorship authority. Bills were introduced for censorship on the federal level in 1914, 1916, 1925, and 1934. All were defeated. As late as 1932, forty civic and religious organizations were still lobbying for a national censor board.

Much of the impetus for this federal push came from the actions of Hollywood itself. In the early 1920s, the movie industry was racked by scandal, and attempted to save its image. In 1921, Roscoe "Fatty" Arbuckle, a popular comedian, was tried for murder after one of his female guests died at an all-weekend party in his hotel suite. Arbuckle was never convicted of the crime, although he stood trial three times. During the first trial, publicity disaster struck Hollywood again as director William Desmond Taylor, rumored to be at the center of a love triangle, was found murdered in his home. Both incidents destroyed the careers of all those involved. Then, Hollywood was struck again when popular, handsome, supposedly clean-cut actor Wallace Reid died of a drug overdose. Hollywood's morals were under siege, prompting producers to run for the safety of collective mea culpas in the form of a public housecleaning to be undertaken by a new movie "czar." Will H. Hays, a squeaky clean, well-connected politico (formerly President Warren G. Harding's postmaster general) and elder of the Presbyterian Church, became the president of the MPPDA, the organization founded by the industry moguls to minimize the damage done by the censorship boards and to keep federal censorship unrealized. Now Hays was set to work to clean up Hollywood's image. Hays and his colleagues began watching the state and local censor boards to determine what they would object to. That list, the "Don'ts and Be Carefuls," was intended as a warning to producers, but it also came in handy as a public relations tool to make the industry look as if it were sincerely trying to clean itself up for the good of the U.S. moviegoing public. In practice, though, this list of no-nos had no enforcement provision, and it was ignored more than followed.

Criticism of movie content continued, and by the 1930s, the movie industry was facing a cacophony of new and more serious woes: overextension of credit for new theater construction and for retrofitting existing theaters for sound equipment; a serious decline in audience numbers as the Depression deepened; and intense pressure from religious leaders, especially Catholics. Because many urban theatergoers were Catholic, and the industry could ill afford to lose any ticket buyers, the church carried a great deal of leverage with the movie moguls. So, when Father Daniel Lord, an adviser to Cecil B. DeMille's 1927 blockbuster, *The King of Kings*, and Martin Quigley, a prominent Catholic and publisher of the *Motion Picture Herald*, offered to write a new code to replace the "Don'ts and Be Carefuls" in 1930, Hollywood jumped at the chance. The code the moguls accepted called for no movie to be produced that would "lower the moral standards" of the viewers. The "sympathy of the audience" was never to be "thrown to the side of crime, wrongdoing, evil, or sin." The code demanded that only "correct standards of life" be presented onscreen, and that the rule of law should never be "ridiculed" but should be respected. Unlike the open-ended censorship statutes passed by the states, the Production Code, as it was named, contained specific lists of proscribed subjects, words, and actions under headings like "Crime," "Brutality," "Sex," "Vulgarity," "Obscenity," "Blasphemy," "Costumes," "Religion," "National Feelings," and "Cruelty to Animals."

The industry was so intent on proving itself worthy of America's respect that it actually used this new code to denigrate its own product. Number one under the "Reasons" for the code was this language: "Theatrical motion pictures, that is, pictures intended for the theatre are primarily to be regarded as ENTERTAINMENT. . . . The motion picture, because of its importance as entertainment and because of the trust placed in it by the peoples of the world, has special MORAL OBLIGATIONS. . . . The latitude given to film material cannot, in consequence, be as wide as the latitude given to book material." Although it might have seemed wise at the time to call off the moral reformers, this language would come back to haunt the industry when it tried to fight governmental censorship in the 1950s.

Initially, the new code was ignored as the financially strapped, Depression-battered studios turned to box office surety: sex and violence. Just three years after the introduction of the Production Code, leaders of the Catholic Church were up in arms again, this time threatening a nationwide boycott. To carry out that threat, an Episcopal council created a new pressure group for lay Catholics to join: they called it the Legion of Decency. The Legion was to review all movies to be shown and rate them either A1 — "approved for all"; A2 — "unobjectionable for adults"; B — "objectionable in part"; or C — "condemned." A rating of "C" could spell financial ruin for a Hollywood movie — theaters would refuse to book it out of fear of Catholic boycotts.

Millions of Catholics took a "pledge" starting in 1934 to patronize only those movie theaters that showed wholesome films and, under pain of sin, to boycott any condemned movies. One priest explained in the Catholic journal the *Sign*, "The pledge is a promise and its binding force comes from the virtue of fidelity." Another related, "At most, this pledge would seem to be only a promise; . . . however, by reason of the matter promised, the fulfillment of this pledge may be a grave obligation, binding under pain of mortal sin." When the pledging Catholics were joined by some Protestant and Jewish congregations, Hollywood faced real trouble.

Confronting such daunting opposition, the industry had to act. It had tried cleanup campaigns several times before, but none had succeeded for long in convincing moral guardians that any real progress was being made. This time the industry needed something with teeth, an enforcement arm. The MPPDA found a way both to silence its increasingly vociferous Catholic critics and hold off any future federal censorship by announcing the creation of the Production Code Administration (PCA), an office that would oversee and strictly enforce content suitability according to the code, backed up by the ability to impose fines and deny theater bookings. From 1934 on, only films with Production Code seals could be shown in member-owned theaters (the majority of the metropolitan first-run theaters). Films denied a code seal were cut off from the source of most of the industry's profits. Now an offending movie producer would face not only the condemnation of the Legion of Decency but also denial of the most lucrative movie theater bookings.

The PCA had another goal besides holding off Catholic protests and federal censorship: to protect member studios by keeping a list of those things sure to ruffle the government censors, a continuation of the earlier "Don'ts and Be Carefuls." Never perfectly able to guess what would rile the censors of a particular area, the PCA's frequently updated lists did offer a rough outline of what member studios should avoid. Judging from the records of New York State's censors, the PCA succeeded: a high of 19 percent reported as "problem films" by the censors in 1932 dropped to just 7 percent in 1937 and hovered around 4 percent during the World War II years.

The person largely responsible for the PCA's success was its leader, Joseph I. Breen, described as "an altar boy with brass knuckles" by Francis Couvares and "a professional Catholic" by Leonard Leff and Jerold Simmons. Breen was an anti-Semite who believed that the mostly Jewish movie moguls needed to be taught a lesson in Christian morality. He became Hollywood's first and most influential chief enforcer, remaining on the job as the industry's moral commissar for two decades.

This collusion between Hollywood moguls and Catholic officials enjoyed popular approval even if people did not understand the underhanded nature of the alliance. Jimmie Fidler, a powerful, conservative Hollywood columnist and radio host, echoed many supporters of the Legion when he declared in 1944 that it had "never been accused, even by producers whose financial toes were stepped upon, of using its enormous power unfairly. It has never censored a cinema that did not deserve censorship. All in all, both the public and the motion pictures have benefited." Historian of American Catholicism Una M. Cadegan puts it this way: "Defenders of the Legion . . . maintained that their program reflected the values of all 'decent' or 'right-thinking' people. They claimed to be speaking for the majority of their fellow citizens, a cultural majority powerless in the face of amoral, monied conglomerates. Further, they were affirming their own right to define midcentury culture against, as they saw it, both Eastern sophisticates and West Coast moguls." As influential as the code was, it is important to note that the intention of the codemakers was different from the intentions of the legislators who had drawn up censorship statutes: the Hollywood codemakers did not intend to censor films; rather, they intended to help producers make films that would not offend various categories of people.

———

Distributors Fight Back

The PCA seal of approval helped to immunize member studios from pressure groups like the Legion, kept governmental censor problems to a minimum, and offered the studios a safe haven from public outcry. But independent and foreign productions were on their own. They faced both the uncertainty of dealing with the various states' censoring whims (which could change in some states with each new administration) and the privilege of paying for it. Each distributor paid an examination fee and waited to find out whether parts of the movie would have to be changed or cut out altogether. For the major distributors who were owned by the Hollywood studios, such fees were a minor cost of conducting business. But for independent producers and distributors, the fees could be a major burden. Small profits from small distribution films became even smaller when distributors were forced to pay their censor bills up front.

Nor did the distributors like the power the censors had over their product. Joseph Burstyn had dealt with the New York State film censors since the 1930s. He hated the idea that every time he wanted to exhibit a motion picture, he had to seek permission from censors who might approve his film and might not. "Every time I had to submit a film for censorship," Burstyn said, "I felt that I was in an illegitimate business and that being in this business was a crime."

Other independent distributors and exhibitors shared Burstyn's feelings, and struck back at censor determinations. Only two years after the nation's first censorship ordinance, the first legal challenge was filed. When Chicago started prescreening films in 1907, theater owner Jake Block decided to challenge their open-ended authority. Although the legal culture of the time routinely accepted ambiguous statutory language without explanations of terminology, Block thought that a censor should have more direction than single words like "immoral." His answer from Illinois Supreme Court Chief Justice James H. Cartwright should not have surprised the movie industry: "The average person of healthy and wholesome mind knows well enough what the words 'immoral' and 'obscene' mean and can intelligently apply the test to any picture presented to him." Cartwright's position, that definitions and standards were unnecessary, and that legislatively empowered experts should have wide discretion, was widely accepted in the legal culture of the Progressive Era. The idea that censors should have broad discretion would prevail in the courts for the next forty-four years.

For those moviemakers not willing to accept this circumstance, and for those who decided to challenge the right to censor, there were two big obstacles. First, as Jake Block had learned, when moral guardians began to advocate control of motion pictures, faith in legislatively empowered public servants was pervasive. Courts routinely practiced "judicial restraint," a philosophy that calls on judges to bow to the legislative will and the actions of the legislatively empowered agents unless there is compelling proof of unconstitutionality or malfeasance. The ascendance of such a philosophy meant that censor rulings would be overturned only if a distributor could prove real abuse. Disagreements over whether the statute had been correctly applied or arguments over the meanings of terminology were likely to go nowhere. The censor, with broad latitude for decisionmaking, would always win.

Second, the judiciary was not interested in claims that a state agency had violated the right to free speech. Before 1925, the Supreme

Court did not consider the First Amendment applicable to state action. According to the Supreme Court's interpretation of federalism and the First Amendment, states were perfectly within their legal rights to police speech. After all, the language of the amendment reads, "Congress shall make no law . . . abridging the freedom of speech, or of the press." It says nothing about state legislatures. This strict dual federalism began to change in 1925, however, when the Court began to take a broader view of individual rights, and began to question whether some of those rights were so basic that they should be protected against state infringement.

The stepping stone that got the justices to this new position was the Fourteenth Amendment passed in 1868. Part of that amendment, written to protect the former slaves from the black codes of southern state governments after the Civil War, reads: "No state shall make or enforce any law which shall abridge the privileges and immunities of citizens of the United States, nor shall any state deprive any person of life, liberty, or property without due process of law." The framers of the Fourteenth Amendment had not limited the language of the amendment to the freedmen, instead using the words "citizens" and "persons." Nor did they spell out what the "privileges" and "immunities" were.

Shortly after its passage, the Supreme Court adopted a limited interpretation of the new amendment despite evidence that Congress intended the Fourteenth Amendment to act as a brake on state legislation violating the "privileges" and "immunities" of such basic liberties as free speech and free press. Scholars still disagree about the intent of the Fourteenth Amendment's framers. Some, like Raoul Berger, argue that their intention was merely to protect the provisions of the Civil Rights Act of 1866 from constitutional assault, but others, like Michael Kent Curtis, maintain that the framers (certainly bent on protection of the freedmen) were also intent on protecting all citizens from state governments that infringed Bill of Rights freedoms like speech.

Nevertheless, the justices' limited interpretation of the Fourteenth Amendment's scope continued through the Progressive Era and into World War I. But when state and federal law alarmingly trampled on the free speech rights of anarchists and communists during and immediately after World War I, some Progressives and some justices began to question whether free speech should be considered one of the fundamental rights that the Fourteenth Amendment prohibited states from abridging.

In a process that legal scholars call *incorporation*, the Supreme Court gradually came to consider many of the original rights embodied in the Bill of Rights as those "privileges and immunities" guaranteed against state infringement by the Fourteenth Amendment. Two of these were the rights of free speech and free press. The justices decided in a 1925 case, *Gitlow v. New York*, that free speech and free press were indeed "among the fundamental personal rights and 'liberties' protected by the Due Process Clause of the Fourteenth Amendment from impairment by the States." Although the Court had begun to consider freedom of speech a fundamental right, the only speech considered worthy of protection was political speech that did not incite to criminal behavior or disrupt public order. Commercial speech, libel, and anything construed as obscenity, blasphemy, or profanity were outside First Amendment protection.

Although *Gitlow* represents a major turning point in constitutional interpretation, it sparked no revolution. It was many more years before the justices added other fundamental liberties of the Bill of Rights to the list of rights protected against state violation. This process of bringing more rights under protection against state infringement — incorporation — was a gradual process. Freedom of religious exercise, for example, was not brought under the umbrella of the Fourteenth Amendment until 1940. Others like the Sixth Amendment's right to counsel or the Fifth Amendment's protection against double jeopardy were not added until the 1960s.

But all this was years in the future and so could not help when in 1913 one distributor, the Mutual Film Company, began a litigation campaign to overturn film censorship statutes in three states based on violation of free speech rights. After losing, rather predictably, all three state cases over the next two years, the case came before the U.S. Supreme Court (not until 1925 did Congress give the Court the right to decide which cases it would consider). The nation's first national medium — film — got its day in court.

But Mutual did not get the answer it wanted. Dismissing the company's arguments in *Mutual Film v. Ohio* that the statutes were too vague, that they burdened interstate commerce, that they violated due process requirements, and that they violated the free speech provisions of state constitutions, Justice Joseph McKenna wrote the opinion for a Court that was unanimous in its concern over the potential for harm from movies. Since movies could be used for "evil" as well as for good, McKenna found their examination prior to exhibition a necessary control. He rejected the idea that movies should be considered part of the press or of the national discourse. They were "a business pure and simple, originated and conducted for profit, like other spectacles, not to be regarded, nor intended to be regarded by the Ohio constitution, we think, as part of the press of the country or as organs of public opinion."

The Court's definition of movies as a business of "spectacle" accorded with popular and elite opinion. Through the early 1920s, theater owners used movies as part of variety shows. Even though, *The Birth of a Nation* had illustrated the artistic potential and popularity of feature-length films, movies were used to attract patrons like other amusements. Throughout the 1920s and into the 1930s, if the idea of movies as art entered the popular consciousness at all, it did so because marketing campaigns sold the experience of seeing a movie. But there was no effort to convince the public of cinema's intellectual or artistic worth. Moviegoing was an attraction; the film and its stars were an experience. Thus the most important battles during the early period of film history focused on reforming the experience of seeing the movie rather than any debate over whether movies were art.

And so, the justices of the Supreme Court had come down squarely on the side of the censors. Considering, as David Rabban reminds us, that no group in the United States was more hostile to free speech claims before World War I than the U.S. judiciary, the outcome of the case should be no surprise to anyone. *Mutual v. Ohio* became a major victory in 1915 for those who favored governmental control of motion pictures. Although today it seems wrongly decided, it made good legal sense at the time for several reasons. Most people of this era would have agreed that movies were not art (even free speech activists did not consider entertainment speech worthy of the First Amendment). Moreover, Americans were accustomed to censoring of theatrical productions, and commercial speech was not considered protected under the First Amendment. Also, people of the Progressive Era had great faith in their legislatively empowered experts, whose jobs were to control harmful things (like movies). And, finally, judges were probably also influenced by the moral panic over movie influence in 1915. The case clearly reflects the thinking of the Progressive Era in which it was made, yet it also far outlasted both the era and the philosophy of the time. For thirty-seven years, legal challenges to film censorship had to contend with *Mutual* as it became a stranglehold on film freedom. Even after the introduction of sound and color, even after motion pictures had become sophisticated works of art and commentary, the legal culture continued to hang on to a position adopted during their infancy. Not until 1952 when *Burstyn* challenged film censorship would the Supreme Court consider the issue of film freedom and the First Amendment again.

Along with defining movies as "spectacles" and profit-making industries not worthy of free speech protection, the *Mutual* decision also reinforced the attitude seen first in Judge Cartwright's evaluation of statutory language in *Block v. Chicago*. It was completely unnecessary, both courts maintained, for the terms under which movies could be banned to be spelled out or defined in any way. Terms such as *educational, moral, amusing,* or *harmless* did not require explanation, the Supreme Court said in *Mutual*, because they get "precision from the sense and experience of men." This phrase — "the sense and experience of men" — justifying the use of nonspecific words, would be used repeatedly to uphold censoring statutes until 1952 when a more modern Court would find that such terms did indeed necessitate some attempt at clarification.

1920s and 1930s Challenges

Although the nation's highest court considered the matter of film freedom settled, the highest courts of several states did revisit the issue of film censorship during the intervening three decades. The *Mutual* decision buttressed the claims of the censors and discouraged any further attempts by distributors to claim that their right to free speech had been violated, but it did not keep independent film distributors from making other legal arguments against censors' interference.

{ *Chapter 1* }

New York bore the brunt of most challenges, probably because its market was the single most important. Just three weeks after setting to work in 1921, New York found its censors challenged by the Pathé newsreel company. Testing *Mutual*'s weight as precedent, Pathé's lawyers argued that New York's statute was unconstitutional prior restraint of a news medium. But New York's highest court declined to buck the Supreme Court. Movie companies throughout the world got the message that *Mutual* was indeed the daunting precedent it seemed. The *Mutual* decision, fortified by New York's *Pathé* decision, was so dispiriting that even trained constitutional lawyers retreated from any appeals to free speech rights for the next thirty years.

In the 1920s and 1930s, state censors faced seventeen cases from disgruntled distributors. But after *Pathé*, none based a case on the constitutional issues of free speech and free press rights. Instead, these distributors argued that the censors had been wrong in deciding that their films were immoral or indecent or inhuman. Such appeals, in an era of judicial restraint, were likely to go nowhere. A Pennsylvania judge reflected the legal culture of the time when he dismissed one distributor's claim that censors had overstepped their bounds: "Every reasonable doubt must be resolved by us," he said, "in behalf of the administrative action, lest we arrogate to ourselves the functions of legislator and administrator." Even after newspapers were freed from prior restraint by the Supreme Court in the 1931 case of *Near v. Minnesota*, prior restraint continued unquestioned by film distributors throughout the rest of the 1930s and into the World War II years. Instead of questioning free speech rights, prior restraint, or due process violations, the challengers squabbled over differences of opinion, statutory definitions, and the interpretation of connotations. In a legal culture that venerated bureaucratic expertise and the legislative will, such arguments were not likely to sway judges.

Movie censorship was so accepted that in the crucial New York market between the mid-1920s and the end of World War II, only thirty-eight of the hundreds of movies denied licenses bothered to appeal to the censors' overseers, the state's Board of Regents. Those who were brave enough to appeal were rebuffed, as the regents reliably upheld the censors. Only six distributors went over the regents' heads and appealed to the courts. All six involved independent productions or foreign films distributed by small companies, and all lost. One of the cases involved a docudrama about pregnancy and childbirth produced in an effort to lower infant mortality rates. Even though the censors clearly overreacted, and dozens of public service groups came forward to insist that the movie be cleared for public viewing, New York refused to budge. And the courts of New York refused to nudge them in a more reasonable direction. Only once in two decades did the Board of Regents overrule the censors, and that exception came after six years of litigation.

Part of the reason for the utter failure of censorship challenges in the 1930s stemmed from supposedly scientific studies of the effects of movies on children. Among the most celebrated and controversial was that conducted by the Reverend William H. Short. In 1929, Short won the support of a wealthy Cleveland family foundation, the Payne Foundation, to fund a study that he hoped would ultimately lead to federal regulation of movies. The final report was titled *Motion Pictures and Youth* (popularly known as the Payne Fund studies) and included twelve studies published in eight volumes between 1933 and 1935. Short and his team pioneered sociological research on the effects of movies on children. Yet the study had two intellectual problems: first, it was conducted by researchers recruited to substantiate Short's overtly negative assessment of movies; and second, its results were repackaged by an author named Henry James Forman, who in 1933 published a skewed summary in an influential book titled *Our Movie-Made Children*. Forman's summary simplified the research and twisted some conclusions of the Payne Fund studies in the hope that his provocative argument would prompt federal censorship. According to historian Garth Jowett, "Short and Forman were crusaders and publicity hounds. They presented the research in a moral context and as a call to action." Yet, even after the complete scientific studies were published in 1935, "There was [still] no spontaneous public outcry for federal action against the motion picture industry. Short had discovered what many other reformers had known since the turn of the century—the general public did not really perceive the movies as a serious threat to society." Yet, the publication of the Payne Fund research generated lots of attention and encouraged people to believe that movies still had that "special capacity for evil."

Here was the irony of film censorship: although it was widespread and generally supported by civic leaders, and even though many believed movies to be dangerous, audiences were ambivalent about it as a social and political issue. Efforts to create federal censorship consistently failed, but the public passively supported other censoring regimes.

Because of popular ambivalence about censorship, it fell to distributors, those most directly affected by censors, to mount an attack against the right of the state to interfere with movie content. In the 1920s and 1930s, a small, unorganized number of distributors, each challenging the banning of a single film, did manage to have some effect. Although they lost every case, publicity from the court proceedings, slight though it was, helped to shed some light on the sequestered work of the censor boards. In 1927, the distributor of a film called *The Naked Truth* tried to convince the New York courts that its message about sexually transmitted disease could serve the public, but the judges refused to consider such a topic fit for public exhibition. For the next twenty years, not one film about syphilis was permitted to be shown in New York State.

In 1934, a Czech-German film about adultery (starring the not-yet-famous Hedy Lamarr) was denied entry by the U.S. Customs Service, which, under a 1930 tariff law, was empowered to ban obscene materials. After court proceedings, *Ecstasy* (1933) was released for U.S. distribution, but New York State would have none of it. Trying an end run around the censors and hoping to capitalize on the money spent in its customs fight, the distributor, Eureka Productions, asked a U.S. District Court to enjoin New York from interfering since the film had been cleared for entry by the federal government. The federal court declined to interfere with the State of New York's authority to ban a film to protect its citizens. Eureka then tried to persuade the New York courts — five times — to overrule their censors, but to no avail. Although their attorneys did not use First Amendment arguments, they did argue that the film was considered a work of art by critics — the first time an appeal to artistic merit and critical evaluation had been used. But in the mid-1930s, films were not considered art, film critics were not the cultural authorities they would later become, and the tactic failed.

Even book reviewers were not considered valuable authorities on obscenity or artistic value by most 1930s courts. Until 1934, the

Hicklin rule (from the 1868 British case *Regina v. Hicklin*) allowed judges to rule as obscene any part of a work (and hence the entire work) that might have a harmful effect on society's most susceptible persons. Such a broad definition of the obscene allowed prosecution for the sale of such classical works as *The Decameron, The Arabian Nights, Moll Flanders,* and *Candide.* In 1934, Judge John M. Woolsey tried to overrule the *Hicklin* precedent. He rebuffed the federal government's assertion that James Joyce's *Ulysses* was obscene and insisted that a work of literature should be judged by the author's intent and the work's effect on an average man rather than its effect on the most susceptible. When the government appealed, Judges Learned Hand and Augustus Hand upheld Woolsey's new test using the average reader. In another obscenity case the same year, Learned Hand found it reasonable to allow published reviews of "qualified critics" when determining obscenity in a jury trial. As other historians have noted, these decisions impressed the literati but had little effect on the judiciary.

Failing to move the New York and federal courts with artistic merit arguments, Eureka also tried to convince the PCA to give *Ecstasy* a seal, but code administrator Joseph Breen was not interested in the movie, which by 1936 had become an international controversy denounced by the pope, the Legion of Decency, and even the Nazis. Without a code seal, *Ecstasy* could not play in the nation's major theaters, and without a New York license, it lost its largest market. Critics were starting to take notice, though; some wondered why the film was allowed to play in some areas without any ensuing societal moral breakdown but was not allowed to play in New York. After numerous edits and further court challenges, the New York Board of Regents finally overruled the censor board, authorizing a considerably watered-down and chopped-up *Ecstasy* to be licensed in 1940.

At the same time as Eureka's protracted litigation, *Tomorrow's Children* (1934), a film about eugenics and forced sterilization, became another test of New York's censorship statute. Although the state court did uphold the censors again, this decision came with a potent dissent. Clearly influenced by the frightening power of authoritarian governments in Europe in these final years before the outbreak of World War II, Presiding Justice James P. Hill compared New York's censors to "ministers of propaganda" and found their assertion that the movie would incite to crime preposterous. "The film no more suggests sterilization as a means of birth control," he wrote, "than a film showing the amputation of a leg would suggest that as a means to prevent persons from walking into danger." But this was just a dissent, and the distributor lost.

Tomorrow's Children was not to be seen in New York, but the decision split the justices of New York's intermediate appellate court, and they were never again unanimous in dealing with prewar movie censorship challenges. Moreover, the lawyers for *Tomorrow's Children* had convinced the judges to watch the movie, a major turnabout from earlier cases, indicating that the judges were now willing to consider matters of interpretation along with the facts of the case. Unquestioning judicial deference to the censors' interpretations, so steadfast in the Progressive Era and the 1920s, was starting to crack, but it would be several more decades before film would be seen as a serious art form worthy of the free speech and free press protections in the First Amendment.

In the 1930s there were four more important challenges. *Remous* (1933), a French film, carried a message about the disastrous results of adulterous relationships that probably would have satisfied as rigorous a moralist as Joseph Breen at the PCA, but it was not acceptable to the censors of New York. A honeymooning bridegroom suffers an auto accident that leaves him impotent. After vainly struggling to be faithful, his young wife succumbs to another man. She agonizes over her infidelity, and when her husband discovers the truth, he commits suicide. The distributor, Joseph Burstyn, and his partner, Arthur Mayer, hired Arthur Garfield Hays, a high-profile corporate attorney and leading member of the American Civil Liberties Union. Hays had successfully represented H. L. Mencken's magazine, *American Mercury*, against Boston's infamous Watch and Ward Society. Despite Hays's impressive liberal credentials, the briefs he prepared for *Remous*'s court appearance in 1939 curiously never mentioned freedom of speech or of the press. Even though such ideals were being used to fight book and magazine censorship cases at the same time, Hays chose to argue that the censors were mistaken.

Ignoring the *Near v. Minnesota* case, which had overthrown prior restraint on newspapers seven years earlier, Hays instead quarreled with the censors, calling them naive and out of touch with current social mores. Hays's tactics seem odd, but Mark Graber's *Transforming Free Speech* offers an explanation. Graber shows that even civil libertarians in the post–World War I years often did not consider restrictions on speech as First Amendment issues. They saw them instead as economic issues. When famed trial lawyer Clarence Darrow defended Eugene V. Debs, who had been arrested for urging workers to leave their jobs, he did so based on the right to strike rather than on Debs's right to free speech.

More surprising, though, Hays failed to mention two recent Supreme Court developments that could have helped Burstyn's case over *Remous*. Two years earlier, in 1937, Justice Benjamin Cardozo suggested in *Palko v. Connecticut* that certain liberties of the Bill of Rights were so "implicit in the concept of ordered liberty" that they should be protected from state interference. One year later, Justice Harlan Stone built on Cardozo's lead and suggested in *United States v. Carolene Products* that the justices should closely scrutinize the legitimacy of any statute that limited the personal liberties of the Bill of Rights. Acting on what came to be called this "preferred freedoms" argument, over the next few years, the Supreme Court would overturn several state laws because they infringed on the rights of radicals, labor organizations, and minority religious groups to speak and organize freely. The evolution toward current speech-protective positions was progressing in some areas, but still lay decades in the future for movies. If even a civil liberties expert like Hays would not make free speech arguments in the New York courts, it is no wonder that the judges of the pre–World War II era would fail to see film censorship as unconstitutional.

When *Remous* was finally cut enough to satisfy the New York Board of Regents in 1940, *New York Times* film critic Bosley Crowther went to see it. It had taken nearly four years of legal wrangling and censor negotiations for the movie to be shown on a New York screen. The censors' scissors were painfully apparent in the final version, according to Crowther's review: "Whatever emotional impact this tortured psychological drama may have possessed before the public's guardians had at it has been manifestly impaired by the most tantalizing interruptions, cuts of critical scenes, and a consequent series of blank transitions which leave one groping desperately for the thread.

. . . Scenes which obviously should have been emphasized . . . have been cut away in chunks." Arthur Mayer later wrote that the cuts made the film incomprehensible. No one could understand "why a man deeply in love with his newly acquired wife refused, after one apparently agreeable night, again to sleep by her side, or why his equally devoted newly acquired wife was so incredibly upset by an auto mishap as to start bestowing amorous glances on stalwart strangers."

When other foreign films faced similar pruning, film critics began to take notice of the effect of censorship, and over the next two decades would become increasingly disparaging of unthinking censors. But in the 1930s, their voices could not compete with the legislatively empowered censors. Artistic merit of films, although starting to become important for written publications, would not yet be a consideration in either the reviewing room or in the courtroom.

Along with snipping immorality, censors had unlimited discretion over what was "indecent." It is difficult to say definitively what the Progressive Era legislators had in mind when they wrote indecency into their censorship statutes, but clearly some censors thought it meant anything outside mainstream political thought. As Gerald Butters has shown, political messages were frequently curtailed by the Kansas censors in the early 1920s. Kansas routinely marked up scenes about drinking, even banning a 1934 newsreel of President Franklin Roosevelt defending the end of Prohibition. In 1937, as Europe descended into war, Pennsylvania used indecency to censor two political message films. Both challenged the censors, and both lost. The first was *Spain in Flames* (1937), a pro-Loyalist semidocumentary about the Spanish Civil War. The second, *The Ramparts We Watch* (1940), showed a "Hitler-like" figure denouncing Americans. Agreeing that the movie might inflame anti-German sentiment, the state's supreme court backed the censors' ban.

The last major censorship case before the onset of World War II shows just how dogged censors could be even when faced with overwhelming public opposition. This was indeed an unusual case since, as we have seen, the public was mostly ambivalent about movie censorship. But this case got lots of attention and lots of input. A semidocumentary sponsored by the American Committee on Maternal Welfare, *The Birth of a Baby* (1937) was intended to lift the secrecy shrouding pregnancy and childbirth in the United States. When the movie was made, few women knew what to expect when they gave birth to their first child, a fact that partially explained the high infant mortality rate, and the American Committee on Maternal Welfare hoped to do something about it by producing a film for theatrical release. But a childbirth scene in the movie was too much for the censors of New York, Pennsylvania, Kansas, and Virginia (even though the mother's anatomy is completely concealed). It was deemed "immoral" and "indecent."

The American Committee on Maternal Welfare was no impoverished distributor: it was a subgroup of the National Academy of Sciences. When the enormously popular and influential magazine *Life* picked up the story and ran thirty-five still photos from the film, the censors' ban became national news. Editors at major newspapers and magazines called for the release of the film and revealed the absurdity of the censors' position to much of the U.S. public. The previously secretive censors found themselves at the center of a national firestorm. The debate over *The Birth of a Baby* revealed the central conundrum of the movie censor: critics, liberals, and much of the public expected the censors to change with changing social mores, yet their most basic function as censors was to serve as a brake on new ideas. Childbirth traditionally had been a private matter, not fit for the public discourse, at least as the censors saw it.

Then the critics jumped in. Ernest L. Meyer's *New York Post* column suggested that the New York censors should change their name to the "Society for the Perpetuation of the Stork Legend." Despite the American Committee on Maternal Welfare's arguments about the vagueness of the censor standards and the desperate need for such a movie, both New York's appellate courts refused to overrule. The producers eventually gave in, revising the movie sufficiently to get an exhibition license in 1941. In the meantime, the movie had been kept from New York screens for more than three years.

The case had drawn national attention but further insight would have to wait until after World War II. During the war years, when importation of foreign films dried up and patriotism rose, challenges to state film censorship determinations dropped significantly.

In the prewar challenges, independent distributors had attacked the censors' determinations (repeatedly), and occasionally challenged the vagueness of the statutory terminology as well as the censors' lack of accountability. But they had not questioned the basis of the statutes: the prior restraint that allowed the censors to work in secret, keeping ideas and actions from the public discourse. Nor had they questioned the qualifications of those appointed to act as society's guardians nor the right of the state to interfere with speech, even though all of the censoring states had free speech provisions in their constitutions. The 1915 decision in *Mutual Film v. Ohio* stood unattacked and seemingly permanent.

This should not be surprising, though. Even eminent free speech activists like Zechariah Chafee and Alexander Meikeljohn saw nonpolitical speech as unworthy of First Amendment protection. Meikeljohn's influential First Amendment theory, for example, held that political speech should be absolutely protected by the First Amendment—no exceptions to who could speak or what could be said. But nonpolitical speech—something like movies—could reasonably be restrained by governmental action under the state's police power. If the state abused that power, Meikeljohn argued, the Fifth Amendment would protect against arbitrary interference with liberty through the Due Process Clause. Indeed, movie censorship statutes usually included the right to appeal. So, for Meikeljohn and many other free speech advocates, movie censorship was not a violation of the First Amendment.

Chafee, too, saw free speech in a narrow light. He was arguably the most influential of the free speech advocates. A 1919 article of Chafee's is largely credited with changing Oliver Wendell Holmes's mind, convincing him of the necessity of protecting speech unless it was clearly and imminently dangerous. Chafee's *Freedom of Speech in the United States* (originally published in 1920 and reissued in 1941) is considered by some the most influential book on law of the twentieth century. A Harvard law professor, Chafee sought to persuade not only jurists but the public through magazine articles and radio and television appearances that free speech was in peril. Chafee's biggest concern was that the United States would repeat the speech repressions of the Espionage and Sedition Act prosecutions during the 1919 red scare. The antidote to such repressive tendencies in the name of security, he argued, was more speech. "The real value of freedom of speech is not to the minority that wants to talk," Chafee wrote, "but to the majority that does not want to listen." But even Chafee saw a clear distinction between political speech and entertainment or commercial speech — the one protected and the other not.

Clearly not concerned with movie freedom in the 1930s, these free speech advocates nonetheless were laying foundations that later justices would adopt as they expanded the scope of expression protected by the First Amendment. Along with Meikeljohn and Chafee, some judges, like John Woolsey, Learned Hand, and his cousin Augustus Hand, were also pushing the legal culture to protect non-majoritarian free speech. On the Supreme Court, Cardozo and Stone were moving ahead in adopting a new speech-protective philosophy, but it would take time before other justices would come around to their insistence on scrutiny of state interference with personal liberties. It would take even longer for such speech-protective ideas to filter down to the state courts. In the meantime, motion picture censorship went on — in Hollywood, in state office buildings, and in city halls.

{ *Chapter 1* }

CHAPTER 2

Origins of Movies as Art

For most of their history, movies have been caught between competing definitions of what they are. Movies have been seen both as a social problem and a force for social uplift, nothing more than crass entertainment and nothing less than the most vital and vibrant art in the world, a commodity to regulate as well as a singular expression of democratic culture.

One thing was clear by the late 1920s, though: movies had become the dominant form of mass entertainment in the United States. A survey published in 1928 by *Film Daily*, an industry journal, reported that upwards of 65 million people attended movies weekly, most seeing at least two movies each week. Statistics such as this one came from the movie industry in order to serve and capitalize better on rising attendance. The numbers also were used to justify a boom in theater construction — from the massive and ornate to the small and nondescript.

The idea that movies represented a coherent form of expression, like the press or art, took a while to evolve. Film historian Lee Grievson points out that by 1915 "the constitutional framework for censorship was set in place, and from then on the mainstream industry pursued the strategy of accepting cinema's role as a provider of entertainment, by and large dropping the strategy of arguing for its social relevance." In other words, the film industry was steering clear of controversy in order to keep profits high. By accepting a conservative legal and social definition of mainstream cinema — that it was a business pure and simple — the industry created an identity for itself that provided the foundation for financial security.

Of course, movies would continue to appear that were socially relevant and politically forceful. *The Birth of a Nation* had been one example. But it was not alone. Other films with social "messages," such as Sergei Eisenstein's *Battleship Potemkin* (1925), Lewis Milestone's *All Quiet on the Western Front* (1930), and even Charlie Chaplin's *Modern Times* (1936) illustrated that movies had the capability to express complex ideas. Moreover, there were radical cultural critics, many of whom wrote for the short-lived *Experimental Cinema*, who argued that movies had the potential to be a great force for social change if those who controlled the movies—both the industry and the censors—allowed them to move beyond mere mindless entertainment. The novelist Theodore Dreiser even sued Paramount Pictures in 1931 in an attempt to redeem the radical message of his book *An American Tragedy* from the much-diluted film version the studio produced. He lost his lawsuit, and the industry, with the support once again of the courts, continued to define movies as entertainment rather than as speech. As the wily producer Samuel Goldwyn once quipped: "If you want to send a message, call Western Union."

The obvious power of movies, therefore, moved censors and the industry to establish limits on the ability of movies to operate as a force for political and social change. At the same time, though, the fact that millions of people went to the pictures each week was something with which critics had to contend. Thus, many early champions of movies wrestled with the implications of this medium to alter the calculus of culture, rather than the sphere of politics. Many pondered how the popularity of movies would affect the definition of culture. As entertainment, movies did not fit neatly into the standard assumptions attached to art—Charlie Chaplin films probably would not uplift the masses. Yet, the fact that the masses loved Charlie Chaplin remade him, and many other stars, into influential cultural figures. Here was a conundrum of the modern era: would movies destroy the pretensions of bourgeois culture or would culture elevate the movies?

In numerous journals from the early twentieth century, critics expressed hope that movies would help spread upstanding cultural values. For example, in 1907 Joseph Medill Patterson contributed a long article to the popular weekly magazine *Saturday Evening Post* on the growth of movies and their worth as a cultural experience. Patterson reiterated what many newspapers and other periodicals had been reporting about the rise of the motion picture industry and the type of audience pictures attracted. But he was especially encouraged by the promise of movies to become a civilizing influence among the masses. "Civilization," he wrote, "has been chiefly the property of the upper classes, but during the past century civilization has been permeating steadily downward." With the introduction of movies, "drama, always a big fact in the lives of the people at the top, is now becoming a big fact in the lives of the people at the bottom." The fine arts had always belonged to the upper class; movies seemed to belong to all the people, thus helping to advance a democratization of culture.

Likewise, an editorial a few years later in the *Nation* argued that "the technique of the theatre is a subject for professionals and 'highbrows.' But the crowd discusses the technique of the moving picture with as much interest as literary salons in Paris and London discuss the minutiae of the high drama." For this reason, "the number of those thus directly interested in the moving picture plays must be enormous. In a very real sense the photoplay has become a truly popular art." But, the *Nation* cautioned, "like the picture magazine," movies required "no thought and little attention."

Randolph Bourne, one of the Progressive Era's most original intellectuals, offered critical insight into the power of this new popular art. Following a trip to the movies, Bourne concluded that although he felt a "certain unholy glee at [the] wholesale rejection of what our fathers reverenced as culture," he did not "feel any glee about what is substituted for it. . . . We seem to be witnessing a lowbrow snobbery . . . as tyrannical and arrogant as the other culture of universities and millionaires and museums." Bourne was justifiably skeptical that a commercial medium made to appeal to (rather than educate) millions of people would somehow also advance intellectual life.

Bourne's concerns were explored more fully in one of the first book-length studies of the effects of movies on U.S. culture. In 1916 Hugo Münsterberg, a well-respected Harvard psychologist, wrote a prescient work titled *The Photoplay: A Psychological Study*. Münsterberg had spent hundreds of hours studying the production and reception of movies. At the end of his experiment, which was the first of its kind, he concluded that the photoplay provided a "satisfaction" and "superb enjoyment" unique among the arts. But he added that if movies take hold of an audience, "such a penetrating influence must be fraught with dangers." What he feared was that movies would undermine culture – that life would be trivialized through "steady contact" during those hours in the dark "with things . . . not worth knowing." In a sense, Münsterberg foresaw a time in which entertainment would "carnivalize" culture. But the future could be different, he insisted, if "an enthusiasm for the noble and uplifting, a belief in the duty and discipline of the mind, a faith in ideals and eternal values" permeated "the world of the screen." In a culture that subscribed to such principles, censorship of its entertainment would be unnecessary. Movies could portray "evil and sin" without worrying about glorifying such actions.

But this hope was predicated on the presumption that movies could assist in the cultivation of popular taste. "Hardly any teaching," Münsterberg believed, could "mean more for [a] community than the teaching of beauty where it reaches the masses." Since the motion picture was "an art in itself," he urged producers to consider that they could cultivate popular taste without the public even realizing it. "The teaching of the moving pictures," he said, "must not be forced on a more or less indifferent audience, but ought to be absorbed by those who seek entertainment and enjoyment from the films and are ready to make their little economic sacrifice." Mass art had the power to be both significant and popular; Münsterberg hoped such a role for movies would be realized in the future.

The National Board of Review of Motion Pictures (NBR), formed in New York City in 1909 largely to stave off federal censorship, became perhaps the staunchest defender of the promise of movies, and took as its basic premise a more pragmatic view than those who expected movies to enlighten and educate. The organization had formed in response to the threat of prior restraint of films, and brought together community leaders – socially conscious elites – who saw in movies great hope for mass culture rather than great peril. In short, this group disagreed with its censoring compatriots. From 1909 through the mid-1920s, the film industry sent the NBR thousands of films in the hope that this group's endorsement would protect films from censorship around the country. This arrangement failed. But the NBR continued to oppose censorship – especially efforts at federal censorship – by helping to forge a mainstream movie aesthetic. If it couldn't compete with the censors, the NBR hoped to educate the public. In this regard it enjoyed some success.

Throughout the 1920s, the NBR made its case for movies in its journal *Exceptional Photoplays*, which was renamed in 1926 the *National Board of Review Magazine*. The group continued to review hundreds of films each year as a service to the public rather than to the film industry, cultivating a view of the inherent cultural worth of movies. This long-term commitment to the newest art yielded a critical approach that took films on their own terms. The editors of NBR's journal argued that movies had significance in large part because they were popular, not because they promised to deliver a fine art experience to the masses. NBR did not expect movie magic to enlighten audiences, only to entertain millions week after week. Progressives scoffed that NBR lacked any identifiable social mission; censors condemned its work as less than effective, naive, and wrongheaded. Of course, for the large audience watching movies, NBR's approach made sense — after all it merged an aesthetic appreciation of movies as dramas with accounting for popular appreciation of those dramas.

NBR's editors and writers were not the only critics thinking along these lines; they were, though, an important part of a movement that offered a way to respect movies despite the opinions of censors. Historian Andrea Friedman explains that such an approach developed in opposition to the kind of logic employed by censors. In place of the absolute moral authority that had dominated the elite opinion of the nineteenth century (and that had been adopted by movie censors), a positive view of movies offered a more "democratic moral authority," to use Friedman's term. An individual's experience with common or mass culture had value in a democratic society because that individual's opinion had worth in a democracy. Therefore, liking movies did not by default lower one's value as a citizen.

The Critics

As organizations such as the NBR labored to legitimize movies as a respectable experience, a generation of critics began to write unabashedly about movies as significant culture. Prior to the 1940s, there really was no such thing as a film critic. There were, though, writers who looked seriously at many different aspects of U.S. culture, and they often focused on the tremendous influence movies had on life. In his recent volume for the Library of America, Philip Lopate offered a compendium of work of film critics from 1915 to the present. His survey of early film critics included writers of considerable talent who also happened to write about movies. In other words, Lopate could not include those who wrote only about movies because those who did so barely registered a byline — they provided plot summaries and not much else. The first forty years of film criticism was actually dominated by poets such as Vachel Lindsay and Carl Sandburg, playwrights such as Robert Sherwood, and essayists such as H. L. Mencken, Edmund Wilson, Gilbert Seldes, William Troy, and, perhaps the first real film critic, Otis Ferguson. These disparate writers did have one thing in common, though — they all took seriously the idea that the movies had introduced a new kind of artistic spark to U.S. culture.

Gilbert Seldes was among the first and most prolific and influential critics to make this case. His first book, *The Seven Lively Arts* (1924), was a collection of ideas about popular culture that he had tried out first in many of the country's most popular magazines, such as the *Saturday Evening Post*. Thus, Seldes himself stood as a critic who bridged different cultural strata — he was a good writer, well respected for his insights into culture, and he argued that one could appreciate both Charlie Chaplin and the paintings hanging in the Metropolitan Museum of Art without betraying any standard of taste. In short, Seldes "got" the movies: he understood the significance of a fleeting moment because he appreciated what it took to create thousands of fleeting moments that entertained millions of people week after week. Timely culture deserved respect as much as timeless culture, if not exactly in the same terms. "We require arts which specifically refer to our moment," Seldes wrote, "which create the image of our lives. We must have arts which, we feel, are for ourselves alone, which no one before us could have cared for so much, which no one after us will wholly understand." Those "fully civilized" could recognize the high seriousness of fine art and also be able to "appreciate the high levity of the minor arts."

Seldes's essays marked the beginning of film criticism as serious cultural criticism. He not only took movies on their own terms but also made the case that movies had opened up a new avenue for criticism. In effect, his writing on movies made it respectable to be a film critic. If it was possible to create a body of film criticism, was it also possible to give movies an artistic past, thus making them a timeless art?

British writer Iris Barry thought so. Two years after Seldes published *The Seven Lively Arts*, Barry developed an approach to movies that both accounted for their social significance and avoided attaching moral weight to their influence. To her, movies were neither good nor bad in a moral sense; one should not expect either uplift or degradation as inevitable or eventual effects of going to the pictures. Barry's criticism echoed many other critics of the 1920s and 1930s.

But unlike most of her compatriots, Barry's view achieved official recognition from the U.S. cultural elite. In the early 1930s, Barry became the first curator (and in that sense) the founder of New York City's Museum of Modern Art (MOMA) Film Library. Her job was deceptively simple: catalog old films by creating a historical context that would justify their preservation. Barry and her husband, John E. Abbott, had convinced the museum's chief benefactor — the Rockefeller Foundation — to back their ambitious film preservation program. As Barry explained, "There is no body of reference available, no 'sources' to inspire, no heritage other than the most accidental and fragmentary. Makers of films and audiences alike should be enabled to formulate a constructively critical point of view, and to discriminate between what is valid and what is shoddy and corrupt." Thus, Barry hoped, by salvaging what was left of the past of motion pictures, a film library would be a positive influence on both sides of the screen. "A comprehensive film library or any library of films at all must become invaluable historically," she added, "and of major importance in raising both the level of production and appreciation. Unless the better films of the past are preserved no standards are possible." By the end of the 1930s, MOMA's film library had become a national treasure — serving scholars, critics, and the public through its archives and rotating exhibitions on the history of film. Barry and her associates had given motion pictures a tangible, artistic past.

Barry's experiment succeeded in part because the movies themselves offered the most compelling argument for respect. From the widespread introduction of sound in the early 1930s through World

War II, U.S. movies grew to dominate the international market. This happened because of a combination of factors: star power, professional directors, great writers, and a studio system that took advantage of a European market ravaged by two world wars to "steal" talent and sell movies. The results were legendary. In 1939 alone, audiences saw *Gone with the Wind*, *Mr. Smith Goes to Washington*, *The Hunchback of Notre Dame*, *Stagecoach*, *Wuthering Heights*, and *The Wizard of Oz*. Two years later, Orson Welles established a new artistic standard with *Citizen Kane*. The period between 1930 and 1946 is known as the Golden Age of Hollywood; a time when the industry commanded 80 percent of the total entertainment dollars Americans spent each year. By 1946, U.S. movies had enjoyed twenty years of unprecedented success. These movies had hit the cultural trifecta: they were financially successful, wildly popular, and artistically accomplished. And yet, they remained the only U.S. art form subject to prior restraint.

Books, newspapers, and the theater had been completely freed from prior restraint by the 1930s. Newspapers, as organs of the press, were granted First Amendment protection against prior restraint by the Supreme Court in 1931. Allegedly obscene books ran into trouble now and then when John Sumner, Anthony Comstock's disciple and successor at the American Society for the Suppression of Vice, found something objectionable. But even when that happened, Sumner had to mount an after-publication suit to claim that a book, such as James Joyce's *Ulysses*, was obscene. Sumner and his cohorts then had to prove to a judge or a jury that the book in question was actually obscene.

This was far different from the prior restraint practiced on movies at the same time. Of course, Hollywood had little incentive to challenge the status quo — stability meant reliable profits; financial success meant happy directors, stars, studios, and bankers. However, such caution grated against the idea that movies (and by association, moviegoers) deserved more respect. Certainly, the industry cared enough about its product to improve it and keep its consumers happy. And even though movies were censored by the industry's own PCA, great movies were made. Was there a direct relationship between strict control over film content and the long-term artistic worth of the movies? There was in the sense that censorship was part of a system that made movies an efficient and effective business enterprise. The PCA had input throughout the filmmaking process, just as studio bosses did. Moreover, unlike the more traditional notion of the creative process where a single soul expresses itself in a singular act, Hollywood churned out art by committee. The result was movies of various quality—from the awful to the brilliant—in order to satisfy the bottom line rather than pay homage to an abstract notion of art or speech.

Thus, movies existed in a curious dualism. They were art but not in the traditional sense of the term. Hollywood was, as Hortense Powdermaker famously wrote in 1950, a "dream factory." In her scathing assessment of the movie industry, Powdermaker likened Hollywood to a totalitarian state: "In Hollywood, the concept of man as a passive creature to be manipulated extends to those who work for the studios, to personal and social relationships, to the audiences in the theaters, and to the characters in the movies. The basic freedom of being able to choose between alternatives is absent." An esteemed anthropologist, Powdermaker dissected the movie industry and discovered that it operated in a constant state of "crises and continuous anxiety," which prevented people "from thinking" or being able to challenge the authority of the dictators charged with keeping the system afloat. "The result of this overelaboration," she concluded, "is business inefficiency, deep frustration in human relations, and a high number of unentertaining second- and third-rate movies."

No other critic of Hollywood had condemned the industry quite like Powdermaker. Her assessment did have validity, though: Joe Breen was the in-house dictator, controlling content with an iron fist; the Catholic Church was the shadow power behind the Production Code, regulating the moral temper of the industry; the studios were smoothly operating bureaucracies that aspired toward commercial success with ideological devotion; and those who worked for the industry had not merely to follow the Production Code but, with the onset of the cold war and the threat of being blacklisted, had also to champion the industry with a kind of patriotic enthusiasm. Moviegoers—the people—accepted the product Hollywood dished out without so much as a peep. But then crisis struck.

Hollywood in Crisis

Revolutions often occur during periods of rising expectations. This happened in U.S. movie culture during the early postwar years. In the first few years following World War II, events conspired against, though not necessarily within, the Hollywood system. In its heyday, Hollywood had vertically integrated by constructing theaters and creating distributing companies as well as producing the product. To maximize profits, the industry created a system called block booking that required theaters, whether studio-owned or independent, to take blocks of movies sight unseen. A strong "sure seater" like a Mary Pickford or Clark Gable movie would be lumped in with several "B" movies, and the theater owner or manager had to take the entire bunch. In the 1930s, the federal government had initiated antitrust proceedings against the major studios and in 1948, the U.S. Supreme Court ruled on Hollywood's restraint-of-trade practices. In *United States v. Paramount Pictures, Inc. et al.*, the Court upheld the government's position and required the companies named in the suit (often referred to as the Big Five and the Little Three) to divest their theater holdings. This decision (leading to a series of similar rulings) was a shock, though not a fatal one, to the practical collusion among Hollywood's studios. In effect, the studios could no longer own the property that showed their films. This meant that it might become increasingly difficult for Hollywood to produce whatever it wanted and force exhibitors to buy it. The supposed cumulative effect of this antitrust ruling was to force studios to sell each film based on its merits.

The *Paramount* case did little to change the basic calculus of production and distribution, though, because big companies still retained the capital to dominate the industry. Yet *New York Times* film critic Bosley Crowther found hope in the *Paramount* case. Because Justice William O. Douglas had written that he had no doubt that movies were part of the press, the case illustrated that the government could see beyond simply the "commercial aspects . . . [to] a concern of the cultural importance of motion pictures." For the first time, the nation's highest court hinted that movies might be cultural expressions worthy of legal protection in their own right rather than something to protect the public from.

The case also seemed to break the paradigm that Powdermaker had identified—it meant that the monolithic hold Hollywood had on the imagination of moviegoers could no longer be assumed. The industry would be forced to compete not so much for the markets where movies were shown but for the minds of moviegoers in those markets, and in doing so the moviemakers would have to compete among themselves. Theater owners would continue to exhibit studio products, but they could also demand the kind of movies the public wanted to see. Such a prospect altered the relationship between the two sides of the screen. Audience taste began to matter in a different way—not that audiences could dictate what Hollywood made, but the industry had to consider who its audience was and how that audience was changing.

Thus, in the early postwar period, Hollywood had to face the prospect that it could lose its audience. Suburban growth and the rise of a new medium—television—also changed the way people physically went to the movies. Operating in a business climate where competition had not been much of a factor for five decades, Hollywood suddenly found itself rethinking how to retain its customers by working to attract moviegoers.

That meant that Hollywood needed to know and understand moviegoers. In November 1946, the *New York Times* cosponsored a public forum to discuss the topic "Have the Movies Failed Us?" Five panelists, including Bosley Crowther and novelist MacKinlay Kantor, concluded that audience tastes in films had changed because of World War II. The panelists suggested that the public was growing dissatisfied with U.S. movies because those movies had grown distant from the needs and expectations of moviegoers.

The sense that the war had changed the audience was a hard notion to pin down, though. In an exchange between Crowther and British film critic Dudley Carew, the point that seemed to underscore this development was the popular desire for reality. Carew argued in his essay "Hollywood Indicted" that "Hollywood must get back to the first principles of film making and remember she is an American town and not a rootless, stateless, dehumanized machine for the production of rootless, stateless, dehumanized motion pictures. . . . The Hays Office, that absurd Hollywood organization which strains at the gnat of the word 'bastard' and swallows camels laden with sex-ridden celluloid would seem much to blame." Crowther offered a retort in "Hollywood Defended." Crowther didn't so much defend American films as promise that they would get better. He conceded that Hollywood deserved Carew's scorn but added that the industry was not completely to blame since the "mass of movie-goers" had passively accepted what they saw. Crowther assured his readers that things were changing and not least because of the effects of the war both on the audience and on Hollywood filmmakers. "It is hard to imagine," Crowther observed, "such directors as Capra, Wyler, Huston, or Kanin going back to Hollywood to make 'rootless, dehumanized' films. And it is hard to imagine new cinematists trained in the fluid 'action' style forsaking their dynamic techniques." Indeed, as all critics and champions of Hollywood had to acknowledge, the industry had produced the best films the world had ever seen — but it had also produced most of the worst. The question became which tradition Hollywood would and could build upon.

Dorothy Jones thought she knew. As head of the Film Reviewing and Analysis Section of the Office of War Information during World War II, Jones had a unique view of the contributions Hollywood directors made to the war effort. After the war, she wrote in the *Nation*, "Traditional ideas about film-making which have so long governed the motion-picture industry are slowly yielding before the progressive forces." She pointed in particular to "the gradual revision of the stereotyped characterization of minority groups [and] the new effort toward a more realistic portrayal of American life for foreign audiences." Hollywood had not, Jones acknowledged, changed so dramatically that it would turn away from its stock features of musicals, comedies, and westerns, but she also believed based on films released in the early postwar period that the industry had accepted that movies with "serious treatment of social and economic problems" could make money, too.

Moviegoers also responded to the new imperatives of the postwar world. In 1947, the *New York Times* received a spate of letters from moviegoers offering "Free Advice to Hollywood." One wrote: "I think it is a good lesson and potent warning to Hollywood that the critics topped their 1946 ten-best lists with foreign films. Hollywood has been sitting on its laurels for too long, and if it doesn't wake up it will soon find the public clamoring for only English and French films." Sounding a bit desperate, the writer pleaded: "No more 'significant' pictures in which the hero finds his Shangri-La." In another long letter reprinted in the *Times*, a reader sneered that "the movies, with their vulgar and incompetent ways, their sniveling concern with luxury and high-priced entertainment, are drifting further away from human behavior and the true ways of our world." Another advised: "American motion pictures should pause to 'clean house,' offering the public sound movies devoid of pretentious emotion, implausible situations, and annoying heroics." Many letters resounded with a clear preference for films from abroad because they offered a dose of reality and felt more relevant. "Why should we be 'tolerant' of an industry that has unparalleled resources in money, technical equipment, and talent — and yet produces hardly six pictures a year that are not an insult to half-adult intelligence?" "What is wrong," a writer declared, "is the asinine restrictions of the Eric Johnston office [Johnston had succeeded Will Hays at the MPAA in 1945] and the Legion of Decency, which water all adult themes down to the ten-year-old level. The cure is for our producers to ignore these two institutions for unreconstructed prudes and to make pictures for grownups."

Johnston recognized that Americans were "growing up and [that] films needed to catch up with that 'phenomenon.'" Polls suggested movies were becoming the preferred cultural experience of the educated classes. Other trends suggested as much. Memberships to film societies grew dramatically in the early postwar period. The nation's most influential movie market, New York City, was home to dozens of such clubs, including the country's largest one, Cinema 16. Universities and colleges began offering courses in film and, using the holdings of museums such as MOMA, developed a generation of cinephiles.

How would Hollywood respond? In the first few years after the war, movies appeared that did depart from the all-too-cheery fantasy world of the industry's golden years. The industry allowed pictures with a darker, more realistic view of human nature and drama. Genres referred to now as *film noir* and social problem films connected with audiences and film critics. James Agee wrote in 1946 about three crime dramas that he found "much better to watch than the bracing, informative, constructive films which are the only kind . . . progressives would allow, if they were given half a chance." This trend offered creative outlets for genuine auteurs such as Alfred Hitchcock and Orson Welles and gave burgeoning independent directors such as Elia Kazan a way to translate the social realism of the New York stage into Hollywood commercialism. And yet, as interesting as this moment was, Hollywood remained a conservative company town. Throughout the late 1940s, the studios responded more to the domestic anxieties of the cold war than to the creative possibilities of their own talent.

However, Hollywood did not have that same kind of control over foreign films and their distributors. From 1946 to 1947, total revenue earned by foreign films distributed in the United States increased from $5.6 million to $8.01 million. Writing for the *New York Times*, Thomas Pryor reported, "Distributors who have been handling such movies for years frankly admit that their market is bigger now than ever before." He attributed the surge in interest to the success of films such as Roberto Rossellini's *Open City* (1945) and the importance of the New York City market. According to *Variety*, runs in New York City represented 60 percent of the total gross receipts any foreign film could expect. Yet they were still restricted to the art house circuit. "Few foreign films have yet to break into the affiliated circuits," *Variety* noted, "and when they do, it is generally because they have more than critical nods."

The industry journal also speculated that the success of most foreign pictures came from advertising that hinted they were more racy and explicit than the typical Hollywood movies. This was true, according to Joseph Burstyn's business partner, Arthur Mayer: "The only sensational success scored by Burstyn and myself in the fifteen years in which we were engaged in business were with pictures whose artistic and ideological merits were aided and abetted at the box office by their frank sex content."

Moviegoers had reason to expect films to become more frank. Book banning, postal censorship, and theatrical program shutdowns were becoming relics of history. In the mid-1930s, as Americans watched the Nazis burning thousands of books, the idea of banning books for all because their content might be inappropriate for some looked antidemocratic and downright authoritarian. A few years later, in the midst of the U.S. war against fascism, the Supreme Court ended Anthony Comstock's reign of freewheeling postal censorship when it freed *Esquire* magazine to be sent through the U.S. mail. The postmaster general could no longer stop publications just because he found them personally offensive. Theater censorship, which had never been conducted in the United States under any system of prior restraint, seemed to fade after the 1920s, with only sporadic attempts to shut down individual performances through the 1940s and early 1950s.

At least partially in response to some moviegoers' quest for more frank and candid films, between 1946 and 1949 the number of foreign film importers and distributors increased from twenty-five to sixty-two. Moreover, some regular theater owners were also taking advantage of the foreign film boom. Charles Skouras, a big-time distributor, owned sixty-two neighborhood theaters in New York City, and by 1947 had responded to changes in audience taste by running foreign films on double bills with Hollywood pictures. The manager of the Bijou Theater in lower Manhattan actually cancelled his booking of the quite popular *Best Years of Our Lives* in favor of a French film. Media historian Barbara Wilensky explains: "Art films . . . were seen to offer two very different alternatives to Hollywood cinema. On the one hand, art cinema was seen as 'noncommercial' and artistically motivated, offering an escape from the brash commercialism of Hollywood. On the other hand, some critics depicted the art cinema industry as actually more vulgar in its commercialism than Hollywood, willing to take advantage of any sexual angle to attract an audience."

Of course, foreign films alone were not going to remake U.S. movie culture, which continued to be dominated by Hollywood. But a storm was brewing in the early postwar period that divided movie culture into two unequal parts. The dominant part of movie culture stayed beholden to the industry mind-set, remaining uncontroversial and lucrative. The other part existed outside the industry, antagonizing the mainstream view of U.S. films by propounding a view that films were art and as such had to serve a different function in society. This secondary movie culture was both related to and discordant with the mainstream industry. This was not the avant-garde or underground cinema, but an alternative movie culture close enough to the mainstream in ideas and function to want to challenge Hollywood's dominance. In an article for the *New York Times Magazine* in August 1947, Bosley Crowther illustrated this point. Crowther noted in an essay entitled "Hollywood v. New York" that "it is reasonably charged that our movies are unimaginative and standardized because the people who make them live concentrated, insular lives." But he suggested that as realism in movies grew more prevalent through the importation of foreign films, especially from Italy and England, the popular audience would come to expect similar content from Hollywood. He concluded that "some decentralization must take place if Hollywood's pictures are not to descend to an even lower level."

Crowther hoped for some creative destruction. He had championed foreign films and decried censorship, whether by the industry or by the government. He cheered when the Supreme Court took on industry collusion in the *Paramount* case, and was appalled by the chilling effect the postwar red scare had on the artistic integrity of the film industry. Yet Crowther was no radical. He liked most Hollywood productions, and praised only those foreign films that appealed to his liberal sensibilities. His positions on issues in movie culture served as an interesting barometer — he was the critic the middle-class, liberal moviegoers liked best. Thus it was no small matter when Crowther began to champion Joseph Burstyn's approach to films. In 1949, a case emerged that brought together all the major elements of the alternative movie culture — a film, its distributor, and a critic who supported them — and revealed the potential for a sea change in mainstream movies.

The Bicycle Thief

Joseph Burstyn bought the rights to *The Bicycle Thief* from Italian director Vittorio de Sica in 1949. Although de Sica's film had little in common with typical Hollywood fare — it was realistic, gritty, and shot in grainy black and white — Burstyn had developed a keen eye for the kind of picture that, with the proper marketing campaign, could score a financial and critical success at least in the New York

City market. The picture opened in December 1949 at Manhattan's World Theatre, and in the first five weeks of its run grossed more than any previous foreign film. In short, audiences loved it.

So did critics, who cheered it as "remarkable and moving." *The Bicycle Thief* tells the grim story of life in immediate post–World War II Italy. Its hero, a day laborer desperately trying to land a steady job in Rome, finally finds work as a poster hanger, but he must have a bicycle or he cannot take the job. Hocking his family's few pathetic heirlooms, he purchases a bicycle and sets off on his first day of work only to have the bike stolen. He and his six-year-old son frantically search for the bicycle thief but to no avail. In a final, terrible act of despair, the father steals another bicycle, losing his dignity, his pride, and, he fears, the love of his son. It was a shockingly realistic movie of postwar European life.

Commonweal called the plot as "realistically simple (and complicated) as life." Its reviewer concluded that "*The Bicycle Thief* is a well-rounded slice of life, and as a movie it is a gem of understanding." John Mason Brown, writing in the popular *Saturday Review*, related that because the film's realism appeared so "unposed and uncontrived," the understated tone of the picture had "power by making everything exceptional in it appear to be average." Such vision eluded U.S. filmmakers, he wrote, because "Hollywood, even in its most courageous moments, approaches our very real, though dissimilar, problems in terms of make-believe. Instead of showing things as they are, it puts on a show."

The success of *The Bicycle Thief* attracted the attention of Warner Brothers, one of Hollywood's movie conglomerates, which hoped to book the film for its theaters in other cities. Like other Burstyn-imported Italian films that had previously enjoyed modest success in the United States, *Paisan* (1946) and *Open City* (1945), *The Bicycle Thief* was a good bet for Burstyn. But with this film Burstyn actually had a shot at national distribution. Burstyn might have been an importer of foreign films, but his ultimate goal was to bring artistic films to a wide audience.

Abiding by the industry's rules, Burstyn mailed a print of the film to the PCA. On January 31, 1950, Joe Breen told Burstyn he had to cut the film, citing two scenes in particular, one that showed the young son attempting to relieve himself on a wall and another of a brief and quite innocent look inside a brothel. These cuts were typical of Breen's style. As Leonard Leff and Jerold Simmons explain in their history of the PCA, Breen "simply believed . . . that if he ever allowed even the most innocent of toilet gags, unscrupulous producers would flood the screen with them." Unfortunately, what he refused to consider was the broader meaning of the scene: for the entire day, the father had been so desperately determined to find the bicycle thief that he had completely forgotten about the most basic needs of his young son, who, not wanting to burden his father further, had taken upon himself the solution to his problem. This was hardly a "toilet gag," but that did not matter to Joseph Breen.

On de Sica's orders, Burstyn refused to make the cuts. A man who valued film art, Burstyn also appreciated what a little controversy might mean to the success of the movie. Throughout 1950, while a contest of wills thrust the small Italian film into the spotlight, Burstyn ran ads in New York City papers capitalizing on the PCA's attempts to censor the film. One advertisement for the film used an oversized cartoon depicting the son in his controversial pose: with his back to readers, he declares, "I'm the kid they tried to cut out of *Bicycle Thief* . . . but couldn't!" Under the film's title are the series of awards won by the film, including an Oscar in 1949, the "Best Foreign Film of the Year" from the New York Film Critics Circle, and the National Board of Review's top prize as the "Best Film of the Year." Elsewhere, ads for the World Theatre presented little Bruno in one of his tragic scenes seeming to look up at a statement that reads "Please don't let them cut me out of . . . *Bicycle Thief*" (with the title in full movie announcement type). This was, the World announced, "the prize picture they want to censor!" But if people came to the World, they would see the "uncensored version!" of the movie playing for its "sixth month!" For anyone living in New York City or anywhere close to it, it would have been hard to avoid knowing about de Sica's film. What had so bothered Breen had not raised an eyebrow among New York's censors. *The Bicycle Thief* had been awarded an exhibition license, and the Legion of Decency had given the film a "B" rating, meaning that it was "objectionable in part" but contained nothing to condemn outright. Even politicians typically hostile to the movies came out in favor of it. Colorado Senator Edwin C. Johnson, who just a few months later would propose federal licensing for people making movies to "protect public morals," said *The Bicycle Thief* was "the most fascinating and engrossing picture" he had ever seen.

With critical and commercial success and tacit approval from other censors, Burstyn challenged Breen's ruling by appealing to the MPAA, the only appeals process available once the PCA had denied a code seal. Burstyn carried with him letters from Bosley Crowther and Elmer Rice, a playwright who wrote to the MPAA on behalf of the American Civil Liberties Union National Council on Freedom from Censorship. Breen sat back and let the officials of the MPAA do their jobs. The industry sided with Breen and quashed a controversy sparked by a small-time distributor over a film that wasn't even American.

That decision provoked Crowther to issue his most public and pointed attack on censorship to date. In many ways it was the article that established Crowther as a genuine defender of what he came to call "freedom of the screen." He wanted his readers to understand that the PCA's refusal to give a seal to *The Bicycle Thief* was indefensible. He acknowledged that Hollywood had entered a difficult time — falling ticket sales, congressional investigations, Court-mandated divestment, and renewed calls for national censorship had studio bosses scrambling for shelter. But Crowther argued that this decision was "indicative of industry thinking" and demanded scrutiny. The MPAA, Crowther declared, "illustrates the sort of resistance to liberalization or change that widely and perilously oppresses the whole industry today. And even though some may think this a minor and unimportant case it plainly is representative of a major attitude. More than a question of morals is involved in *The Bicycle Thief.*"

Indeed, Crowther had picked up on the way the controversy over *The Bicycle Thief* operated not just in opposition to Hollywood but despite Hollywood. The reception of the film was an indication that control over movie culture did not necessarily rest exclusively within Hollywood. The movie industry knew that its dominance came in part from popular apathy — audiences accepted what Hollywood produced. But what if audiences chose differently? What if other options appeared — as they had begun to in the postwar period — and audiences simply disregarded mainstream cinema? Although a complete turnabout in popular tastes was unlikely, any successful challenge to the status quo in movie culture would have sharp reverberations. Joseph Breen knew this.

Breen was in fact stung by the fight with Burstyn. Hollywood's chief censor sensed a dangerous development brewing in his motion picture world. An associate of Breen's reinforced those suspicions: "*The Bicycle Thief* is a trial balloon rather than a case in its own right," Fred Niblo believed. "Evidently it has the backing or blessing of some people in the studios who have lent themselves, consciously or stupidly, to the role of boring from within. It may well be that this is only the first round of a bigger fight." Joseph Burstyn and his new ally Bosley Crowther certainly hoped so.

CHAPTER 3

The Miracle on West 58th Street

If *The Bicycle Thief* was a rehearsal, Burstyn's next import was the real thing. Who was this man bedeviling Joe Breen and the Production Code?

Joseph Burstyn was a Polish immigrant who believed passionately in U.S. democratic ideals. He had come to the United States in 1921 as a diamond polisher, but he had too much entrepreneurial spirit to follow that trade for long. So he started moonlighting as a publicity agent for the Yiddish theater. The day his ambition meshed with movies, he found his niche. In 1930, he borrowed $500 and rented the Folk Theater to show *A Jew at War*. After a sixteen-day run, he had cleared $2,500 in profit: the seed money to start his own film importation business. Over the next six years he was to learn, though, just how weak the U.S. market for foreign films could be. But he slowly and carefully built both his business and his reputation. In 1936 he joined forces with the irrepressible Arthur Mayer, a New York theater manager, and by the late 1930s, they were highly respected in what Burstyn called the "heartbreaking and fascinating" business of film importation. Interested only in fine foreign films over his twenty-year career, Burstyn imported many prizewinners, including *Club de Femmes, Open City, Paisan, The Bicycle Thief,* and *Miracle at Milan.*

Burstyn passionately loved movies, and hoped to produce his own someday. Film critic Thomas Pryor described him as "a short man, slight of frame, [with] finely chiseled features topped by a shock of wavy gray hair." He had, said Pryor, "a passionate affection for the film medium and a philosopher's outlook on life." Mayer used similar language to describe Burstyn as "a man absolutely enamored of film" and "a very fine judge of film art." Mayer also revealed that Burstyn's adoration of movies led him to adopt some unusual business methods. Typically, according to Mayer, he would "fall in love with a picture, and when he was in love with that picture, it was like being in love with a woman; nothing else mattered." His devotion to the film of the moment was so intense that he would, to Mayer's dismay, ignore other movies in their inventory that were still capable of making money. When Burstyn was smitten by a particular film, Mayer had to "tiptoe around the stricken lover trying to carry on a hushed business having to do with matters out of his current world: trivia such as rival pictures which were competing with us, pictures which we were contemplating handling (or had been contemplating before Cupid conked him on the head), and pictures which Burstyn had once been in love with and which, with a little attention, were still capable of paying box office returns." Clearly, this was a man to whom film art was important, someone who would take censor interference as an insult to be fought.

In 1948 Burstyn fell in love with *Il Miracolo* (*The Miracle*). Roberto Rossellini and Federico Fellini's short but powerful film had been a flop in Italy. But that would have been of little concern to Burstyn; he loved it and that was all that mattered. Burstyn's purchase of the U.S. distribution rights gave the filmmakers a second chance at breaking even. Based on what Rossellini had to say about the controversy later, he had not foreseen that *The Miracle* could be denounced as godless, communist, anti-Catholic, antiwoman propaganda. Nor did Rossellini or Burstyn imagine that the movie had the power to become the central character in a religious-cultural-political brawl that simultaneously ended the thirty-seven-year roadblock of the *Mutual* decision and opened a thirteen-year legal struggle over prior restraint and the scope of the First Amendment.

While Burstyn was discovering *Il Miracolo* in Venice, back home in the United States a new era of speech restriction had begun. In the first half of the twentieth century, Americans had had a roller coaster relationship with the ideal of free speech. During World War I, free speech came under attack. Congress and the president instituted a rampage of speech restriction under the Espionage Act that continued at the end of the war and was strengthened during the ensuing red scare with the addition of the Sedition Act. Thousands of radicals were arrested — many on flimsy evidence of their potential harm — and at least 1,000 were convicted for the expression of dissident opinions. Hundreds were deported. Restriction on speech, which in the Progressive Era had seemed such a good idea — a democratic ideal for the benefit of society — began to look downright antidemocratic by 1920. When the excesses of these red scare prosecutions calmed down, many Americans performed a sort of civic soul searching and reconsidered whether government should be in the business of suppressing countermajoritarian views. At this point, free speech became what Paul Murphy has called "a fine, generally disembodied shibboleth in which everyone believed." In the next decade, however, the rise of repressive, fascist regimes in Europe caused many to view U.S. free speech rights in a new light, and to disavow intolerance of dissent. Widely publicized Nazi book-burnings illuminated the need to watch for such tendencies at home. When strikes broke out across the United States in the early years of the Depression, the response was a call for tolerance rather than repression. In fact, as Reuel Schiller has shown, a tactic often used to encourage state courts and the Supreme Court to protect individual rights against the police power of the state was to raise "the specter of totalitarianism." This new atmosphere had a profound effect on the Supreme Court. Both a majority of the justices and the populace seemed to favor expansion of free speech rights. The defense of free speech assumed the level of a "national cause," according to Richard Steele. So, when the Court offered to serve as a national monitor over free speech issues, some significant advances were made toward the protection of individual liberties during the New Deal decade. But with the end of World War II and the rapid expansion of the Soviet Union into the countries of Eastern Europe, many became convinced that the Soviets were bent on worldwide domination. A second red scare began, tolerance of dissent again weakened, and the Court retreated from its speech-protective role.

Hoping to appear tough on infiltrating communists, President Truman ordered a new loyalty oath program for government employees in 1947. Not to be outdone, three years later Congress passed the McCarran Act, a bill that required registration of all subversive groups (so designated by the Senate Internal Security Subcommittee and the Federal Bureau of Investigation [FBI]). Free speech activists such as Zechariah Chafee grew alarmed. Since both the president and Congress had fallen into communist hysteria mode, Chafee looked to the courts as the last hope. When in 1951 the Supreme

Court upheld a 1940 law that made it illegal to advocate the teaching of communist philosophy, Chafee despaired even of that last resort. As Professor Ralph Brown wrote in 1958, "of the majority that had exalted the freedoms of the First Amendment death had removed three (Stone, Murphy, and Rutledge), time had modified the convictions of two (Frankfurter and Jackson); only Justices Black and Douglas pursued an unswerving course." The First Amendment now meant, Chafee wrote, that "Congress shall make no law abridging the freedom of speech and of the press unless Congress does make a law abridging the freedom of speech and of the press." Freedom of speech was not at a high point in U.S. legal culture when Burstyn returned home with *The Miracle.*

Back in New York City, Burstyn did what all movie distributors did to get theater bookings: he submitted the film to the New York State censors. It passed. But for some unknown reason, Burstyn did not book the movie. A year later, he dusted it off and packaged it with two other shorts—Marcel Pagnol's *Jofroi* and Jean Renoir's *A Day in the Country*—and titled the triptych *Ways of Love.* The censors had no problem with *Ways of Love* or any of its three components and duly issued the necessary license. Burstyn settled in for what he expected to be a modestly profitable run at New York's Paris Theatre.

After opening night on December 12, 1950, most critics praised *Ways of Love*, and some particularly praised *The Miracle.* Making no mention of possible interpretational problems, Wanda Hale of the New York *Daily News* called *The Miracle* "Forty-one minutes of unrelieved tragedy. . . . Artistic and beautifully done." Frank Quinn of the *Daily Mirror* called Magnani's performance as the homeless woman "phenomenal." Seymour Peck of the *Daily Compass* thanked Burstyn for "two hours of uncommon fare." *Ways of Love* was, he said, "an unusually intelligent and fascinating experience in moviegoing." The *New Yorker*'s reviewer said it was a picture that "almost everyone will enjoy."

A few reviewers, though, mentioned almost parenthetically that to some religious groups, the film might appear a mockery of the virgin birth. Even the laudatory Bosley Crowther was concerned. Although it seemed to him "just a vastly compassionate comprehension of the suffering and the triumph of birth," he also noted that the story "with its symbolic parallels, might by some be considered a blasphemy of the doctrine of the Virgin Birth. . . . It might also be considered a mockery of religious faith." An anonymous *Newsweek* reviewer worried that it would be "strong medicine for most American audiences." That, as it turned out, was putting it mildly. Within days powerful Catholics in New York City, including the license commissioner and the Legion of Decency, attacked Burstyn's little film.

Alerted by the Legion of Decency, Commissioner of Licenses Edward T. McCaffrey went to see *The Miracle* and was horrified. He notified the management of the Paris Theatre on December 22 that he found *The Miracle* "officially and personally blasphemous," and ordered that it be removed from *Ways of Love* or the theater would lose its operating license. New York's license commissioners had been able to make and carry out such threats for decades. Although there was no specific statutory authority for the license commissioner to police movie morals, it was understood that a theater could be shut down for immorality or offense to the public good. Local courts had always backed up the license commissioners when this authority had been questioned.

McCaffrey and some other Catholics viewed *The Miracle*'s plot as a mockery of the virgin birth. But much of the virulent reaction also stemmed from American Catholic fury at its maker, Rossellini. A year before, while filming *Stromboli*, he had had a well-publicized affair with Americans' favorite film nun, Ingrid Bergman. When Bergman left her husband and child to have Rossellini's baby, it became a major international scandal. The uproar was so intense that state and local film censors were besieged by letters demanding that *Stromboli* be banned (although there was nothing remotely objectionable in the movie itself). The threat of federal censorship loomed once again as Colorado Senator Edwin Johnson called for legislation that would have required federal licensing of all filmmakers and actors. Appalled by news stories about Rossellini and Bergman's adultery, Johnson called for an investigation into Hollywood's "exploitation of immorality." The senator demanded "a method whereby the mad dogs of the industry may be put on a leash to protect public morals." Clearly, 1950 was no time for a Rossellini film that American Catholics might interpret as insulting to their faith.

McCaffrey's threat to shut down the Paris Theatre was a major blow to Burstyn, a small distributor with a large financial investment in *Ways of Love*. He conferred with the managing director of the Paris, Lillian Gerard, who had reluctantly removed *The Miracle* from *Ways of Love* for two scheduled performances the afternoon of McCaffrey's threat. When Burstyn reminded her of their contract, she happily agreed to restore *The Miracle*, and it was shown twice that night. That got McCaffrey's attention, and he suspended the theater's license.

McCaffrey was messing with no ordinary theater, though. The Paris had been built two years before by the Pathé Company, a French film producer and distributor, as a venue to showcase the best European films. Its audience, according to Gerard, consisted of "snobs," those who disdained U.S. films, and who demanded art when they went to the movies. The Paris was a taste leader in the city that was the trendsetter in foreign film viewing. Its managing director, Gerard, was more than someone who unlocked the doors and turned on the projector. She was a confirmed cinephile with a degree in English literature, completely devoted to the study of motion pictures as art, and just as completely dedicated to fighting censorship.

McCaffrey's action just seemed wrong to Gerard and to Burstyn. The difficulties with Breen over *The Bicycle Thief* had involved the private censoring arrangements of the MPAA. But *The Miracle* was duly licensed by the censors of New York State — twice. Burstyn was deliberative by nature, rarely prone to rash acts. According to Gerard, who knew him well, "he would worry himself into acute anxiety before he made a move, and when he did move, he moved like the chess player who always expects defeat." Although Burstyn's lawyers urged caution, Gerard was itching for a fight and was grateful for the attention of a *New York Times* reporter named Richard Parke. He and his editor wanted to know why *The Miracle* had been removed from the screen, and Gerard wanted people to know about the license commissioner's interference. So she revealed what had happened.

The next day, Christmas Eve, 1950, readers found a front-page story in the *Times*: "Rossellini Film Is Halted by the City: *The Miracle* Held Blasphemous." As Gerard later related, "New Yorkers learned from this front-page story that the license commissioner, a man who issued licenses to bowling alleys, laundries, . . . and newlyweds, had taken it upon himself to become a film critic." As Gerard put it, "he had decided that *The Miracle* was unfit for the eyes of all other New Yorkers and thus declared it verboten."

On Christmas Day, Burstyn got a one-two punch: first McCaffrey extended the license removal threat from the Paris to any theater that might consider booking the film; then the Legion of Decency published its rating of *Ways of Love* — C for condemned, the first film the Legion had designated as sacrilegious. As if jumping to its feet in reaction, the New York Civil Liberties Union (NYCLU) offered its considerable legal aid to any theater willing to defy McCaffrey's ban. But no one else stepped forward.

Burstyn, joined by the Paris Theatre, initiated legal action to enjoin McCaffrey's ability to strip theater licenses for showing *The Miracle*. The NYCLU and the New York film critics association were both eager to chip in. The NYCLU contributed an amicus brief for Burstyn's challenge in the New York Supreme Court. The film critics, after a thirteen-to-three vote, sent Mayor Vincent Impellitteri a telegram: "The New York Film Critics protest the suppression of the film *The Miracle* by the New York City Commissioner Edward T. McCaffrey. The suppressive action, we feel, is symptomatic of a growing tendency toward dangerous censorship of the content of films." The critics' next contribution was to name *Ways of Love* the best foreign film of 1950.

But this move set off another uproar and more Catholic pressure. Prominent lay Catholic Martin Quigley knew that the film critics were planning to hold their annual awards ceremony at Radio City Music Hall. Quigley told the management that if it allowed the hall to be used for the New York Film Critics Circle awards, it would incur the disfavor of the Catholic Church and could expect a boycott. The Right Reverend Monsignor Walter P. Kellenberg, reached by phone for comment, backed up Quigley's assertion. Not wanting to damage Radio City, the film critics voluntarily changed the location for the awards ceremony. Accepting the award at the hastily rescheduled ceremony at the Rainbow Room, Burstyn acknowledged the ruckus he was causing. He managed to keep his cool, but his message was blunt. He told the critics and stars, "Perhaps I should apologize. Perhaps I brought some embarrassment to some of you. I'm not sorry, but I apologize anyhow." Then he jabbed at McCaffrey,

Kellenberg, and Quigley: "I accept the award as a tribute to the integrity of people who really care about films, as a symbol of the truth cherished by all Americans."

At first it seemed that Burstyn was not alone and that the motion picture industry was gearing up to help tackle the license commissioner. Luminaries such as actor Vincent Price, director/producer King Vidor, and screenwriter/director Joseph Manckiewicz spoke out against McCaffrey's act. The trade publication *Variety* reported that "industryites were unanimous over the long Christmas weekend in promising support to the theatre and Burstyn in a 'full-scale legal fight.'" But no support materialized, and the possibility of a unified industry—namely the Motion Picture Association of America (MPAA)—facing off against the Catholic pressure and the license commissioner was not to be.

Film critics and newspaper editors, though, were determined to help Burstyn's cause, and began churning out columns and opinion pieces. "The issue," the *New York Post* editorialized, "is not whether the film is a triumph or a turkey; the issue is whether the city License Commissioner is empowered and/or qualified to decide what films are fit for the eyes of New York." The *New Republic* took issue with McCaffrey's allegation that the movie was blasphemous: "To blaspheme is to revile or curse the Deity, and *The Miracle*, whatever its shortcomings, is a powerful statement of the mercy and peace that God bestows on His most unhappy and forsaken children. If the Commissioner is setting himself up as a one-man inquisition, he should consult a dictionary before handing down any more bulls." Max Lerner of the *New York Post* found the real blasphemy in McCaffrey's assumption of "Godlike powers of decision for the rest of us."

Burstyn got a temporary injunction, and *The Miracle* resumed its place in *Ways of Love* at the Paris. Lines snaked around the block despite the wintry weather. The audiences came, Gerard reported, "as if we were giving away a glass of champagne with each ticket." That week the Paris accommodated more patrons than it ever had or would again until it showed *The Exorcist* in 1973.

If Gerard and Burstyn thought they could relax, they were badly mistaken. On December 31, all the major New York City papers carried official words of condemnation from the Archdiocese of New York. Monsignor Kellenberg denounced *The Miracle* as "an open insult to the faith of millions of people in this city and hundreds of millions throughout the world." When Legion reviewers had first seen Rossellini's film in Venice, at the same time Burstyn did, they had found it blasphemous. According to Alan Westin's account of the *Miracle* case, the Legion reviewers had warned Burstyn in Venice against any U.S. distribution of the film. Now it seemed that warning was proving prophetic.

Five days into the new year of 1951, New York Supreme Court Justice Aron Steuer stopped McCaffrey by granting Burstyn's request for an injunction. In doing so, Steuer overturned decades of precedent in favor of the license commissioner's power over movie content. Only once in thirty-five years had a New York City court failed to uphold the license commissioner's authority to shut down a film he found objectionable. Just four years before *Burstyn*, a similar case had come before the same court courtesy of the flamboyant maverick filmmaker Howard Hughes. His notorious film *The Outlaw* had been shut down by order of McCaffrey's predecessor, Benjamin Fielding. Judge Bernard Shientag at that time ruled that Fielding had been perfectly justified when he threatened the license of any theater that dared to show *The Outlaw*, despite its Motion Picture Division license. In doing so, Judge Shientag was following a long tradition of upholding New York City's license commissioners' interference with movies.

Six months after Shientag's decision, a similar case reached another New York Supreme Court judge in Rochester. There, the city's commissioner of public safety had shuttered a theater that was showing another duly licensed film, *Forever Amber*. But the Rochester justice's ruling was the opposite of the New York City ruling. Justice Warner disagreed with Shientag's position and found the situation quite clear-cut. He ruled unequivocally that state law necessarily supersedes local regulation: "Where any conflict exists between the licensing by the State of New York of any motion picture and the regulation and direction thereof by any Ordinance of the City of Rochester, that Ordinance must, as a matter of law, yield to the provisions of the statutory law of the State and that the Laws of the State shall have preference and supersede local ordinances."

Relying on the precedent of the upstate court, and noting that the state legislature had recently prohibited criminal prosecution for exhibition of a licensed motion picture, Steuer ruled that only the state censors had the authority to decide the fitness of any film and that the license commissioner had overstepped his bounds. With the commissioner's censorial wings clipped, *The Miracle* continued to play to overflow crowds. But Steuer's opinion would prove to be a mixed blessing for Burstyn. Although Steuer had stopped McCaffrey, he had also opened the door for an appeal to the regents to revoke the license. Indeed, the opinion even suggests such action. Steuer ended with nods to both sides of the controversy over *The Miracle*:

> The commissioner of licenses is not the protector from affronts of a large portion of our citizens or even of all of them. They can protect themselves first by ignoring the exhibition, and secondly any individual can seek to have the Board of Regents revoke its permit, or if he can show that the license was granted through an abuse of power, he will find the court just as ready to relieve against such an abuse as it is to restrain this one.

Burstyn won, the license commissioner lost (despite an appeal), and *The Miracle* was replaced in *Ways of Love*. But all was not well. Twenty-three years later Lillian Gerard wrote an article about the *Miracle* controversy. She never could have guessed at the time, she wrote, what lay ahead, "what ugliness, what fury, what duplicity would envelop us all in the name of patriotism, all rooted in Puritanism, an Armageddon to prove the inviolability of censorship."

The "fury" was, indeed, just beginning. Two days after Steuer's ruling, the real attack on *The Miracle* began. That Sunday, January 7, 1951, Cardinal Spellman wrote a pastoral letter to be read in all churches of the diocese condemning *The Miracle* as a "diabolical deception" that was insulting to Italian women. Spellman called on all 26 million American Catholics to boycott the movie and any theater that dared to play this piece of "art at its lowest." Calling *The Miracle* a "despicable affront to every Christian," he asked "all right-thinking citizens" to join him in working to change the law that allowed the Board of Regents to license such a "perversion."

This was early 1951, the height of the cold war — two years after the "loss" of China to communism, after the United States had lost its atomic monopoly and the Soviet Union was developing a nuclear arsenal. The United States was embroiled with (and losing to) North Korean communists and worried about internal communists and Russian spies. Spellman made sure to equate *The Miracle* with "atheistic communism," the goal of which was to "divide and demoralize Americans so that the minions of Moscow might enslave this land of liberty." The movie that had so captivated Burstyn two years earlier had now become the center of anticommunist propaganda in his home city of New York. It had become the perfect vehicle for Catholics to proclaim their patriotism through anticommunist rhetoric.

That evening, picketers surrounded the Paris Theatre with signs reading "Don't enter that cesspool," "Don't look at that filth," and "Don't be a communist — all the communists are inside." Others read "This picture is an insult to every decent woman and her mother," and "From the cesspool of Italy comes *The Miracle* of blasphemy." And another, "Communists hate religion. Communists like this picture." Passersby were handed catechism-like flyers:

Question: Can you give me one good reason why I shouldn't go see the picture?

Answer: What now happens to us may someday happen to your Belief. If you give your O.K. to antireligious pictures by patronizing them, then don't be surprised if a picture is made attacking your own religion.

Question: I saw the picture and I didn't see anything wrong with it.

Answer: Nobody knows the Catholic religion better than Catholics themselves and they are therefore better able to know what is attacking their Belief.

Question: I am a Catholic and I like the picture.

Answer: You are evidently either ignorant of the teachings of our Church or you are actually defying our Church and are then not a real Catholic. Since the Church has condemned the picture, you are therefore disqualifying yourself as a Catholic by acting contrary to what the Church has told you.

The picketers, often 200 at a time (mostly members of the Catholic War Veterans, of which McCaffrey was a national commander) remained on the sidewalk in front of the Paris Theatre for three weeks. Altogether, 15,000 had pledged to serve on the picket line. Sometimes they were joined by two pro-*Miracle* picketers whose signs read "Jesus taught compassion, not condemnation," "Let him who has not sinned cast the first stone," and "We protest censorship: Let the people decide!" On one Sunday, January 14, nearly 1,000 members of the Union of the Holy Name Society joined in. To Crowther, the picketing was the worst part of the ever-widening controversy. It was growing loud and ugly. Hoping for an injunction against the picketers, Burstyn and his attorney, Ephraim London, planned to film and tape-record the sounds one night, but when they arrived with their equipment, there were only a few silent pickets. London was convinced then that their phones were being tapped.

Protestors found other ways to interfere. The Paris Theatre received several anonymous bomb threats starting on January 20, 1951, each time causing the theater to be emptied and searched only to find no bomb. And by the last two weeks in January, the harassment became official. The theater was repeatedly hassled by city officials, along with the fire department, looking for any minor infraction. The *New York Post* editors were appalled: "When fire chiefs become movie censors, we can all start running, not walking, to the nearest exit."

Some of this newfound official interest in the Paris Theatre no doubt came from Spellman's connections within city government. Spellman's biographer John Cooney sees nothing surprising in the city fire department's new zeal for safety at the Paris. The fire chief was Catholic, the mayor was Catholic, the frustrated license commissioner was Catholic. City officials, Cooney writes, "flew to Spellman's causes like pigeons to bread crumbs." Catholics had been in control of the city's government "for as long as anyone could remember." When Spellman called for a boycott, it was certain that city officials would do whatever they could to assist.

City interference also may have been inspired by a press conference Burstyn called the day after Spellman's command to boycott. The press conference was well attended and well reported. In prepared remarks, Burstyn pointed out that if *The Miracle* was sacrilegious, it had not appeared that way in Italy where it had been passed by the Italian censor board (which was responsible both to the

Catholic Church and to Italy's 99.6 percent Catholic population). Moreover, a review of the film in the Vatican's own newspaper had categorized *The Miracle* as having "passages of undoubted cinematic distinction," and concluded, "We continue to believe in Rossellini's art and we look forward to his next achievement." Burstyn waved an affidavit from the director of the Venice Film Festival stating that he saw no blasphemy in the film. "In the twenty years that I have been engaged in the distribution and presentation of foreign motion pictures to the American public," Burstyn said, "my primary consideration in the selection of films has been the artistic merit of the picture. That was my sole criterion in the selection of *The Miracle*." Moreover, he said, his opinion had been validated by the critics. He went on to praise Steuer's decision against the license commissioner because it removed the threat of "one-man rule" over films, and he concluded, "If we permit one person or one group to direct us what to see or not to see, then our basic constitutional liberties will have been abridged." During questioning, Burstyn insisted that both Spellman and the Legion of Decency had the right to express their views on any picture, but, he said, they did not have the right to demand increased governmental censorship or to set themselves up as censors. "There seems to me to be a motive behind this big ado," Burstyn continued. "The Legion has been quite harsh — quite tough — on films coming in from Europe. It is my impression that the Legion is trying to establish itself as the official censor of the City of New York." He went on to accuse the Legion of "completely disregarding the culture of other countries and . . . the intelligence of the American people." Such language would not have been well received in certain circles of the city's government.

Burstyn may have gone on the offensive against the cardinal, but not so Rossellini. He sent a "deferential" telegram, expressing "profound sorrow" that Spellman had so strenuously condemned his film. Trying to explain his purpose in making *The Miracle*, he said that the film shows that "men are still without pity because they have not gone back to God. But God is already present in the faith, however confused, of that poor persecuted woman and since God is wherever a human being suffers and is misunderstood, the miracle occurs when at the birth of the child the poor demented woman regains sanity in her maternal love." Spellman was not moved.

Although many were publicly jumping on the anti-*Miracle* bandwagon, some groups in the city were refusing to accept Catholic pressure. A few Protestant ministers spoke out against Spellman's intimidation attempt. The Reverend Karl M. Chworowsky of the Flatbush Unitarian Church issued a blunt retaliatory statement: "As a Protestant and as a religious liberal of the Christian persuasion, I resent a public statement calling the Catholics of the nation 'the guardians of the moral law,' and I further and deeply resent the insinuation of the Cardinal that everyone not sharing his opinions regarding *The Miracle* is thereby classified as an indecent person." Two days later, prominent Protestant clergy and laypeople sent a telegram to the Motion Picture Division, now under pressure to rescind Burstyn's license for the film. The Protestants' message insisted that "the Roman Catholic Church has no legal or moral right to attempt to force its views on the state as a whole." Another telegram signed by playwrights, novelists, theater producers, and members of the Authors' League of America (including Eugene O'Neill and Henry Steele Commager) urged the censors to stick with their original determination on *The Miracle*.

These telegrams came, no doubt, in response to a new tack taken by the church. In the previous month, as we have seen, the Legion of Decency had tried to shut down *The Miracle* by rating the movie "C" for condemned. Spellman and much of the Catholic press had tried to get the film pulled, but the Supreme Court of New York had thwarted those attempts. The Catholic War Veterans had tried to intimidate people from seeing *The Miracle*, but had succeeded only in boosting box office receipts. So now the political arm of the church went to work. The Catholic Welfare Conference, the church's lobbying organization, announced that it was turning its considerable attention to the New York State legislature, asking for a stronger censorship statute. Spellman and many others demanded public input in censorship decisions. Perhaps responding to Steuer's recommendation, some of the later placards at the Paris read, "Write to the Board of Review [*sic*] in Albany to remove the license of this picture."

How had the board, specifically charged by statute to keep "sacrilege" out of New York theaters, failed to see any sacrilege when it twice reviewed *The Miracle*? Motion Picture Division Director Hugh Flick sent a detailed memo to the deputy state commissioner of education to answer that question. On first screening, Flick explained, three of the four reviewers thought *The Miracle* was about people's unthinking persecution of nonconformists. The villagers' heartless treatment of the pregnant woman was seen as the major theme of the movie, not any satire or mockery of the virgin birth. The reviewers saw "the cold cruelty of a community toward a misguided and mentally disturbed member." The reviewers had not seen any disrespect. As Flick explained to his boss, "If the reviewers had considered the picture a calculated insult to the Christian religion in general and the Roman Catholic Church in particular, the license would not have been granted." But, after Spellman's criticism, Flick was reevaluating his stance. He now realized, he wrote, that there were complicating factors—Rossellini's personal life and his recent negative publicity, the film's debut at Christmas, a "problematic" title "in bad taste," the publicity that kept ticket buyers flowing and blew the controversy out of proportion—all seemed to suggest to Flick that there was a need for some sort of public appeal process.

Perhaps he was also motivated by the amount of mail his office had been receiving. The Motion Picture Division reported receiving hundreds of letters opposing *The Miracle*. They also received other letters supporting the public's right to see *The Miracle* (supportive letters from prominent Jewish and Protestant clergy had also poured in), but this fact went unmentioned. Later court documents filed in Burstyn's case included letters, affidavits, and sermon excerpts from thirty-eight Protestant and Jewish clergy, including several representing the Princeton Theological Seminary (which seems to have taken a real interest in the case). Much of the attention, though, focused on the negative.

More pressure hit when the 400-member Catholic Press Institute called on Governor Thomas E. Dewey to intervene and rescind *The Miracle*'s license. With even the state's head censor considering retreat, along with the mounting cacophony of political pressure on the Board of Regents, it was only a matter of time before the roof would cave in on Joseph Burstyn. On January 19, 1951, it did. He received notification to appear eleven days later at a hearing to determine why *The Miracle*'s license should *not* be revoked. Burstyn would have to bear the burden of proof and explain to the state why it should not rescind a duly issued license. Actually, this backward burden of proof, as odd as it sounds today, made some sense. It was always the distributors who bore the burden of proving that their films were not harmful. The system of prior restraint on movies had been stacked this way since its beginning back in 1907.

And so, in this virulently anticommunist, anti-Rossellini, anti-*Miracle*, procensorship atmosphere, Burstyn and his lawyers prepared for the unprecedented situation of defending before a regents' committee a license issued by its own censor board. But the circumstances grew even more stacked against Burstyn than they seemed already. The regents' committee that was to hear Burstyn's argument that the movie was not sacrilegious — one Jew, one Catholic, and one Protestant — had already seen the movie, and had gone on record as having decided that it was, in fact, sacrilegious. That hardly augured well for an impartial review.

At the show-cause hearing, John Farber, one of Burstyn's attorneys, tried to convince the three regents to recuse themselves as biased. When that failed, Farber walked out, refusing to acknowledge the legitimacy of the hearing. (Such a move would preserve his right to argue that the committee hearing was extralegal: had he stayed, this tactic would be difficult.) The committee then refused, despite the purported purpose of the hearing, to allow Burstyn's other attorney, the well-respected Ephraim London, to speak. Nor would its members hear any of the twelve Protestant clergy members and divinity professors who appeared on Burstyn's behalf. All together, eight groups and twenty-four individuals who expected to be heard were turned away and allowed only to offer written statements. As Lillian Gerard later wrote, the committee "had earlier promised to 'hear' all interested parties. . . . Now the committee was proceeding without 'listening' to anyone."

After the hearing, all thirteen of New York's regents watched the movie, and predictably, they revoked *The Miracle*'s exhibition license two weeks later. This was an unprecedented move, clearly motivated by Catholic pressure. Justifying their decision, the regents told Burstyn that "the law recognizes that men and women of all faiths respect the religious beliefs held by others. The mockery or profaning of these beliefs that are sacred to any portion of our citizenship is abhorrent to the laws of this great State. To millions of our people the Bible has been held sacred and by them taught, read, studied, and held in reverence and respect. Generation after generation have [*sic*] been influenced by its teachings. This picture takes the concept so sacred to them set forth in both the Protestant and Catholic versions of the Bible and associates it with drunkenness, seduction, mockery, and lewdness."

All the screens of the indispensable New York State market were now off-limits to the seemingly inconsequential Italian movie Burstyn had imported. The struggle that ensued and its consequences, though, were anything but inconsequential.

A Major Shift in Jurisprudence

In 1925, twenty-six years before Joseph Burstyn found himself entangled in New York's judicial system, the U.S. Supreme Court had embarked on a new era in constitutional interpretation when it incorporated free speech into the liberties protected against state action by the Fourteenth Amendment. Six years later, the Court overturned a Minnesota statute that permitted prior restraint on newspapers, and in the process incorporated the right to a free press within the privileges and immunities of the Fourteenth Amendment.

But as the Supreme Court slowly added more liberties to the list of rights protected by the Fourteenth Amendment after 1925, and as it gradually added to that list more and more sources of speech — leaflets, picketing signs, phonographs, loudspeakers, magazines, and radio — those who objected to prior restraint on movies began to take heart. What they were seeing was a major shift in U.S. jurisprudence. By the 1940s, the legal culture was becoming more receptive to the right to communicate ideas and less tolerant of state limitations on free expression. But it would take more challenge cases before the right to communicate freely through movies would be considered constitutionally necessary by the standards of state constitutions or the U.S. Constitution.

As the anticensorites watched the Supreme Court gradually expand the right of free communication to other media throughout the 1930s and 1940s, they began to hope that movies might be next. Independent distributors and producers, civil libertarians, and film critics who opposed censorship got a big dose of hope in 1948 when the Supreme Court decided a long-running antitrust case against the MPAA. When the Court ordered the industry to divest itself of its theater outlets in *United States v. Paramount Pictures*, Justice Douglas parenthetically added that "we have no doubt that moving pictures, like newspapers and radio, are included in the press whose freedom is guaranteed by the First Amendment." Because this was a monopoly case in which movie freedom was not at issue, and Douglas's comment was *dictum* (a statement made that did not directly bear on the issues of the case), the statement carried no real weight. But it did indicate that at least some of the justices were ready to rethink the *Mutual Film* decision. That 1915 bottleneck, the stare decisis case upon which the constitutionality of motion picture censorship rested, that had restricted much film freedom for more than three decades, seemed, at least for some on the Court, open to challenge.

Although in the late 1940s the anticensorites faced what seemed like a more sympathetic Supreme Court, and although they began to gather support from film critics and other cultural liberals, they faced a political culture growing increasingly hostile to anything not 100 percent patriotically "American." As the cold war grew progressively more frightening, pressure grew for conformity of opinion, exactly the type of thing state and local censors had been set up to safeguard. Early cold war tensions and the fear-mongering of the McCarthy era played directly into the hands of those who favored censorship. Many people were convinced, including U.S. senators and representatives, that communists had invaded Hollywood and were spreading their messages through movie scripts. In 1947 and 1951, the House Un-American Activities Committee (HUAC) held hearings that ruined the careers of many Hollywood figures and resulted in prison sentences for ten influential movie writers, directors, and producers who refused to cooperate. These years of fear gave censors a boost. Both the Production Code Administration (PCA) and the government censors appeared to many Americans a necessary protection against communist infiltration into the entertainment world. But to others, like Burstyn, London, and the ACLU, they were impediments to artistic freedom.

In pursuing an appeal against the regents' decision, Burstyn clearly faced the courts and the public at a time of great legal, political, and cultural flux. Since its 1937 change of direction toward close scrutiny of liberty-restrictive laws, the Court seemed more sympathetic toward free speech claims, finding in favor of the rights of radicals, labor organizations, and minority religious organizations. In the ten years preceding Burstyn's case, the Court had overturned speech-restrictive state statutes concerning peaceful picketing, public discussion, argumentative speech, religious proselytizing, and licensing for public speech. But the Court also cautioned that the First Amendment was not absolute: that there were two layers inherent in speech — expression protected by the Free Speech Clause and expression excluded from it. In the long run — in the years since the late 1930s — the Court seemed to be moving toward expansion of protected speech. In the short run, however, with the rising temperature of the cold war since 1948, the Court had shifted direction again, upholding new government restrictions on speech and expanding the size and scope of unprotected expression. Where an individual case might fall within these two categories in 1951 and 1952 was anybody's guess.

Where the Court was going remained unpredictable, but the direction of the political culture was clear: moving toward repression of dissident or nonconforming ideas. Somewhere in this erratic legal culture and the constricting political culture were the movies — inching toward new thematic treatments and artistic maturity, yet restricted by the law.

A Shift in Film Culture: The MPAA

Burstyn was not the only industry person hoping to free movies from restraint. Even some Hollywood producers and directors had begun pushing for greater artistic freedom after World War II. Producers, particularly those independent of the major studios, knew that U.S. audiences were hungry for the types of movies being made in Europe after the war. Influenced by these less formulaic, more realistic European films, U.S. movie audiences applauded when Hollywood delivered films such as *The Best Years of Our Lives* (1946) about the realities that confronted returning veterans, *Gentleman's Agreement* (1947) about anti-Semitism, *Home of the Brave* (1949), and *Intruder in the Dust*

(1949), both about race relations. Box office success for these movies (*The Best Years of Our Lives* won seven Oscars) not only encouraged independent producers to tackle more mature themes but also convinced some of the MPAA movie moguls that both their own censorship and the government version needed to loosen.

But things were not so simple for the MPAA, which encountered a dizzying array of problems in the postwar years. In the rapidly intensifying cold war environment, the HUAC hearings had been and were a continuing public relations disaster. To counter their effect on Hollywood, the MPAA tried to build an impeccably patriotic reputation. Challenging government censors in court to gain greater artistic freedom to make more mature-themed movies may have been appealing to some, but could not have found a place high on the MPAA's agenda, beset as it was by communist conspiracy charges. After all, the MPAA's mission was to protect the business environment so films could be made, distributed, and exhibited profitably. Bucking societal and political trends was not in the organization's best interest.

More bad news was hitting the industry in the form of increasing competition from television, foreign films, and the enforced divestiture of the studios' movie theater holdings. This last problem was a double whammy leading not only to lowered profits but also to an increased number of screens for yet another competitor, independently made movies. Things looked glum all around for the movie industry in the late 1940s. In earlier hard times, the industry had always turned to its surefire ticket sellers, sex and violence. But, with the Catholic Legion of Decency firmly entrenched in Hollywood's back pocket, that approach would not work this time.

Eric Johnston, like his predecessor Will Hays, needed the backing of the Catholic Legion of Decency, especially now that the movie industry was under such dire attack as a communist haven. For the beleaguered movie industry, Catholic support was as good an anticommunist credential as could be found. So Johnston, a well-respected and progressive businessman, was no more likely to want to cross the Legion or tangle with government censors than Hays had been. But Johnston also had a slightly different agenda, one stemming from his personal politics as well as his position on the Board of Directors of the NAACP.

Johnston was under significant pressure from the NAACP to reduce racial stereotyping in U.S. movies. Before the 1950s, blacks in U.S. films had always been servants (or servile), children (or child-like), or criminally inclined (or criminals). But, as much as Johnston might want to change that, he knew that censors in Virginia and in southern cities such as Atlanta and Memphis were skittish about any nonstereotypical views of African Americans, and would surely ban movies that represented them as capable or educated or like whites. Johnston thus found himself torn between his job — to reinvigorate Hollywood's image as patriotic after the HUAC trouncing — and his personal contacts at the NAACP urging him to improve black imagery on film. But if the movie industry were ever to mature to produce racially progressive entertainment, southern censors would have to be confronted.

This left Johnston in a bind: he wanted to see censorship of serious race-themed movies loosened, yet he needed to tread carefully lest his organization's patriotism be questioned or its self-censorship mechanism be attacked. The situation not only frustrated Johnston but also led the MPAA to an inconsistent public position on the issue of censorship. Prodded by some of its members, Johnston and the MPAA had begun making public statements about combating state censorship in the name of artistic freedom, yet there was little concrete action. Indeed, when approached by the ACLU in 1947 about teaming up to fight censorship, the MPAA ignored the offer. Again, when Morris Ernst of the ACLU urged the MPAA to take the leadership role in fighting censorship in 1948, it waffled and hedged, concerned, its leaders said, about how to get started in the "correct procedural manner."

So Johnston and the MPAA took baby steps into the battle with state censors. Johnston had to pick his fights. He soon realized that one area where he might take an aggressive anticensorship stance (keeping his progressive producers happy) was on race-themed movies (keeping his NAACP colleagues happy). This way, he could placate some of his restless members in the MPAA, and appease both the ACLU and the NAACP. And so, the MPAA's first forays into legal challenges of censorship came over three movies with racial content: a 1947 light comedy called *Curley*, censored in Memphis, Tennessee, because it showed an integrated classroom; a 1949 film called *Lost*

Boundaries, censored in Atlanta because it showed a black family passing for white; and a 1949 film called *Pinky*, censored in Marshall, Texas, because it showed a black woman bucking the racial system in the South. Each was a good choice for censorship tests for the MPAA: *Lost Boundaries* and *Pinky* to prove that it had matured and was giving U.S. audiences thought-provoking movies, and *Curley* because its banning was so outlandish. But some of the MPAA's hopes were dashed when the Supreme Court declined to hear cases brought on behalf of *Curley* and *Lost Boundaries* in 1950. *Pinky* was still alive as a legal challenge, although it was stalled in the Texas courts.

And then there was Joseph Burstyn and *The Miracle* in New York. After Burstyn's badgering of Breen and the PCA the year before in the *Bicycle Thief* fracas, hope of getting MPAA support was dim. Moreover, as far as the MPAA was concerned, *The Miracle* had more liabilities than possible benefits. First, it was a foreign film distributed by an independent. Foreign films were direct competitors to Hollywood studios in the major metropolitan centers. Second, some attorneys for the MPAA believed that because *The Miracle* had been banned for "sacrilege," a court decision might strip New York of the ability to censor only for that one term — and that would be only a minor victory. Third, if *The Miracle* lost, and there was a very real possibility of that, the MPAA attorneys feared that it might encourage lawmakers to introduce new censorship statutes. Finally, some industry attorneys were convinced and were saying publicly that the Supreme Court in 1951 was less likely to rule in favor of movie freedom than it had been when it handed down the *Paramount* decision three years before.

At that time, only Justices Black and Douglas had said that they wanted to extend First Amendment protection to films. Although Black and Douglas were still on the Court, two staunch civil libertarians, Wiley Rutledge and Frank Murphy, were gone, replaced in 1949 by two more conservative men, Sherman Minton and Tom Clark. So, if anything, the bench had shifted to the right. When the 1950 Court refused to hear either of the MPAA's cases, it seemed that the pessimistic MPAA attorneys might have been right.

Not only did the timing look inauspicious, *The Miracle* actually presented Hollywood a big red flag: because the ban had been demanded by the Catholic Church, any MPAA support of Burstyn would have directly challenged the hegemony of the Catholic Church over movie content. Having worked with the Catholics for twenty years, the MPAA was not likely to cross it in the communist-hunting atmosphere of 1951. David O. Selznick had learned this lesson when, even with a Production Code seal, his *Duel in the Sun* (1946) got no assistance from the industry because the Legion condemned the film.

The MPAA was not about to tackle the Legion. Ephraim London specifically invited the MPAA to file an amicus brief in February 1952, but it declined. Instead, it chose to support *Pinky* by getting behind William Gelling, the manager of a Marshall, Texas, theater who had shown the movie despite a ban by local officials. The case became known as *Gelling v. Texas* as it ground its way through the lower courts.

Unfortunately, the MPAA would later learn that *Gelling* was not a better case. Although the MPAA worried that the religious controversy in the *Miracle* case would muddy the legal waters, it actually made *Burstyn v. Wilson* the better test case. *The Miracle* presented the justices with a whole lot more to sink their juridical teeth into: a separation-of-church-and-state controversy, a void-for-vagueness question, and the prior restraint issue. Indeed, the case centered on whether the U.S. Supreme Court would allow a church to dictate propriety in religious messages and use the apparatus of the state to enforce its decrees — this was nothing short of a heresy issue. And the case came at a time of serious cultural questioning of the role of religion in civic life. As Alan Westin wrote in his 1961 case study, *The Miracle Case*, "there was a feeling in the air that powerful changes in the American law of church-state relations might be in the offing."

Neither of the MPAA's chosen test cases, *Gelling* (*Pinky*) or *RD-DR Corporation v. Smith* (*Lost Boundaries*) contained any new legal questions. And *Curley* was out of the picture, dismissed on a technicality. So, by the end of 1951, the MPAA, for all its talk about fighting censorship, was backing only one Supreme Court challenge case, and that had been brought reluctantly. (According to a *Variety* article from February 27, 1952, neither the MPAA nor William Gelling's bosses had been eager to bring the case before the Supreme Court.)

The Miracle Reaches the Courts

The ACLU, however, was ready to go to court. Its lawyers had been soliciting a case actively for several years by the time *The Miracle* was shut down by Commissioner of Licenses McCaffrey. In 1946, the organization had supported Howard Hughes in his attempt to buck the New York City commissioner's authority to keep *The Outlaw* from the screen. In 1947, it had backed another New York State test case over a French film called *Amok*. ACLU lawyers wrote amicus briefs for both *Curley* and *Lost Boundaries* and offered to aid *Gelling*. And, in 1950, the group had offered help to any exhibitor willing to make a test case of the censorship of *The Bicycle Thief* in Oregon.

In addition to censorship, the ACLU was interested in fighting what it called pressure groups (today they are called special interest groups). One of the organization's main targets was the Catholic Legion of Decency, which not only influenced the films MPAA member studios could make through its unofficial control of the PCA but also was growing more vocal attempting to control foreign films. The *Miracle* case presented the ACLU and its local affiliate, the NYCLU, two active targets: censorship of a film brought about by one of the most powerful pressure groups of the day and a good, solid, prior-restraint-of-speech case.

Joseph Burstyn was clearly ready. Film critic Alton Cook called him "a small man with small fame outside movie trade circles. But within them," Cook wrote, "he is regarded with a combination of amazement and awe." Burstyn's imports gave him an impressive record of critical success, winning the New York Film Critics Association's Best Foreign Film of the Year award five times between 1947 and 1952.

Burstyn's aversion to censorship was clear as far back as 1936 when he and Mayer had tangled with the New York censors over their French film *Remous*. Mayer and Burstyn had taken the board to court, losing two rounds over three years of litigation before running out of money. And with *The Bicycle Thief* in 1949, Burstyn's reputation had been secured: a man who disliked interference with film whether it came from the MPAA or the government.

When *The Miracle* was attacked by McCaffrey, Spellman, and then the Board of Regents, but supported by the Paris Theatre, the film critics association, and the NYCLU, Burstyn decided to go ahead with a legal challenge. Advised to hire Catholic attorneys, Burstyn also chose to use his personal lawyer, the man who had helped defend *The Bicycle Thief* in Oregon, Ephraim London. Together, London and Burstyn went on to work as a team, fighting, in the phrase of the day, for freedom of the screen.

London came to Burstyn's case as a committed civil libertarian. At thirty-nine, he was twelve years younger than Burstyn, yet the two became fast friends. When he signed on to represent *The Miracle*, London was just on the cusp of a distinguished career that would place him before the justices of the Supreme Court in nine civil liberties cases, all of which he would win. Tall, well-spoken, imperturbable, and likable, he was an exceptionally good litigator, and he tirelessly fought for the cause of the anticensorites. This proved to be no easy task.

So the anticensorship cast was set: Burstyn, London, the NYCLU, and the film critics. But one critic wanted to know why the MPAA was not willing to help. On February 22, 1951, Crowther typed up his column and asked the association why it was silent about the regents' action. Why, he wrote, would an industry that claimed to oppose censorship not work to reverse such a dangerous precedent, one that would probably encourage other pressure group action? Why would the MPAA accept censoring on such a nebulous term as *sacrilege*, and why were its leaders not worried that other religious groups would show up demanding that their view of a religious work of art be accepted by all? Hoping to prod the foot-dragging movie industry, Crowther warned, "If there ever was a clear case on which to challenge censorship, this is it."

In addition to regular columns like this, Crowther was working on an article for the *Atlantic Monthly*. This article was intended as a frontal assault on Catholic movie censorship dominance. Crowther argued that the church had successfully locked down Hollywood content and was now trying to extend its control to foreign films. Its target, the centerpiece of this premeditated showdown, Crowther wrote, was *The Miracle*. Burstyn's movie had become "the recognized issue for a calculated test of strength." Still the MPAA remained silent.

To get *The Miracle* back into *Ways of Love* now that its license had been revoked by the New York Motion Picture Division, Burstyn and his lawyers prepared for oral arguments before the New York Supreme Court Appellate Division. Here they would have to convince the justices that the politically powerful Board of Regents had been wrong in revoking the license. No gambler would have bet on Burstyn: legal precedent was solidly contrary to his position that movies should be free of prior restraint. Since the 1915 *Mutual* decision, the only way to win a court battle against censors had been to prove abuse of "discretion"—to prove that the censors had acted maliciously or arbitrarily. Since the New York legislature had specifically authorized the Motion Picture Division to look for sacrilege, its doing so would be considered appropriate.

Nevertheless, Burstyn filed two briefs with the appellate division: one for his business and one for him personally. His personal brief centered on the arbitrary denial of his property rights in contravention of the First, Fifth, and Fourteenth Amendments to the U.S. Constitution and of the New York Constitution. Burstyn contended that the court could not rule on whether *The Miracle* was sacrilegious since there were diametrically opposing viewpoints on that very issue. The court could rule, though, and should rule, he insisted, on whether those who want to see the movie should have their wishes restrained by the pressures of a "minority group."

The brief filed for Joseph Burstyn, Inc., argued that the regents had no authority to revoke his license, that the state's censorship statute violated separation of church and state by taking the religious views of one group and fastening them "with the force of law on the backs of all citizens," and that New York's censorship was prior restraint, which violated both the First Amendment and the New York Constitution. The brief reminded the justices that according to Supreme Court Justice Douglas's 1948 *Paramount* dictum, movies deserved First Amendment protection. An amicus brief from the NYCLU tried to convince the appellate division justices that despite its recent speech-restrictive decisions, the U.S. Supreme Court was indeed moving in a more speech-friendly direction.

The Motion Picture Division and the regents were represented by Charles Brind, a dedicated anticommunist who believed that motion picture censorship protected New York's citizens. Brind, counsel to the state's education department, brought a personal passion to his procensorship arguments. Within two years of his appearance in *The Miracle* case, he would publicly call for New York's censorship statute to be expanded so it could be used to ban "subversive" content. But in 1951, he defended the regents' action on *The Miracle* by arguing that sacrilege was not an ambiguous term. Despite all the public disagreement among religious leaders in the preceding months, he claimed there was "common agreement" that *The Miracle* was "sacrilegious per se." He countered Burstyn's argument that the license revocation was illegal by asserting that it would be "inconceivable" if the Board of Regents could not oversee the administrative actions of its subordinate departments. Finally, he did significant damage to the NYCLU's argument that the Supreme Court was moving toward recognition of movie freedom by drawing attention to the Court's recent refusal to hear two movie censorship cases. It was only the year before that the Court had refused to hear the *Lost Boundaries* case.

The appellate division justices withdrew after oral arguments to watch *The Miracle* and deliberate. It did not take them long to strike down the best efforts of Burstyn, London, Farber, and the NYCLU. In May 1951, the appellate division unanimously decided that its courtroom was not the appropriate forum to overturn *Mutual*, the long-standing precedent of the U.S. Supreme Court, particularly since that Court recently had been presented with the opportunity to hear movie cases but had refused to do so. Justice Sidney F. Foster, writing for the court, had no problem upholding movie censorship for sacrilege since movies were not legitimate "organs of expression" like the press. Foster agreed with Brind that the Board of Regents had ample authority to rescind a license when its subordinates, the censors, had made a mistake. The purported sacrilege of *The Miracle* was clearly a proper area for the censors' and the regents' authority. The "conflict of views is proof," he wrote, "that the issue is one of judgment to be resolved by the administrative body which has it in charge." Clearly, the majority of this court had not lost faith in legislatively empowered experts. Nor, without any clear direction from the U.S. Supreme Court, was its interest in film freedom growing.

But Burstyn and London were not about to give up. They immediately began to prepare for the Court of Appeals, New York's highest court. Each side recycled its major points, and the NYCLU used this second opportunity to ramp up its argument that the court needed to free movies from prior restraint by scuttling *Mutual*. "It is now the duty of this Court to . . . lay the ghost of that precedent, and to vindicate the fundamental constitutional principle *that every vehicle of ideas is shielded from such censorship*" [emphasis in original]. *Mutual* was a dinosaur, the NYCLU argued, decided during the infancy of the movie medium and when the free speech and free press provisions of the First Amendment had not yet been incorporated and applied against state infringement. Then the NYCLU went straight after the church-and-state issue: because banning the movie answered criticism that came only from Catholics, the license revocation could be seen as an impermissible state support of one religion. But this was a risky argument: three of the seven Court of Appeals judges were Catholics, and at the briefing stage, neither the NYCLU nor London could know which of the seven possible judges would actually hear the case. (In New York's Court of Appeals, five judges constitute a quorum, with the concurrence of four necessary to reach a decision.) As it turned out, all seven judges sat on Burstyn's case, an indication of how seriously they took the issue of movie censorship and the enormous controversy that had been raised by New York City's Catholics.

London's brief argued that the regents had no statutory authority to revoke a license, that the statute violated the constitutional guarantees of religious liberty and separation of church and state, and that it served as an unconstitutional restraint on free expression. He closed with jabs both at the license commissioner and the censors by repeating U.S. Supreme Court Justice Robert Jackson's oft-quoted 1943 phrase, "If there is any fixed star in our constitutional constellation, it is that no official, high or petty, can prescribe what shall be orthodox in . . . religion or other matters of opinion."

The NYCLU's pumped-up amicus had company. A brief from the Metropolitan Committee for Religious Liberty (the New York chapter of Protestants and Other Americans United for Separation of Church and State) intemperately referred to the Catholics who lobbied against *The Miracle* as "holy rollers." Artists Equity Association and the American Jewish Congress were more circumspect but added little to the constitutional arguments.

The state spent most of its brief arguing that *The Miracle* was "sacrilegious per se" and that the regents had not only the power but the duty to revoke its license. The activities of the Motion Picture Division violated neither free speech rights nor religious liberty. Interestingly, though, the state left out any defense of the charge that it was promoting one religion over another and therefore acting to establish a religion.

Still, it probably came as no great surprise to anyone when New York's highest court upheld the Board of Regents and ruled against Burstyn's First Amendment appeal. The majority was happy to accept the *Mutual*-era contention that movies presented a "unique problem" with a "potentiality for evil, especially among the young." The court dismissed London's contention that the regents could not revoke a film's license, saying that such authority was "implicit." On the issue of separation of church and state, the majority had little sympathy. Judge Charles W. Froessel, writing for the majority and citing an 1892 Supreme Court case, concluded that "we are essentially a religious nation of which it is well to be reminded now and then." That some benefit might accrue to one religion he found to be "immaterial from the constitutional point of view if the statute has for its purpose a legitimate objective within the scope of the police power." Then, reflecting what had been happening in the U.S. Supreme Court in the previous three years, the New York Court of Appeals interpreted recent speech jurisprudence not as a gradual expansion of individual liberties but as the constriction of free speech rights: "If there is any one proposition for which the free speech cases may be cited . . . it is that freedom of speech is not absolute, but may be limited when the appropriate occasion arises." It was clear to this majority that banning *The Miracle* was just such an occasion.

But Burstyn could take heart: the Court of Appeals opinion revealed some dissension on this point. Two on the Court of Appeals refused to go along with the five-judge majority. In a lengthy dissent, Judge Stanley H. Fuld, joined by Marvin Dye, agreed with the NYCLU that the Supreme Court was clearly moving into a more speech-protective position, a doctrinal change they welcomed. Moreover, these two judges proved themselves no devotees of judicial restraint: that philosophy of bowing to the legislative will made little sense to Fuld, who expected legal interpretation to change with the times. New York's censorship statute was clearly too broad because it imposed a "general and pervasive restraint on freedom of discussion of religious themes in moving pictures, which cannot be justified on the basis of any substantial interest of the state." Rather than relying on *Mutual* as the majority had done, Fuld took up the NYCLU's call for *Mutual* to be laid to rest. "The *Mutual Film* case should be relegated to its place upon the history shelf. Rendered in a day before the guarantees of the Bill of Rights were held to apply to the states, and when motion pictures were in their infancy, the decision was obviously a product of the view that motion pictures did not express or convey opinions or ideas. Today . . . some would deny protection for the opposite reason, that films are too effective in their presentation of ideas and points of view. The latter notion is as unsupportable as the other." Fuld took the NYCLU's cue and ended his opinion by repeating Jackson's famous "any fixed star in our constitutional constellation" quotation. Fifteen years later, in an interview with the Albany *Times-Union*, Fuld revealed, "I just favor free speech and I oppose any limitation on it." The *Miracle* case had given him a platform.

———

To the Supreme Court

Burstyn and London had now lost two rounds in New York State's appellate courts. Burstyn took no time to decide what to do next. The day the Court of Appeals handed down its decision, he announced an appeal to the U.S. Supreme Court. Getting the case heard, though, required convincing at least four justices that the case had broad constitutional significance, by no means a certainty. In the 1951 term, 1,107 cases applied for review and only 200 were accepted. Moreover, despite the 1948 *Paramount* tease, the Court had not shown itself eager to reconsider constitutional issues of movie censorship; it had just denied certiorari to hear either the *Lost Boundaries* or the *Curley* case.

Nevertheless, Burstyn went ahead. In October 1951, he announced that he had support from several civic, civil liberties, and entertainment groups, but he declined to reveal who they were. One group that definitely would not be joining Burstyn's appeal: the MPAA.

After his bout with Burstyn the year before over *The Bicycle Thief*, Breen had no sympathy for Burstyn's case. In fact, he was quite convinced that Burstyn's "latest attempt to stir up trouble," as he put it in a January 1951 letter to MPAA attorney Kenneth Clark, might get the association "into a situation by which we shall be made to suffer very much." Breen was concerned that a Court loss would rile up what had been a mostly reasonable censor board in New York.

Eric Johnston was not interested either. Despite Johnston's personal interest in seeing censorship attacked, industry attorneys still were not convinced that the time was right. The lawyers were convinced that the only thing to be gained from a suit regarding *The Miracle* would be play dates in New York. They believed that since the central question in Burstyn's case was whether New York could censor for sacrilege, any decision from the Supreme Court, even if positive, would be limited to the religious issue. Industry attorneys, according to a February 27, 1952, *Variety* article, preferred to wait for a broader case, like the one brewing in Texas, the *Gelling* case over *Pinky*. This caution would have come as no surprise to Burstyn. After all, the MPAA was not in the business of fighting censorship: it was in the business of making the economic climate more profitable for moviemaking. A Supreme Court case that might lose, or at best, might only strike out sacrilege as a permissible censoring standard, was not very appealing to industry lawyers. So Burstyn, London, and the NYCLU were on their own.

The Supreme Court and *The Miracle*

The Supreme Court before which Burstyn would present his case against New York State and Catholic pressure was not, by most accounts, a collegial bench. Court historians Herman Pritchett, Melvin Urofsky, William Wiecek, and others have written about the failure of comity during the Vinson years. In fact, Urofsky titles his book about the Stone and the Vinson Courts *Division and Discord.* With several prima donnas, several hostile relationships, and without a chief justice who could calm troubled waters, this was at times an internally divided court. Although eight of the nine justices had been New Dealers, they had little else in common.

The Justices

The 1951–1952 Court was composed of seven Protestants, one Jew, and one Catholic. Considering the religious affiliations of Americans at the time, this was a fairly representative body. To mirror U.S. religions more perfectly (which, of course, there is no constitutional necessity to do) the Court would have needed to shift only one justice: one less Protestant and one more Catholic. So the Court that would hear Burstyn's case was close, but not perfectly representative of the religious affiliations of the U.S. populace.

One of the seven Protestants on the Court was Chief Justice Fred Vinson. Son of a rural Kentucky jailer, he worked his way through college and law school, played semipro baseball, and then went to Congress, where he served on the powerful Ways and Means Committee during the New Deal. Vinson resigned his House seat when Roosevelt appointed him to the federal bench in the District of Columbia. A superb organizer, during World War II he headed the

Office of Economic Stabilization, then the Office of War Mobilization, and later he served as Truman's secretary of the treasury. But even his exceptional organizational skills could not help him when he inherited a badly fractured Court from former chief justice Harlan Fiske Stone in 1946. It didn't help that Associate Justice Robert Jackson believed he had been promised the chief justiceship or that Felix Frankfurter considered Vinson a second-rate legal mind. Vinson's job was to use his patience and conciliatory manners to corral the Stone Court's "wild horses"—the deep animosities between Frankfurter and Douglas as well as between Black and Jackson, bitter fights over recusals, and a deepening ideological split between Frankfurter and Black. Healing these festering wounds may have been an impossible task, and today Vinson is listed frequently as a failure as chief justice. As a jurist, he was pragmatic and respectful of strong central government, never voting to overturn a congressional statute or presidential action. When most of his brethren voted to disallow Truman's attempt to seize steel mills during the Korean War, Vinson voted to uphold Truman's unprecedented action. Urofsky sums up Vinson's decisions as nearly always favoring "the power of the federal government over that of the states, and the power of the government in general over that of the individual."

Hugo Black, a southern Baptist, graduated first in his class at the University of Alabama Law School, then served brilliant careers both as a prosecuting and defense attorney. He represented Alabama for two terms in the U.S. Senate, where he staunchly supported Franklin Roosevelt's New Deal policies, and was rewarded with the Supreme Court nomination in 1937. Because he had been a senator, his confirmation by the Senate was a mostly foregone conclusion, but he began his judicial career under a cloud as allegations sprouted that he had been a member of the Ku Klux Klan—charges he never denied or confirmed. After the dust settled, Black became a solidly liberal justice. According to Urofsky, Black was no slave to precedent, and was perfectly willing to overturn even long-standing cases if he believed a new situation demanded new interpretation. This augured well for Burstyn, especially since Black treasured the First Amendment, which he saw in absolute terms. "Congress shall make no law," he famously wrote, "means Congress shall make no law." Black became the leader of a liberal bloc that would later see its philosophy ascend during the Warren Court years of the late 1950s and 1960s.

Stanley Reed, another Kentuckian and another Protestant, studied law at the University of Virginia and at Columbia but never received a law degree. He served in the Kentucky House of Representatives and as counsel to the Federal Farm Board. Although a political moderate, he firmly believed that the supremacy of the national government and its commerce powers permitted broad authority to regulate the economy, and so he became a loyal New Dealer. After Reed served in the Hoover administration, Roosevelt named him solicitor general, where even his considerable abilities could not help save many New Deal programs from legal attack. Reed was easygoing, respected, and congenial, and Roosevelt hoped that he might be more use to the government on the bench. The president nominated Reed in 1938, and he was easily confirmed by the Senate. More a judicial restrainer than a judicial activist as a Supreme Court justice, Reed consistently voted to sustain New Deal powers, but he also sympathized with organized labor, protected the rights of picketers, and often voted to extend First Amendment rights. He saw the Court as a necessary arm to protect Americans from "gusts of popular frenzy" that could "sweep away the rights of the individual."

Felix Frankfurter was both the 1952 Court's only immigrant (born in Vienna) and its only Jew (although he is widely believed to have been either an atheist or an agnostic). He is one of the legendary justices of the Supreme Court. His family emigrated to the United States in 1894, and he grew up amid the infamous tenements of New York's lower east side, graduating at the top of his class from City College and then Harvard Law School. After several stints with the federal government, Frankfurter taught at Harvard Law School, where he established himself as an expert in constitutional law and federal jurisdiction and trained dozens of promising young lawyers who would go on to service under Roosevelt's New Deal. In 1938, Roosevelt named the brilliant Frankfurter to the Supreme Court, where he was expected to be a solidly liberal jurist and a committed civil libertarian. He surprised many legal commentators frequently, however, because he adopted a firm (some would say too firm) policy of judicial restraint: he decided that judges should not, no matter how illiberal or unfortunate the outcome, contradict the legislative will unless a law was clearly unconstitutional. A sharp debater and prolific writer, Frankfurter was one of the great scholars of the Court. But he was also one of the most annoying justices. He was temperamentally compelled to try to convert opponents to his side. And he had something to say on almost every issue. Even when he agreed with the result of the majority, he often wrote concurring opinions, producing hundreds during his career on the Court. By comparison, his colleague Stanley Reed wrote only about one per year.

William O. Douglas, son of a Presbyterian minister who died when Douglas was just six, lived much of his early life in poverty, working long hours to help his family make ends meet. Despite holding three jobs to put himself through Columbia Law School, he managed to graduate second in his class. He taught law both at his alma mater and at Yale and then went on to great acclaim as the head of the Securities and Exchange Commission during its crucial early years in the New Deal era. When appointed to the 1939 Supreme Court at the age of forty-one, he became the second youngest associate justice in the Court's history, and he would stay longer than any other justice — thirty-six years. In his first decade of Court service, he seemed a mainstream New Dealer, but the speech restrictions of the early cold war era caused his jurisprudence to shift radically, and he became a staunch supporter of First Amendment freedoms. Like Hugo Black, he came to believe that the Fourteenth Amendment incorporated the entire Bill of Rights. And like Black, he became a "liberal absolutist" on the issue of free speech. Precedents, even long-standing ones, were of little concern to Douglas. His goal was to get the right result.

Robert H. Jackson was raised an Episcopalian. He was a brilliant lawyer despite having had only one year of law school when he passed the bar in his native New York State. He practiced law in New York until tapped to join the Roosevelt administration as legal counsel to the Internal Revenue Service, then solicitor general, and then attorney general. Roosevelt appointed Jackson to the Supreme Court in 1941, from which position he also served as chief U.S. prosecutor at the Nuremberg war crimes trials at the close of World War II. Like Frankfurter, Jackson believed in judicial restraint and wrote brilliant prose, but he had no clear judicial philosophy, and his jurisprudence is often considered erratic. But, on the whole, as William Wiecek writes, "he could be counted on the side of order in its contest with freedom." Jackson would not likely vote to end censorship and free movies from all restraint.

The last three justices of the 1951–1952 Court, Burton, Clark, and Minton, were Truman appointees. Harold Burton, a Unitarian, was born and raised near Boston and graduated from Bowdoin College and Harvard Law School. After serving as mayor of Cleveland, he went to the U.S. Senate in 1940 as a Republican denouncing much of the New Deal. Once in office, though, he moderated his views and served on the influential and effective Truman committee that kept a close reign on government wartime spending. Truman was pleased with Burton's work and nominated him to the Court, hoping to cement his political base with moderate Republicans. Although a Republican, Burton is considered to have been the most liberal of Truman's four appointees. Burton's conduct on the Court earned him a reputation as open-minded, one who considered all aspects of an issue before making a decision. One of his clerks described Burton as a man who "tried to divest himself of every prejudice before working out his positions by himself." One of Jackson's clerks later told Richard Kluger, "If I had my life at stake and wanted to come before the fairest judge in the world, Burton would be my choice." Although laudable in theory, such open-mindedness also meant Burton was a real wild card for those trying to predict case outcomes.

Tom Clark, son, grandson, and brother of successful Texas lawyers, was born into a devout Episcopalian family. His attendance at Sunday school was reported to be perfect, and Clark became one of the country's first Eagle Scouts. When he married at age twenty-five, he adopted his wife's denomination, Presbyterianism. Completing both college and law school in just three years at the University of Texas, he practiced law and became an active Democratic politico. He joined the U.S. Department of Justice in 1937 and rose quickly through the ranks. After a turn as Truman's attorney general, where he oversaw the federal antitrust action that led to the *Paramount* decision, he was elevated to the Supreme Court in 1949, where he was expected to be a conservative. Clark was a practical man, not given to philosophizing like his colleague Felix Frankfurter. As a lawyer, he was interested more in the correct application of law than in theory. As attorney general, he was a vigorous antitruster and a dedicated cold warrior who backed stringent laws on spying ("trying to deal with people who are trying to destroy the United States"), requested wiretap authority in espionage cases, and tried to establish a system that would enable the FBI to track every alien in the country. But he was also forward-thinking in some important respects: he became, as Urofsky puts it, "a warm friend of the emerging civil rights movement," and he favored increased rights for African Americans. But once on the Court, he proved of little assistance to civil liberties claimants, voting against them 75 percent of the time in his first year. As the years went on, his position softened. He moved toward the center and away from the conservative side of the Court. But even as late as 1969, Clark did not believe that freedom of speech or of the press were among the "preferred freedoms" that had been espoused three decades earlier by Justices Cardozo and Stone and were actively promoted by Douglas and Black.

Sherman Minton of Indiana, like Douglas, had been raised in poverty and worked his way through college and law school. Yet he was superbly educated and had amassed an impressive resume displaying service in all three branches of the government, including one term in the Senate where he sat next to the senator from Missouri, Harry Truman. Both staunch New Dealers, the two became fast friends. Minton served eight years on the U.S. Court of Appeals, and Truman elevated him to the Supreme Court in 1949. He was the Court's only Catholic. With no clear legal philosophy, he proved difficult to pigeonhole. Like Frankfurter, he thought judges should defer to the legislative will and the findings of bureaucrats, and he prized precedent. He had been considered a true liberal in his Senate years, but his record shows no sympathy for a free press. In fact he was so angered by newspaper attacks on FDR that he introduced a bill that would have punished the knowing publication of false information as a felony. Unlike Black and Douglas, he saw nothing absolute about the free press or free speech protections of the First Amendment. In the end, he failed to distinguish himself in his seven years of service and had little effect on the Court's direction. As Wiecek put it, "The Constitution would not have been noticeably affected if Sherman Minton's chair had been occupied by a stuffed teddy bear from 1949 to 1953."

A widely divergent group, the Court did not lend itself to easy predictions, particularly on civil liberties issues. A glance at the Supreme Court justices' voting records in 1951 would not have held out much promise for those like Joseph Burstyn seeking relief from civil liberties violations. Those inclined to see the glass as half empty would have noted that in the previous five years, six of the nine justices had voted against the claim of a civil rights violation more than half of the time. Chief Justice Vinson's negative voting record on civil rights claims was the second highest at a whopping 85 percent. He was outvoted only by Justice Minton, who denied such claims 89 percent of the time. Reed weighed in at 84 percent, Burton at 75 percent, Clark at 74 percent, and Jackson at 72 percent. In the previous two years, the picture had gotten even worse: only three – Black, Douglas, and Frankfurter – had voted to uphold civil rights claims even half of the time, a bloc not nearly big enough on which to pin any constitutional hopes.

The Supreme Court would come to champion free speech in the 1960s, a time when most Americans were willing to go along. But Burstyn was headed to a different Court in the red scare days of 1952, one that in many respects reflected the concerns of the public – less interested in the rights of the individual and more interested in protecting the nation from disloyal behavior.

Burstyn and London's Strategy

In their petition for review by the U.S. Supreme Court, Burstyn and London pulled out all the constitutional stops: they argued that the film had been incorrectly banned, that the New York law violated both the Free Exercise Clause and the Establishment Clause of the First Amendment's freedom of religion guarantee, that it violated the Free Speech Clause of the First Amendment, and that it violated the Due Process Clause of the Fourteenth Amendment.

For their first argument, that the film had been incorrectly reviewed, their petition maintained that the film was not sacrilegious, that it was "the story of a simple-minded, deeply religious woman who is taken advantage of by a stranger she believes to be St. Joseph. When the woman learns she is with child, she imagines it was

96 { *Chapter 4* }

immaculately conceived. There is nothing in the dialogue or action or acting in the picture that would suggest that it is to be given anything other than a literal meaning, or that it was intended as anything more than the story of the abuse of a deep and simple faith. That was the intent of the writer, the producer, the director, and professional cast, all of whom are devout Roman Catholics."

London also argued that New York's ban of *The Miracle* violated the First Amendment's prohibition of religious establishment. This argument had been ignored by the New York courts, but London believed that the regents' action had clearly favored one religious group over others. It was, after all, a minority group within the Catholic Church that had objected to the picture, whereas Protestant leaders had expressed approval. If the regents intended to show neutrality toward religion, surely they had stumbled when they caved in to Catholic pressure. Were they correct that such protection was a legitimate exercise of a state's police power to protect the public welfare?

London added three more constitutional questions he had already tried in state court; first, whether the censoring standards were so vague as to violate the Fourteenth Amendment's guarantee of due process; second, whether the statute violated the free exercise of religion as well as the nonestablishment of religion; and, finally, whether it violated the guarantee of free expression. Presenting so many constitutional questions, London knew, would make it harder for the justices to refuse the case.

For these additional constitutional questions, London was banking on recent jurisprudential developments. Arguing that the statutory terms were too vague looked particularly promising. Just a few years earlier, in a case called *Winters v. New York* (1948), the Court had held that a New York statute prohibiting "true crime" magazines and newspapers was overly vague and therefore void. A statute limiting freedom of expression, the Court insisted, had to give "fair notice of what acts would be punished." If a statute was so vague that "an honest distributor" could not know whether he was violating the statute, it could not stand. *Winters* established what came to be known as the "void-for-vagueness" doctrine. Having to determine what the State of New York meant by *sacrilege* could certainly be considered unfair since there was no "fair notice" of what the word meant. The disagreement among clergy of different sects as to what was sacrilegious and what was not provided ample evidence for this argument.

Winters held further promise: in that case, Justice Reed had written that "the line between the informing and the entertaining is too elusive" to be a factor in First Amendment cases. With this sentence, he may have, in the words of a 1949 *Yale Law Journal* article, "sounded the death knell of the idea-entertainment dichotomy." This dichotomy, of course, had plagued movies since their invention and had formed the basis for the *Mutual* decision. Movies still were not accepted by the judiciary as legitimate vehicles of expression, but with the *Winters* precedent, London and Burstyn found solid traction for their attempt to break new legal ground and put movies into the "informing" category. The *Paramount* decision four years earlier had made it clear that some of the justices were moving in that direction. Perhaps they were waiting for the right case to come along to nudge them into overturning *Mutual*.

There were fresh precedents to use in the area of religion as well. In 1940 the Supreme Court had incorporated the Free Exercise Clause of the First Amendment to state action, and recognized the Establishment Clause as a freedom guaranteed by the Fourteenth Amendment against state action seven years later. State legislatures were now held to the same religious freedom standards as Congress. London certainly could argue that the regents' response to Catholic pressure showed the state eager to accommodate the views of one particular religion, thus violating the Establishment Clause. He also could argue that interference with Burstyn's right to show the film and the public's right to view the film violated the Free Exercise Clause.

Moreover, the 1940 case that had incorporated the prohibition against religious establishment, *Cantwell v. Connecticut*, also reiterated that prior restraint on expression is unconstitutional. When Jesse Cantwell, a Jehovah's Witness, was arrested for playing an anti-Catholic phonograph record on a street in New Haven, a unanimous Supreme Court held that no statute could interfere with the right of expression unless it was clearly worded to protect against a well-defined clear-and-present danger. Did exhibition of *The Miracle* represent a clear-and-present danger sufficient to muzzle the right of free speech? Here London had another promising tool.

Like freedom of expression and freedom of religion, freedom of the press had been the subject of several recent Supreme Court cases. Press freedom expanded in 1941 when the Supreme Court heard the case of *Bridges v. California*, involving newspaper editorials critical of state judges. State courts had allowed the suppression of the editorials, but the Supreme Court said that without evidence that an editorial could materially harm a trial in progress, its suppression violated the First Amendment. The newspaper had to be free to publish. Five years later, the Court found that the Florida courts also had overstepped their bounds by squashing similar newspaper editorials. In both cases, the message was clear: newspapers could not be silenced unless the danger their publication posed was both "clear and present" and "of high imminence to the administration of justice." Unlike movies, which could be prevented because of a general and unproven threat, newspapers were given wide latitude. That newly codified freedom augured well for London and Burstyn as they prepared their briefs.

The first sign that the Court would revisit the issue of film freedom versus film restraint came on February 4, 1952, with the Supreme Court's grant of review. For the first time since 1915, the Supreme Court would listen to arguments about the voices of filmmakers and distributors as well as the right of audiences to choose the source of their entertainment. Burstyn was thrilled, saying that it was "a step forward in the long struggle to free the American screen from censorship." A newspaper headline read, "Interest Is Widespread," and Bosley Crowther used his column to encourage the Court to establish a "turning point in the destiny of American films."

This case was a first in another respect also, one usually overlooked. It was the first time the U.S. Supreme Court, or any U.S. court, had considered sacrilege as a censorable idea. None of the states that had included sacrilege as a censorable item had bothered to define what the word meant, including New York's Board of Regents. Burstyn's challenge would demand such definition.

Burstyn was now supported by the ACLU (which had taken over for the NYCLU), the American Jewish Congress, the Metropolitan Committee for Religious Liberty, the International Motion Picture Organization, and the National Lawyers Guild. As it turned out, however, Burstyn would be limited to two amicus supporters and

New York State to just one. Amicus participation rules allowed attorneys for each side to object to the filing of amicus briefs supporting the other side. A group so barred could petition the Court to be included. But in the late 1940s and early 1950s, responding to some high-profile cases that had attracted voluminous amicus requests, the Court was, according to legal professor John Frank, "extremely strict in the barring of amicus briefs," a practice he found disturbing because it limited the range of arguments available for the judges' consideration. In Burstyn's case, this meant that New York Solicitor General Wendell Brown would have to agree to Burstyn's amici, and Ephraim London would have to agree to New York's. After protracted negotiations on this issue (Alan Westin's 1961 book, *The Miracle Case*, has all the details), the state agreed to allow the ACLU brief (and whoever would join it) and one other. London agreed to one amicus for the state — it had chosen the Catholic Welfare Committee. London's agreement to the Catholic group's participation makes sense because he intended to argue that New York was violating both the Establishment Clause and the Free Exercise Clause by authorizing its censors to screen out sacrilegious movies. How much clearer could his argument be when the state came to Court with the Catholics by its side? The Catholic Welfare Committee's brief, which had been written by the legal adviser to Cardinal Spellman, would help to prove London's point that the state was too cozy with the Catholic Church.

Burstyn and London were delighted with the news that a new dissident Catholic group calling itself Catholics for Cultural Action wanted to join Burstyn's side. The group had just been organized by some Catholic writers, lawyers, and educators who worried that Spellman's recent acts of activism smacked of cultural bullying. Even before the *Miracle* episode, there had been attempts by some Catholics to shut down what they found offensive. A group of Catholic War Veterans had demanded the boycott of a New Jersey television station because it had scheduled a film by Charlie Chaplin (notoriously atheistic). A Metropolitan Opera production of Verdi's *Don Carlos* had been picketed because it portrayed a priest assisting in an assassination. Dismayed at this type of activity, a group of liberal Catholics drafted a brief and circulated it to "like-minded Catholic laymen throughout the country." The letter invited these others to show that they were not on "the side of censorship and suppression" by taking public stands on "controversies involving 'politics, art, or education.'" Worried about what it called "cultural intolerance," the Catholics for Cultural Action organized to counteract Catholic pressure against *The Miracle*. They wanted to demonstrate that Catholic opinion was neither monolithic nor unanimous.

London desperately wanted this amicus brief because it would counterbalance the Catholic Welfare Conference's brief for the state and prove that even Catholics disagreed about the sacrilege of *The Miracle*. Unfortunately for London and Burstyn, the archdiocese reigned in the new splinter group, persuading its members to withdraw their amicus support by insinuating that they were undercutting Spellman, and by promising to consider their views in any future censorship issues. London's hopes were dashed—the only Catholic voice heard in the Supreme Court would be that of the decidedly conservative Catholic Welfare Conference. It would have to be countered by the American Jewish Congress and the Metropolitan Committee for Religious Freedom, both of which had joined the ACLU brief.

Those writing the ACLU amicus brief for *Burstyn v. Wilson* were some of the organization's brightest stars. The brief carried the names of Arthur Garfield Hays, one of America's most famous trial lawyers; Osmond Fraenkel, considered the ACLU's best litigator with fifteen Supreme Court appearances under his belt; Morris Ernst, who had successfully defended James Joyce's *Ulysses* from obscenity charges; Emmanuel Redfield, another familiar face at the Supreme Court; and Shad Polier, a noted civil rights attorney and counsel to the American Jewish Congress.

Their arguments were based on New York's violation of free speech and its establishment of religion. The brief read like a summary of all the increasingly familiar arguments: first, that *Mutual* could not possibly be controlling any more since it had been decided ten years before the Court had held states accountable for violations of free speech in the *Gitlow* decision of 1925; second, that *Mutual* "was as anachronistic as the nickelodeon" because movies were far from mere entertainment, and even as such, they still should be accorded full constitutional protection (citing *Winters*); third, that prior restraint violated freedom of the press; fourth, that motion picture censorship clearly was influenced by the whims of "pressure groups" and reflected the "suppression of ideas"; fifth, that in seeking to protect against sacrilegious messages, in reality the state was acting to suppress heresy, which once begun "requires a boundless inquisition into religious views" and would lead to protection of a single religious view; sixth, that New York had no reason to suspect that exhibition of the film would cause any of the kind of societal damage it had the duty to prevent; and, finally, that the statute was "so vague that men of common intelligence must necessarily guess at its meaning." It was a most comprehensive brief.

On the other side, the Catholic Welfare Committee's amicus for the state insisted that because the New York courts had found censorship of *The Miracle* a permissible use of police power to protect the public welfare and not an establishment of religion, the Supreme Court should accept the state court opinion. "Neither the regents nor the New York Courts have attempted to decree that anyone must accept or subscribe to any religious views concerning the Nativity of Christ. They have simply enforced a moderate statutory limitation on the means by which a caricature of those views may be expressed in an entertainment spectacle." The group also took a more narrow, legalistic route and asked the Court not to allow Burstyn to attack the constitutionality of a statute of which he had availed himself many times. Quoting a 1947 Supreme Court case, they wrote, "It is an elementary rule of constitutional law that one may not 'retain the benefits of the Act while attacking the constitutionality of one of its important conditions." However, this argument neglected the important consideration that Burstyn's legally issued license had been revoked—hardly the same thing as attacking a statute under which one has expected to gain.

At the Supreme Court

On April 24, 1952, Chief Justice Fred Vinson and Associate Justices Hugo Black, William O. Douglas, Stanley Reed, Felix Frankfurter, Tom C. Clark, Robert Jackson, Sherman Minton, and Harold Burton assembled to hear oral arguments in *Burstyn v. Wilson*. It was a historic moment: only the second time that the Court would deliberate

{ *Chapter 4* }

the amount of freedom to be constitutionally accorded to movies. It was also the first time that justices of the Supreme Court had watched a movie as part of a proceeding. (They were shown *The Miracle* the day before the oral argument. As they filed out of the temporary movie theater in the Supreme Court building, Justice Minton was overheard saying that if he had paid any money to see the film, it would have been too much. The other justices have left behind no clue as to their evaluation of Rossellini's work.)

As he stepped to the podium to make Burstyn's case before the nine justices, London must have been nervous; it was his first appearance at the Supreme Court and he faced the justices alone, whereas New York had sent both the regents' counsel, Charles Brind, and Solicitor General Brown. London stepped to the podium and began with the mandatory phrase, "Mr. Chief Justice and may it please the Court," launched into his carefully prepared argument, and tried to get as much in as possible before the first inevitable interruption by a justice. London had one full hour to make his case (today each side gets only half an hour).

London had boiled down Burstyn's case to just two questions: the broad issue of whether the statute was an unconstitutional abridgment of the right of free communication, and the more narrow, more likely winnable issue of whether censoring for sacrilege was unconstitutional. The charge of sacrilege was unconstitutional on three grounds, he argued; first, because the statute's vagueness nearly guaranteed differing interpretations by reasonably intelligent people (as indeed had happened in this case); second, because censoring for sacrilege violated the separation of church and state; and third, because allowing the Board of Regents, a governmental body, to determine the definition of sacrilege was a violation of the freedom of religious expression. He added that *The Miracle* itself could not be considered sacrilegious since neither the Italian Ministry nor the Vatican had made any religious objections. He managed to get this far through his presentation before he was interrupted by Vinson. The chief justice wondered whether the Italian officials had had any other objection, to which London happily answered "no." He was able to add that *Ways of Love* was recommended by the American National Board of Review and that it had been named best foreign film of 1950. (He had dropped the argument that the regents had no authority to revoke the license because the state's highest court had said that it did and there the matter necessarily ended.)

The justices must have wondered where London was heading when he started off his next argument, "We do not say that there may be no censorship of motion pictures. We believe that censorship of motion pictures is proper, but we believe that the only proper remedy where a picture is obscene or indecent is criminal prosecution, not prior restraint, not licensing. . . . Any licensing system, such as we have here, which provides that no picture may be shown in the State unless it is first approved by a censorship board, and the censorship board, in effect, is answerable to no one, is an abridgment of the right of freedom of communication."

Here, in pure form, was the argument against prior restraint: if movies are to be censored, it needs to be done after first exhibition. Then, if necessary, arrest and prosecute the exhibitors for obscenity or indecency, London urged, but not before the films had been seen by no one other than a bureaucrat. "We say," continued London, "that the same standards apply to motion pictures as apply to magazines and other media of the press. I think there is no question but that magazines cannot be licensed; and that periodicals and books cannot be licensed in advance. And I submit that the same rule applies to motion pictures." This brought a question from Justice Burton about the television situation, giving London an opening to talk about the "curious anomaly and absurdity in the law. A picture," he went on, "that is refused a license for exhibition in theaters may still be shown in the State over television. A limited audience is prevented from seeing the film in a theater while a huge audience may see the banned film over television."

London next countered an argument in the state's brief that motion picture censorship was necessary to maintain what it called the public peace. "I do not believe," he began, "there has been a case in which an attempt was made to ban a film on the ground that it would create a public disturbance." Frankfurter, known to be a tiger during oral arguments, pounced: "Do you think that it would make a difference if . . . the legislature of New York had added, 'because all of these tend towards the breach of the public peace?' Do you think that would have made a difference to you?" London was forced to answer that it would not have made a difference, otherwise he would have been caught admitting that prior restraint might be acceptable. Frankfurter had scored a point. But London fired back. "It played in New York for three months. There was never any disturbance. There were some pickets walking outside very peaceably . . . but there was never any breach of the peace, never any question of that. . . . My opponents will have to concede that the preservation of the public peace was not the motive in banning this film." Justice Reed then joined in, offering London a chance he jumped on: "Would you say that it was the preservation of public morals?" London replied, "No, Your Honor. I say that the reason given was that it was offensive to the religious sensibilities of Roman Catholics."

He then went straight to the heart of the matter and asked the justices to overturn *Mutual*. Because that case had been argued on the free speech provisions of the Ohio Constitution, before the Court had begun to "virtually incorporate" the First Amendment through the Fourteenth Amendment, it had to fall, London repeated.

Since the state's brief had relied heavily upon *Mutual*'s holding that motion pictures were not vehicles of communication, London used his oral argument time to attack that idea. Reminding the justices of their recent *Winters* decision and repeating Reed's own reasoning in that case that it was impossible to distinguish between entertainment and information, London turned to a list of movies currently playing in New York City, showing that most, although entertaining, were also communicating ideas. *Les Miserables, Viva Zapata*, T. S. Eliot's *Murder in the Cathedral,* and *Rashomon* were just four of the movies he used to prove his point. "The communication of ideas by means of media that is also entertaining is the most effective means. . . . No tract was ever quite so effective as *Uncle Tom's Cabin,* so far as the dissemination of an idea was concerned."

New York had also relied heavily (and unwisely) on the second main line of reasoning set down by the 1915 Court in *Mutual:* that movies were nothing other than a business and therefore deserved no special First Amendment consideration. This was an argument that by 1952 was clearly outdated. Newspapers and magazines were certainly big businesses, said London, yet they were not subject to prior restraint.

Finally, he attacked the state's last major argument: that the success and attractiveness of movies made them dangerous enough to require control. "The mere fact that a communication is effective," London charged, "does not mean that it should be denied the freedom guaranteed by the Constitution. If that were the rule, the freedom means absolutely nothing." A seemingly incredulous Minton asked London whether movies could not legitimately be censored even for obscenity. Although we have no audiotapes of the proceedings, it is clear from the words of the written record that London's answer was passionate intransigence: "Not even for obscenity, not censored in advance, not licensed, not subject to a licensing arrangement, Your Honor, even for obscenity."

Returning to the vagueness issue, London revisited the *Winters* precedent. "I think this case affords a classic illustration of a statutory provision about which men of common intelligence must necessarily differ. . . . Here you have virtually 100 ministers of many sects, from the Episcopal to the Unitarian, all agreeing that this film is not sacrilegious. . . . What is sacred depends on the individual's beliefs." The state's brief had insisted that *The Miracle* controversy was not religious. How could it not be? London pointed to the Catholics who adamantly believed the film to be sacrilegious and the large number of Protestants who insisted that it was not. That was clearly a religious controversy into which the regents had stepped, "banning the film and declaring at the same time that its action has nothing whatever to do with religion." This brought London neatly around to the separation of church and state issue. "If a government official judges according to a religious doctrine he violates the constitutional warranty that the church and state shall be separate."

London finished by "pleading" with the Court to decide the case on the broad constitutional ground that prior restraint was unconstitutional. Foreshadowing movie censorship litigation over the next thirteen years, London closed, "I think to avoid a multiplicity of suits the question ought to be finally laid to rest." All in all, London had been relatively free to make his arguments with little interruption by the justices.

Then it was Brind's turn for New York. He stepped to the podium and began by insisting that the statute was "very narrow." According to Brind, the regents did not rely on their own opinions when deciding whether a movie fell into one of the proscribed categories of the statute. His circuitous, rather torturous language pressed

Frankfurter to interrupt repeatedly, trying to figure out how the regents determined whether a motion picture was "sacrilegious." Brind finally had to admit that they used their own personal judgments, not that of any authoritative religious institution.

Then, in a misguided attempt to prove the "narrowness" of the statute, Brind opened a dangerous avenue: he told the justices that in New York State only movies shown for profit were censorable. That got the discussion centered on the hypothetical issue of whether a church group, showing a movie without charging admission (hence exempt from review), could be told it could not show a sacrilegious movie. Brind danced around the issue but really did not know the answer. The justices seemed to bait Brind as if they were the professors and he the first-year law student. Finally, Jackson tried to get to the bottom of the issue: "Is this a correct statement of your view of the New York law? That the New York law prohibits sacrilegious for pay, but permits sacrilegious for its own sake?" Brind sidestepped again. Then, in what must have been great relief, he turned the podium over to Solicitor General Brown, who had to begin his presentation by admitting that Brind had been incorrect earlier when he had told the Court that certain educational movies did not need licenses (an error that led to the state sending the Court an explanatory letter a few days later). This could only have been a most uncomfortable moment for both representatives of New York State at the podium.

Brown then did his best to bring the Court back around to the question of overturning *Mutual*. He attempted to undermine London's argument that *Mutual* was antiquated by pointing to numerous decisions that had relied on *Mutual* since 1915 and by quoting Frankfurter's dictum from a speech case just four years earlier: "Movies have created problems not presented by the circulation of books, pamphlets, or newspapers, and so the movies have been constitutionally regulated." But, the chief justice interrupted Brown, the Court had recently made different statements. Quoting directly from the *Paramount* case, Vinson repeated the phrase, "We have no doubt that moving pictures, like newspaper and radio, are included in the press whose freedom is guaranteed by the First Amendment." Brown must have been uncomfortable — here was the chief justice making the opponents' case. So, Brown wisely reminded the justices about the *Eureka Productions* case in which the Supreme Court had used

Mutual as its rationale for upholding a federal court procensorship ruling in 1938. Pointing to the influence of movies, which if anything had grown greater in 1952 than it had been in 1915, and to the much larger "relaxed, receptive audiences" (which he skillfully pointed out often included children and "teenage boys and girls in darkened theaters"), Brown contended that a state needed the power to regulate movie expression. After appealing to peoples' fears about the effect of movies, he moved on to counter London's television argument by noting that the Federal Communications Commission could revoke licenses for inappropriate broadcasts.

Then he struck a low (but effective) blow: "Counsel [London] has given the impression that the motion picture industry in this country is very much opposed to censorship. I doubt very much that this is so. Certainly there is nothing before this Court to establish that fact. I am informed the industry was requested to participate in this case and refused to do so." Of course, that was true, and as a statement of fact could have been damaging. So London used his brief rebuttal time to contradict Brown and dispel the idea that the industry actively opposed Burstyn's case. Surely the industry could not be seen as accepting censorship, London replied, as evidenced by the MPAA's participation in a second censorship case the Court had just agreed to consider—the *Gelling* case from Marshall, Texas. But Brown had been able to score significant points when he read from the MPAA's Production Code: "Theatrical motion pictures . . . are primarily to be regarded as entertainment. . . . The latitude given to film material cannot, in consequence, be as wide as the latitude given to book material or to newspapers or to plays on the legitimate stage." Those words had been written in 1930, when the industry was eager to prove its patriotism and its desire to clean its own house to stave off federal censorship, but the industry had never repudiated the idea. Brown was able to finish strong, building on this damaging idea by reminding the Court gently that not one, but two appellate courts of New York State had found *The Miracle* sacrilegious and worthy of banning. Brind, Brown, and London stepped back. It was up to the justices now.

When the justices met to discuss Burstyn's case two days later, there was only partial agreement about what to do. According to Tom Clark's conference notes, all wanted to release *The Miracle* from

{ *Chapter 4* }

its New York ban but there was considerable disagreement as to how. Four wanted to take the narrowest possible route: reverse the New York Court of Appeals on the ground that sacrilege was too indefinite to stand as a constitutional censoring standard. Two, Black and Douglas, were ready to reverse because they saw the entire statute as unconstitutional prior restraint. They were not alone in wanting to relegate *Mutual* to Fuld's "history shelf." In this, they were joined by two of the more conservative justices, Chief Justice Vinson and Tom Clark.

Douglas and Black's views about an absolute right to free expression under the First Amendment were well known. Vinson, however, a relatively conservative justice, seemed an odd convert to the *Mutual*-must-go group, especially since he abhorred overturning long-standing precedents. But Vinson viewed censorship of movies as he did censorship of newspapers. Because the Supreme Court had protected newspapers from prior restraint since 1931, Vinson (no matter what his views on movies might have been) voted to extend the First Amendment to movies as well. Apparently, Clark agreed. Both justices saw *Near v. Minnesota* as the controlling precedent.

But there were two justices who were not ready to go that far. Robert Jackson and Harold Burton initially argued against overturning *Mutual*. Jackson was willing to accept the vagueness argument, and that censoring for sacrilege violated religious freedom, and he certainly did not see *The Miracle* as sacrilegious, but he was worried about striking down movie licensing laws. Governmental censorship had been around a long time, he noted, and he was not ready to "release this lawless industry from censorship."

The Decision

Despite their differences, over the next four weeks the justices managed to negotiate their way to a unanimous decision that allowed *The Miracle* to be shown. On May 26, 1952, the Supreme Court delivered the opinion, and it did prove to be the turning point predicted by Bosley Crowther. More significant than that, this was a unanimous decision from a Court that had grown infamous for lack of unanimity. Before 1935, most Court terms had concluded with about 85 percent of the cases decided unanimously. But by 1943 more than half were split decisions, gradually rising to the highest ever to date in 1952, with 81 percent nonunanimous. This rare unanimous opinion for Burstyn was written by Tom Clark, a surprising choice considering this was a decision that both overturned a long-standing precedent and stretched the First Amendment. Clark was famously reluctant to vote to overturn precedents, and he was no First Amendment absolutist like Black and Douglas. He opposed such thinking, as he later wrote, "I do not believe that the First Amendment's commands are absolutes." Clark was, moreover, so staunch an anticommunist that some even believed he had little respect for the First Amendment. At his confirmation hearings just two years before, he had been accused of being an "oppressor of unpopular political faiths," and a "nonrespecter of free speech." These charges probably reflect Clark's actions as Truman's attorney general when he had compiled the first list of subversive organizations and conducted the first loyalty board investigations. However, he did favor free political speech, even for nonmajoritarian ideas; in 1946 he had written, "Even the enemies of liberty and tolerance — our noisy pro-Fascists and race bigots — must be allowed free speech. Granted that they would suppress our liberties if they could, that is no excuse for us to beat them to the punch by suppressing theirs first."

Clark may have been chosen to write the opinion because in 1952 he stood midway between those like Black and Douglas who wanted to overturn censorship entirely, and those like Jackson and Burton who were happy to see *Mutual* remain so that states could police the movie moguls. Since he was in the overturn-*Mutual* group at the justices' conference, but was less extreme than Black and Douglas, Clark was a natural choice in the eyes of the chief justice, who obviously did not want to write the opinion himself.

Both Clark's pragmatic judicial philosophy and the lack of agreement among the justices about how much freedom movies deserved are evident in his majority opinion. The reasoning was crafted to find in favor of Burstyn but in narrow terms. In straightforward language, Clark's opinion held that because New York State had violated both the free speech and the free press guarantees of the First Amendment by banning *The Miracle* on the vague ground of sacrilege, it was not even necessary to visit the other major argument, that

{ *Chapter 4* }

censoring for sacrilege violated the constitutional guarantee against establishment of a religion. But to say that New York had violated freedom of speech and freedom of the press, Clark had to wrestle with the ghost of *Mutual*. This he did by agreeing with London and the ACLU that *Mutual* had been decided in a different legal culture—fully ten years before the Court began the series of decisions that safeguarded speech from state action. The *Miracle* case, then, was the first time the justices had taken the opportunity to consider whether motion pictures should be considered part of the press or proper subjects for the free speech protection of the First Amendment. Of course, two other cases had knocked on the Supreme Court's door within the previous three years, but the Court had not shown any interest. Now, though, in 1952, it was ready. Clark answered the *Mutual* precedent that movies were not worthy methods of expression: "It cannot be doubted that motion pictures are a significant medium for the communication of ideas. They may affect public attitudes and behavior in a variety of ways, ranging from direct espousal of a political or social doctrine to the subtle shaping of thought that characterizes all artistic expression. The importance of motion pictures as an organ of public opinion is not lessened by the fact that they are designed to entertain as well as to inform." Citing *Winters v. New York*, Clark repeated that "the line between informing and entertaining is too elusive" to delineate, so such distinctions provided no basis for interfering with the right of a free press.

Having taken care of one argument against movie freedom, Clark moved to demolish another—the notion that because movies were made for profit, they were not legitimate organs of the press. "That books, newspapers, and magazines are published and sold for profit does not prevent them from being a form of expression whose liberty is safeguarded by the First Amendment. We fail to see why operation for profit should have any different effect in the case of motion pictures." Here was truly new ground: even free speech advocates often drew a distinction between political speech (which was, they felt, absolutely necessary to the functioning of a representative democracy and should be protected absolutely) and entertainment speech or commercial speech. As dedicated to expanding the First Amendment as Alexander Meikeljohn was, he believed that nonpolitical speech did not fall under the First Amendment because it could find whatever protection it deserved under the Fifth Amendment's guarantee against loss of liberty without due process. If a movie was censored, Meikeljohn would not have been perturbed because judicial review was available. But here the justices of the Supreme Court were moving ahead, using Burstyn's argument to carve a broad swath in First Amendment jurisprudence by adding movies to the protected category previously enjoyed only by nonentertainment speech. (Commercial speech would not be added to the protected categories of speech until 1976, and even then its protection would be limited.)

Clark then dismantled the third argument against movies: even if movies were capable of greater "evil" than other means of communication, that did not justify the "substantially unbridled censorship" in New York's ban of *The Miracle*. Such evil, if it existed, would be relevant but only in determining "the permissible scope of community control," presumably prosecution under penal statutes. "We conclude," Clark continued, "that expression by means of motion pictures is included within the free speech and free press guaranty of the First and Fourteenth Amendments." This was not dictum, as the *Paramount* concurrence had been: this was the real thing. *Mutual* was overturned. It was what the anticensorship forces had waited decades to hear. It must have been a sweet moment for Burstyn, London, and the ACLU.

But whatever euphoria they might have felt faded as Clark continued reading the opinion from the bench. "To hold that liberty of expression by means of motion pictures is guaranteed by the First and Fourteenth Amendments, however, [does not mean] that the Constitution requires absolute freedom to exhibit every motion picture of every kind at all times and all places." London's insistence that after-the-fact prosecution could protect the public had not persuaded the justices. Clearly, Clark and the Court were not about to turn the movie industry loose on the public. (This, perhaps, was a bow to Justice Jackson's argument in conference.) The Court was willing, however, to place limits on prior restraint that, as Clark noted next, since 1931 the Court had upheld for other media only in "exceptional cases." (Here he was talking about the *Near v. Minnesota* case, which had overturned prior restraint on newspapers.) So Clark put the State of New York on notice that if it intended to continue censoring movies, it had better be prepared to accept "a heavy burden" to prove that such restriction had been done only in "exceptional" cases. What would constitute an exceptional case, however, he did not say.

Clark next turned to the vagueness issue. Here he completely agreed with London and the ACLU that the New York courts' "broad and inclusive definition" of sacrilege was impossibly ambiguous. "New York's highest court says there is 'nothing mysterious' about the statutory provision applied in this case. 'It is simply this: that no religion, as that word is understood by the ordinary, reasonable person, shall be treated with contempt, mockery, scorn, and ridicule.'" But this was far too vague for Clark. It set the censor "adrift upon a boundless sea amid a myriad of conflicting currents of religious views, with no charts but those provided by the most vocal and powerful orthodoxies. New York cannot vest such unlimited restraining control over motion pictures in a censor." The part about "powerful orthodoxies" must have been welcome to Burstyn and Lillian Gerard, who had born the brunt of so much Catholic censure at the Paris Theatre.

Noting that censoring for sacrilege *might* violate both the Establishment Clause and the Free Exercise Clause of the First Amendment, Clark restricted the decision to free speech and free press because they were all the justification the Court needed to strike down New York's statute. If the state had violated separation of church and state (which Clark clearly thought was the case), it was unnecessary to consider that issue because its violation of free speech and free press as well as its impermissible vagueness were sufficient to strike down the ban on *The Miracle*.

So far, the Court was on the side of the anticensorites and all was clear: prior restraint on movies violated the free speech and free press guarantees of the First Amendment, and sacrilege was too vague a topic to pass constitutional muster. But then the decision became murky.

Since the term "sacrilegious" is the sole standard under attack here, it is not necessary for us to decide, for example, *whether a state may censor motion pictures under a clearly drawn statute designed and applied to prevent the showing of obscene films.* That is a very different question from the one now before us. We hold only that under the First and Fourteenth Amendments a state may not ban a film on the basis of a censor's conclusion that it is "sacrilegious." (emphasis added)

So ended Clark's concise opinion. But what did that last paragraph mean? Did it mean that states and cities could now only censor movies for obscenity? Or was that just an example and states could still censor for other matters provided the statute was "clearly drawn"? If movies were now under the protection of the First Amendment, how could censors continue to practice prior restraint? Such questions were to bedevil constitutional scholars for years to come. Some, like John T. Ford, were downright disappointed: "Students of the subject have been awaiting the overruling of the anachronistic *Mutual Film* case for so long that somehow the great day should be introduced with a legal equivalent of the rolling of drums; one hoped for an opinion in the grand style. Justice Clark treats the case as just another job in a work-a-day world. . . . For all one's gratitude for what is served, the taste is a little flat."

But Clark's opinion was not the final word on *Burstyn*. A seventy-six-word concurring opinion by Justice Reed (who normally refrained from such explications) went mostly overlooked by Supreme Court commentators. But had they paid attention they would have seen that Reed had been compelled to write additionally because he had spotted a big problem with the Court's majority opinion. The ever-practical Reed foresaw the logical conclusion to Clark's opinion and what was to come in the relationship between the Court and movie censors. Because the decision did not "foreclose" all governmental censorship, it would necessarily fall to the justices to decide, case by case and movie reel by movie reel, whether the First Amendment had been violated by state censors. A moderately astute anticensorite would see this statement as an open invitation to litigate whenever a censor ban interfered with profit potential. How much influence this had on later distributors and their decision to sue is uncertain, but Reed's concurrence seems not to have attracted much notice at the time.

A much longer concurring opinion did attract a great deal of notice: Justice Frankfurter (joined by Jackson and Burton) was distressed by New York's loose use of the word *sacrilege*. New York's highest court had relied upon a *Funk & Wagnall's Dictionary* definition that, to Frankfurter, was a most unhelpful tautology: "The act of violating or profaning anything sacred." Sacrilege, according to the New York Court of Appeals, meant defiling something sacred. And who was to decide what was sacred, Frankfurter wanted to know. Always a stickler for judicial precision, Frankfurter must have been paying close attention when Burstyn and London applied for certiorari the previous December. Long before the briefs came in, he set to work on the meaning of the words *sacrilege* and *blasphemy*. Frankfurter sought guidance on this question from George La Piana, a historian at Harvard University, who affirmed Frankfurter's hunch that sacrilege had no immutable meaning across time. When London remarked during oral argument that obscenity had been repeatedly defined in numerous court cases, yet sacrilege had never been spelled out, he was playing directly into Frankfurter's hands.

"Well-equipped law libraries are not niggardly in their reflection of 'the sense and experience of men,'" Justice Frankfurter wrote, "but we must search elsewhere for any which gives to 'sacrilege' its meaning." What La Piana, Frankfurter, and his clerk found when they searched elsewhere was that sacrilege had always meant the physical desecration of religious symbols or church property. But when used "at large," Frankfurter noted, the word had come to mean "the basis for punishing deviation from doctrine." This, indeed, was how New York had used it, and Frankfurter devoted twenty-two pages of the *Burstyn* opinion to setting the legal record straight. He showed that in ecclesiastical matters since the Middle Ages, sacrilege had never been considered synonymous with apostasy, heresy, or blasphemy, although these three terms were clearly closer to what the New York legislature had meant when it passed the motion picture censorship statute. New York's Court of Appeals then compounded the situation by agreeing with the legislature's erroneous connotation. Frankfurter accused them of trying to "fetter the mind" with language that was both imprecise and impossibly vague. What New York had done, Frankfurter was certain, was not to ban something *sacrilegious* but to ban something *blasphemous*.

Looking at the weakness of the statutory language enabled Frankfurter to put his pen directly on the main controversy at issue over

The Miracle: "To criticize or assail religious doctrine may wound to the quick those who are attached to the doctrine and profoundly cherish it. But to bar such pictorial discussion is to subject nonconformists to the rule of sects." Frankfurter recognized that each sect would delineate what was sacred to it. Where that became problematic was when the state used its authority to protect such ideas from criticism or ridicule.

Although the Supreme Court was bound by legal custom to accept a state court's interpretation of its statutory language, Frankfurter saw such imprecision as proof that the statute offended due process. Back in 1915, the *Mutual* justices had insisted that words such as "moral, amusing, or harmless" got meaning from the "sense and experience of men." But, said Frankfurter, that could not be the case with a word such as *sacrilegious* because, as his research had shown, that word's meaning had varied over time and with its context. "The impossibility of knowing" what movies would be considered sacrilegious made the term "unconstitutionally vague." All in all, it was a lengthy concurring opinion that showed off Frankfurter's considerable homework on the meaning of sacrilege, but its only real point was that New York's statute was too unspecific (which the majority opinion had already said) and its courts had used a commonly accepted but incorrect connotation. However, for Frankfurter's threshold of constitutionality, this second point was critical. He was one of the strongest advocates in the Court's history of judicial restraint, particularly in cases involving long-accepted statutes (like New York's censorship law) and long-standing precedents (like *Mutual*). For him to feel any ease in overturning both, it had to be clear that the law at issue was incorrect. New York had used *sacrilegious* when it should have used *blasphemous*. Only with this point of law established could Frankfurter see his way clear to freeing *The Miracle*.

Striking the accusation of sacrilege for vagueness was great news for Burstyn and the future of his film, but Frankfurter's concurrence also carried better news, especially for film critics. Quoting from nine reviews, Frankfurter had found critics' opinions of great importance. After thirty years of censoring without concern for art, the states had been put on notice by one Supreme Court justice that film had artistic value and that film critics were the best judges of that value.

Moreover, Frankfurter's concerns were not just about vagueness and censorial discretion; he also worried about the effect such imprecision would have on the making of films. The industry, he feared, would pay more attention to what might cause offense to various sects than it would to the art of the film. "The effect of such demands upon art and upon those whose function is to enhance the culture of a society need not be labored." Although Burstyn and Hollywood had cause to worry over Clark's opinion, which allowed prior restraint to go on although under a heavy burden of proof, Frankfurter's final words must have offered real comfort. The Court had not only overturned *Mutual*; Frankfurter had written a concurring opinion that was the diametric opposite of Justice McKenna's insistence that movies were mere spectacles.

News of the decision made the front pages of both the *New York Times* and the New York *Herald-Tribune*. The *Times* considered the case important enough to devote a thirty-seven word summary as its headline: "Court Guarantees Films Free Speech: Ends "Miracle" Ban — Opinion Unanimous — High Tribunal Reverses State Appeals Bench in Sacrilege Case — Overturns Own Decision — Denies, as Held 37 Years Ago, That All Motion Pictures Are 'Business Pure and Simple.'"

Burstyn and London were elated. *The Miracle* would be shown in New York. But those pessimistic MPAA lawyers had been right: this was not a sweeping destruction of prior restraint. Sacrilege was out, but a narrowly drawn statute could still suffice to keep a film from the public until a government agency cleared its way.

However, there was much for anticensorites to celebrate. *Mutual* had been overturned, motion pictures had been brought under the free speech protection of the First Amendment, vague standards that had stood legally invulnerable for forty years were now open to question, states could no longer enjoin communication for purposes of religious orthodoxy, and the legal burden of proof had shifted (at least theoretically) — from the distributor to the censor. And the Legion of Decency had lost its bid to take over control of foreign films.

Contemporary and later commentators have remarked on the Court's refusal to declare movie censorship unconstitutional. It is shortsighted to see this opinion as insufficient or unsatisfactory.

Instead, it should be viewed as the beginning the was. Throughout its history, the Supreme Court has consistently balked at deciding cases on broad constitutional grounds. Clark's cautious opinion was really nothing more than a predictably restrained decision.

Yet, although its restraint was normal, the decision itself deserves to be seen as a remarkable turnabout. This was a Court in the throes of what most Americans believed to be a national security crisis. This Court, which had ruled so frequently against claims of civil liberties and in favor of subversives lists and loyalty oaths, not only had taken a speech-protective stance but had done so for a medium still considered potentially dangerous. Even more surprising, it had done so unanimously during the term noted for having fewer unanimous decisions than at any time in the Court's history.

At a press conference a few days later, Burstyn basked in the spotlight, calling the opinion that now bore his name "a victory of the first magnitude . . . clearing the way for the motion picture to take its rightful place as a major and adult art form and as a medium of expression and communication of ideas on all facets of our life and society." The decision marked "the beginning of adult days for the film industry."

The MPAA, which had refused to help Burstyn, also exulted, reprinting in digest form the positive comments of thirty-seven newspapers and magazines from across the nation. *Burstyn* was, Johnston said, "a giant step forward toward removing all the shackles of censorship from the screen." The ACLU had a double victory to celebrate: "The most striking blow the courts have dealt censorship in years," and a jab at the power of one of the most influential pressure groups the union had been targeting for years — the Catholic Church. *Burstyn* was a warning, they said, to "all pressure groups . . . that bans on expression of opinion will not be defended in a democratic society because they run counter to democracy's fundamental concept of unfettered free speech."

Spellman declined comment, but much of the Catholic press despaired. The *Tablet*, which a year before had accused the ACLU of aiding communism by supporting *The Miracle*, called the decision "a victory for the vendors of smut . . . the vicious assailants out to destroy the Christian religion are free to go and do their worst."

Justice Clark got lots of mail about his opinion, much of it pats on the back from other legal colleagues. But much of it also came from average citizens who were appalled. One particularly disgruntled woman from Missouri sent him a little poem:

> There are nine men in Washington.
> To folly much inclined
> They sat to judge a movie
> Though all of them were blind.

The negative letters presaged what was to come in the wake of *Burstyn:* a major clash between those who longed for film freedom and those like the letter writer above who feared for the nation's morals should movie producers gain full access to the rights of the First Amendment.

After reinstatement of *The Miracle* at the Paris Theatre, the lines that had wound around the block during the boycott demonstrations returned. The audience excitement lasted five weeks and then the crowds dropped off. Few noticed when the film closed.

When things quieted down, the International Motion Picture Organization and the Metropolitan Committee for Religious Liberty honored Burstyn at a luncheon in New York City with 310 people attending. The two groups were grateful, they said, for Burstyn's work, which led to the "reaffirmation of their civil and religious freedoms." Burstyn tried to explain why he had gone to so much trouble for a forty-minute movie. "I felt that it was about time to try to restore a little dignity. I think we have now achieved this." Arthur Garfield Hays, also being feted for his amicus participation with the ACLU, spent much of his speech praising Burstyn. The ACLU lawyers had merely been "backseat drivers," Hays insisted. As for the MPAA, the movie industry "with all its money couldn't accomplish what Burstyn and London did." Noting that it had been a long fight, Hays continued, "In this kind of cause, you win sometimes, but you never lose."

Although Burstyn's characterization of the case as "a victory of the first magnitude" might have seemed a bit boastful at the time, over the course of the next fifteen years, his words would prove accurate. Free speech advocates and some judges had labored for decades to expand the interpretation of the First Amendment to include nonmajoritarian ideas, and by the 1940s, they were making some head-way. Now the justices of the Supreme Court, prodded by Burstyn, London, and the ACLU, had included movies within those commu-nications deserving protection from restraint.

But it was certainly not a victory for all: those like the Catholics who worried over public morality, those who fretted over impres-sionable children, and those who valued social stability certainly did not share Burstyn's view. Those who favored free speech, however, who wanted to see movies grow into a mature art form, and who had grown tired of faceless censors deciding what could and could not be seen applauded Burstyn and his anticensorship ally, Ephraim London.

In the law reviews, *Burstyn v. Wilson* met with near universal approval. Only one legal analyst questioned the decision's direc-tion—Howard Newcomb writing in the *North Dakota Law Review* argued that the Court had thrown Christian morality out the legal window. Not even a single issue of the *North Dakota Law Review* went by, though, before Charles Alan Wright, a law professor from the University of Minnesota, blasted Newcomb and insisted that the Court had done nothing other than maintain governmental neutral-ity on religious dogma. It only made sense, Wright argued. If a statute could outlaw sacrilege, then anything offensive to any of the "313" denominations in the United States could be banned. "The same law which prohibited the showing of *The Miracle*," he wrote, "would prohibit the showing of *The Robe*. . . . The result, of course, would be that nothing touching on religion could appear in any movie, nor presumably, could it be communicated by newspaper or radio or books or television."

John P. Frank, who wrote annual Court summaries for the *Univer-sity of Chicago Law Review*, noted that it was about time for the jus-tices to overturn *Mutual*. He predicted that the biggest impact would be on Hollywood, which was, as he wrote, "under attack from any-one with a loud voice." He hoped that the decision would, "in the long run," contribute "a little courage to a TV-scared, pressure-group-scared, Un-American-Activities-scared industry." Other legal analysts mostly saw the decision as a "logical and desirable step."

The law review articles were important, but not nearly so influen-tial with the public as another Burstyn contribution. Through his dogged determination not to bow to Catholic pressure and not to allow his license to be revoked, Burstyn managed to accomplish something other anticensorites had tried but failed to do. He had pushed the issue of film censorship onto the front page. For more than three decades, inconspicuous censors had been having a conspicuous effect on movie screens, banning movies they found offensive, hacking apart movies they found menacing, and approving only those they found innocuous. Except for the controversy over *The Birth of a Baby*, all those distributors who challenged censorship in the 1930s had managed to force little light on the subject. News of their efforts had been buried back on page forty-three. But in 1951 and 1952, Burstyn, London, and the ACLU forced the censor manipulations into the spotlight both in the New York newspapers and in the national media. Tom Clark's "boundless," uncharted "sea" upon which the censors had been drifting, answering only to "the most vocal and powerful orthodoxies," was now visible for all to see.

Looking at the case more than fifty years later, it is easy to slip into the fallacy of appraising it as an inevitable development. As foreign films became more popular, as TV pushed Hollywood to make more daring movies, as popular culture responded to the broadened influences of the postwar world, it seems that the demise of motion picture censorship was inevitable. But, we must remember also that there was little reason for optimism when Burstyn and London applied for review. This was the heyday of the red scare, when conformity in both popular culture and political opinions was valued and when the U.S. Supreme Court was as likely to find against civil rights cases as it was to favor them. The 1951–1952 Court that heard Burstyn and London's appeal is noted for some notorious decisions. This bench had little sympathy for an Italian immigrant who was threatened with deportation because he had briefly flirted with Communist Party membership twenty years earlier. It upheld the 1940 Smith Act against allegations that it violated the First Amendment's guarantee of free speech in the *Dennis v. United States* case. It upheld the Immigration and Naturalization Service's policy of putting aliens in jail indefinitely without bail. It also upheld the right of a school board to find a teacher guilty by association, and it approved the right of the government to wiretap suspected subversives. The Court that would zealously protect free speech rights against state and federal infringement was the Court of the 1960s. Its movement into civil liberties was backed by public opinion as many Americans came to favor expansion of individual rights. The *Burstyn* case, however, was heard years before by a Court with a different chief justice and in an era when political speech was limited to majoritarian ideas and entertainment speech was viewed as second-class communication of ideas. Perhaps, then, the way to view this unlikely victory is to see that movies had arrived, legally and intellectually, through the back door—they were taken just seriously enough to deserve constitutional respect but not enough to be set completely free. That would take another thirteen years and a lot more litigation.

There might have been many things to be afraid of in the early cold war, the Supreme Court suggested, but *The Miracle* was not one of them.

Burstyn's Progeny

Although Burstyn and London could not have known it at the time, the Supreme Court was setting out on a new course. It is, of course, clear in hindsight, but it was by no means obvious in 1952 that the Court was moving to enhance movie freedom. It had reversed its 1915 position that movies were of no benefit to societal discourse and, as a business like any other, were subject to regulation by the state. In 1925, when the Court first applied the First Amendment to state actions, and in 1931, when the Court held that newspapers could not be subjected to prior restraint, the justices had taken the first steps toward an expanded scope of free speech and free press. Then, in the mid-1950s, the Court freed some publications by venturing into the problematic business of defining obscenity. But motion picture censorship with its statutory prior restraint stood in stark contrast with such evolving interpretations of the First Amendment. Fear of societal harm from movies was still so great that it could and did trump constitutional issues and kept movies from the freedom accorded to other media.

What had been crystal clear to the justices in 1915 about movies was becoming much less certain by the 1950s. As movies became more mature as an art form, it was evident that the *Mutual* decision was outmoded—a relic of much earlier and increasingly irrelevant jurisprudence. As one 1953 law review put it, "*Mutual* did not square with either the judicial treatment accorded other communication media or the true character of the modern movie." After all, in 1915 the movies—and the culture surrounding them and interpreting them—were a far cry from the movies that emerged through the 1930s, 1940s, and 1950s.

The Court was shifting from its thirty-seven years of indifference toward movies to what political scientist Richard Randall termed "libertarian supervision." With the *Burstyn* decision, the Court moved into a new role of actively surveilling the nation's censors. Just as Justice Reed had predicted in his *Burstyn* concurrence, the Court would assume the role of supercensor, evaluating case by case and film by film whether bureaucrats had overstepped their statutory bounds.

Before the end of the 1950s, the Court agreed to hear seven more movie censorship cases, each time finding in favor of the distributors, each time chipping away at the censors' domain. Between *Burstyn* in 1952 and the last major prior restraint film censorship case in 1965, the Court overturned the censoring of seventeen out of eighteen films brought to its attention by independent distributors who followed Joseph Burstyn.

In fact, it took only one week after *Burstyn* was decided for the Court to embark on this new guardianship of movies. The case into which the MPAA had put all its hopes, the race relations movie *Pinky*, had finally broken clear of the Texas courts and was granted review by the Supreme Court in March 1952, just before oral arguments in *Burstyn*.

But the justices remained tight-lipped about their intention in taking the case, and they heard no oral arguments. On June 2, the justices handed down a per curiam decision in *Gelling v. Texas* that read: "The judgment is reversed. See *Joseph Burstyn, Inc. v. Wilson* and *Winters v. New York*" (the case that had established the void-for-vagueness doctrine). Industry insiders had been certain that because the justices were reviewing a second case, the Court was ready to declare all film censorship unconstitutional. As it turned out, only one justice was ready to go that far on the record. William O. Douglas, who had written the *Paramount* decision four years earlier with its famous hint that movies were part of the press, was the only voice heard in *Gelling*. He issued a lone concurrence holding that all film censorship was unconstitutional, a position he would maintain steadfastly thereafter. After describing the prior restraint of the Marshall, Texas, ordinance as "evil," Douglas went on, "If a board of censors can tell the American people what it is in their best interests to see or to read or to hear . . . then thought is regimented, authority substituted for liberty, and the great purpose of the First Amendment to keep uncontrolled the freedom of expression defeated."

And so the Court had spoken twice in the space of one week after thirty-seven years of silence, but its message was mixed: films belonged under the protection of the First Amendment, and prior restraint was highly suspect, but governments could continue to keep film messages from the public provided such restraint came from definitively worded statutes that should be limited to obscenity (but that was not clear). It was all quite confusing. Although Clark's opinion in *Burstyn* had called for censors to bear a "heavy burden" of proof to carry out prior restraint on films, the onus for questioning that burden of proof still rested on the distributors' shoulders—not on the government's. The burden of proof was still opposite the norm of U.S. law. This was a bizarre legal conundrum: filmmakers and distributors could claim free speech rights, but they also still could be forced to suffer prior restraint.

Legal commentators, attorneys general, censors, distributors, and moviemakers were unsure what to make of all this. Although, as we have seen, legal comment was almost universally positive, it was also somewhat perplexed. John White Valentine writing in the *Mississippi Law Journal* wondered what the justices most objected to in the New York and the Texas statutes: "Is it the *vagueness* of the restraint . . . or is it rather the *nature of the restraint?*"

Maryland's attorney general seemed the only positive voice. He was so sure that the *Burstyn* decision had overruled all censorship except for obscenity and indecency that he notified his censor board to stop banning films for any other reason. But, when the Maryland censors learned five days later that the New York Court of Appeals had upheld its censors' ban on the French film *La Ronde* for immorality, they decided to ignore their attorney general and carry on business as usual.

Burstyn v. Wilson surely left some legal loose ends, but one thing was clear to anyone who read the decision carefully: movie distributors henceforth would stand a better chance of getting their cases before the Supreme Court. The legal climate had changed since the days two years earlier when RD-DR and United Artists had tried to get their cases heard. The justices now recognized that rapidly escalating contention over motion picture freedom deserved legal resolution, and they had indicated their readiness to be of service.

Even before the justices could finish *Burstyn* and *Gelling*, two new cases were on the way, one through the New York courts and the other from Ohio. Just one year after the *Burstyn* decision, the Court readily agreed to hear both. By accepting what were to become the third and fourth movie censorship cases, the Court again raised the hopes of the anticensorites. Surely, they reasoned, if the justices were willing to take two more cases so soon after *Burstyn*, they must be ready to rule decisively and would soon clarify the legal environment of film. When the two cases were bundled together for hearing and decision, it seemed clear that something big was on the way.

The Ohio case (*Superior Films v. Ohio*) involved a 1951 movie titled simply *M*. This was a remake of the highly regarded 1931 Fritz Lang–Peter Lorre movie by the same title. About a child murderer, the new version faithfully adapted the original story, complete with its overtones of pedophilia. Although New York's censors had had no issue with the movie, Ohio was convinced that "the showing of this picture . . . might quite likely result in the criminal molestation or even the murder of a helpless child." The state felt constitutionally correct in its decision to keep the movie from Ohio screens. The situation, Ohio censors argued, clearly fit the exception "which, under the *Miracle* decision, may be legitimately carved out from the realm otherwise devoted to freedom of expression." Ohio was hoping the justices would see the movie as the "clear-and-present danger" they had seen. *M*'s distributor, Superior Films, decided to challenge the ban, claiming that the Supreme Court had struck down every instance of prior restraint it had heard since 1925, and that Ohio's censorship fee was an unconstitutional tax on free speech rights.

The ACLU joined Superior Films, seeing this Ohio case as an opportunity to open a new line of argument: the indirect effects of censorship. "For each picture rejected," the ACLU asked, "how many more were not submitted through fear of adverse decision?" This, the union argued, could "effectively stifle all discussion of political, social, or philosophic significance," reducing motion pictures to "intellectual pabulum." Although the ACLU lawyers were, of course, talking about the governmental censors, they might also have been speaking directly to the Production Code Administration (PCA), which had so successfully stifled significant themes for decades. (Indeed, some members of the ACLU had been pestering the MPAA to scrap or at least modernize the code since 1948.)

{ *Chapter 5* }

Here was a promising test case for both sides of the censorship issue. Did, as the Ohio censors insisted, the movie represent the exceptional case allowed censorship by the terms of the *Burstyn* opinion, or was it, as the ACLU and Superior Films argued, a clear case of interference with a constitutionally protected right of communication? Whether films could be banned for their potential to instigate antisocial behavior became the heart of the argument in Ohio.

The case from New York over the French film *La Ronde* (1950) also presented the justices something new to consider (*Commercial Pictures v. New York*). *La Ronde* is a clever, sassy film whose shorthand moral might be "What goes around comes around." It was based on a play by Arthur Schnitzler. The setting is Vienna in 1900, and its theme is the romantic games people play. In the first scene, a streetwalker propositions a soldier; in the next scenes the soldier seduces a servant girl who in turn ensnares a young student who then sets his sights on a beautiful young wife who then seduces her reluctant husband. We learn in the next scene that the husband has been uneager because he is having an affair with a young gold digger. The wife then goes after a dreamy young poet who seduces an actress who charms a count who winds up in the apartment of the streetwalker from the first scene. From first scene to last, no visual hint of the actual impropriety is ever shown. Both the playwright, Schnitzler, and the film director, Max Ophuls, were careful to show only the verbal intimacy involved, although only the most innocent viewer would miss the point. *La Ronde* had a most distinguished cast and a lavish production, complete with a charming original Oscar Strauss waltz. Before coming to New York, it had played to rave reviews in Paris, London, Washington, D.C., and several other major U.S. cities. There had been no outcry.

When the New York censors banned *La Ronde* because it was "immoral," the question necessarily became just what did that word mean? The movie can be interpreted upon superficial viewing as a series of seductions leading to casual sex. A closer look, however, reveals its true theme — the dangers of such encounters. The censors had banned the movie because of its ten scenes of seduction, but the majority of critics praised both the movie and its moral tone.

Although anticensorites had long argued that film critics' opinions should be considered in censorship battles, judges had ignored that contention. In the New York case over *La Ronde*, however, the justices found both sides arguing in favor of critical opinion. Usually it was the challenger who argued that film criticism should be considered in censorship decisions, but in *La Ronde*'s case, the state just could not resist a few reviews that had discussed *La Ronde*'s "naughtee" [*sic*] nature. As it turned out, however, the state should have abstained from this new and dangerous line of reasoning, for it opened the door to the idea that movies were indeed artistic, that they had important messages, and that artistic merit should be a consideration in any censoring. In the *La Ronde* litigation, both sides came to do battle with film reviews as ammunition.

After gathering reviews favorable to *La Ronde*, the distributor, Commercial Pictures, and its attorney, Florence Perlow Shientag, reprised one of London's arguments, one that had come up during the oral arguments in *Burstyn*: why was it constitutional to exercise prior restraint over movies shown in theaters but not those shown on television? Whether this rehash of the TV argument or New York's argument that film critics should be consulted impressed the justices will never be known because just eleven days after oral arguments on both *La Ronde* and *M* in January 1954, the Court issued another frustratingly unclear per curiam opinion, citing only *Burstyn* as precedent. Anticensorites' hope for further clarification from the Court was dashed. The only text available for analysis from these two cases came from another concurrence by Justice Douglas, this time joined by Justice Black. As he had in the *Gelling* case, Douglas took the absolutist view of the First Amendment. He argued that the First Amendment made no distinction between the various media, so prior restraint on movies could not be constitutional. But because no other justices had signed on, the only thing that was clear was that Black and Douglas were alone in their opposition to all movie censorship. Where the other justices stood on the extent of permissible censorship remained a mystery, no clearer in 1954 than it had been in 1952 after *Burstyn*. The only thing that was clear was that New York could no longer censor on the ambiguous ground of immorality, and Ohio could no longer censor on the even more indefinite ground it had used for *M:* harmfulness.

The confusion was evident in the wildly varying commentary on the case. The *New York Times* legal reporter and film critics saw the

Superior Films decision as a blow to censorship. This was one of the few instances when the Catholic clergy and Bosley Crowther would agree, both viewing the decision as a severe limitation on the censors' authority. Crowther predicted that the Court would soon overturn all censorship. A "moral atomic bomb" is how the auxiliary bishop of St. Patrick's Cathedral described it. Another *Times* critic, Thomas M. Pryor, called the ruling "a staggering blow to state and municipal censor boards." The ACLU was not so sure—so uncertain, in fact, that it issued no press release.

But Ohio Attorney General C. William O'Neill was certain. Based on the Supreme Court's jurisdiction, O'Neill saw the ruling as completely unambiguous. Writing to Ohio's chief censor, he warned that it was much more than a slap on the censors' wrists for incorrectly banning *M* or *La Ronde*. Using a narrow view of the Court's authority, O'Neill argued that the justices had no jurisdiction over how a state court interprets its own laws (whether Ohio, for example, had correctly censored *M*). The only thing they could do in such a challenge case was to examine the state law for constitutionality. Because the justices had found in favor of Superior Films and Commercial Films and against the censors of New York and Ohio, O'Neill argued that Ohio's ability to ban any movie as "harmful" was clearly overturned as was New York's use of "immoral." But even the ever-so-certain O'Neill was uncertain whether censoring for a specific type of harm or immorality (like incest) would be upheld.

Two more cases petitioned and were heard by the Court over the next three years, putting the total of *Burstyn*-spawned progeny to date at five. The first involved a dialogue-heavy romantic comedy called *The Moon Is Blue* that had been censored in Kansas (and was also embroiled in controversy between its producer and the PCA. See Chapter 6). The case, *Holmby Productions v. Vaughn*, produced another per curiam opinion, which overturned Kansas' ban on *The Moon Is Blue* but did little else. However, since the only question that had come before the state courts was the constitutionality of the entire statute, the Supreme Court's thumbs down should have sent the Kansas censor board into early retirement. However, thanks to a legislative fluke in the bill to repeal the censor statute, the censor board lived on until 1966.

The second case came from an archly anticensor distributor, Times

Film Corporation. Chicago had banned its French film called *The Game of Love*. Again, the Supreme Court issued a per curiam decision, refusing to overturn motion picture censorship as unconstitutional. Neither decision came with any explanation beyond the cases cited as precedent. In each case, the Court merely reversed the lower court and disapproved the censor action without including any legal justification that might have clarified the situation. The justices seemed to have settled into their recently adopted role as super-censors, accepting the proposition that films still could be subjected to prior restraint so long as adverse determinations were open to legal oversight (no matter how long that process took). These five post-*Burstyn* cases, one from New York, one from Texas, one from Ohio, one from Kansas, and the last from Chicago, show a Supreme Court that had taken a major step toward freeing all moviemakers but was still hesitant to declare censorship unconstitutional, accepting instead a supervisory role in questions of how free film content could become. This situation filmmakers and distributors were not likely to accept for long. More motion picture censorship cases were on their way as the 1950s ended and the 1960s began.

The State Courts

But censorship was not a federal issue—it was a state and local one. So the real action in questioning statutory motion picture censorship happened not in the Supreme Court but in the state courts. In the 1950s, there was much state court activity on motion picture censorship, and all of it was based on *Burstyn*.

1955 was a particularly busy year for censorship cases in state courts. First, an Ohio court decided not to wait for a definitive pronouncement from the U.S. Supreme Court. Based on what it had heard from the High Court in *Burstyn*, *Gelling*, and *Superior Films* and on how it interpreted its state constitution, Ohio invalidated its entire censoring statute. To reach this first-in-the-nation position, the Ohio court reasoned that *Burstyn* and the per curiam opinions that followed had invalidated prior restraint on movies by inference. The Ohio censoring statute was, the court wrote, repugnant to "the sacred Bill of Rights" and, in its present form, had to go. A legislative attempt at revival backed by the governor failed to pass, and Ohio ended its thirty-two-year censoring stint. The Ohio censor board was finished in July 1955.

That same year, Massachusetts also overturned its statute that had allowed local officials to ban films shown on Sunday. In *Brattle Films, Inc. v. Commissioner of Public Safety*, the Massachusetts Supreme Court found its "Lord's Day" statute unconstitutional "in light of the controlling decisions of the Supreme Court of the United States."

Next to go was Pennsylvania one year later. The first-in-the-nation state censorship statute (passed in 1911) became the third overturned by state court action in *Hallmark Productions, Inc. v. Carroll* (1956). Faced with an exploitation production about marijuana addiction called *She Shoulda Said No* (1949), the Pennsylvania Supreme Court preferred not to bother with the facts of the case. It was time, these judges thought, to stop hashing over movie after movie and get to the constitutionality point. They found that the U.S. Supreme Court was slowly moving toward overturning all censorship. So, Pennsylvania unanimously declared its censor board unconstitutional. A majority of Pennsylvania's legislators were unhappy with the decision and managed to reinstate the law in 1959, only to have the state supreme court again nix the idea of motion picture censorship by overturning the new statute two years later. Pennsylvania was then out of the censoring business for good.

By 1961, then, three states had followed parallel paths, using *Burstyn* and the ensuing per curiam opinions to invalidate their censoring laws. But attitudes toward motion picture censorship were anything but consistent or predictable: four other states continued censoring, even though their state courts had heard the same pronouncements of the Supreme Court and even though all four had free speech provisions in their constitutions. But their state courts did not invalidate their censor statutes, and motion picture censorship went on. Born of the Progressive Era, bolstered by World War II patriotism, strengthened by the fervent anticommunism during the cold war, but picked apart by the Supreme Court and three state courts, censorship still found allies on the benches of the four remaining states.

New York kept censoring. After losing the *La Ronde* case in 1954, the state realized that it could no longer censor for immorality because the term was too vague. But the legislature did not like that idea and revised the statute to define clearly and distinctly what it meant by the word *immoral*. So, statutorily propped up, the Motion Picture Division censors continued to ban what they considered immoral movies.

In 1956, they banned a French film version of D. H. Lawrence's infamous novel *Lady Chatterley's Lover*. Even though it was based on the expurgated version of the novel, and even though no sexual activity was shown, the film was banned. The problem, as far as the censors were concerned, was not the sexual activity that was suggested, but that it was taking place in an adulterous relationship. This, said the censors, violated New York's law because it depicted such sexual activity in a positive light (the plot suggests that sometimes adultery might be reasonable). Edward Kingsley, who owned the film rights, like Joseph Burstyn, was a small-time foreign film importer. And, like Joseph Burstyn, Kingsley hated censorship.

When the New York censors banned *Lady Chatterley's Lover*, Kingsley turned to Ephraim London, who by this time had earned quite a reputation for bothering censors. Kansas, for example, considered him its "*bête noire*," according to historian Gerald Butters Jr. London saw immediately that the regents' rationale in upholding the ban was a gift: the regents said that the movie should be banned because it "glorifies adultery and presents the same as desirable, as acceptable, and as proper." It was clear that the movie was banned because it presented an idea the regents did not like. As attorney Charles Rembar put it, "The regents were running blindly, headlong into the barriers of the First Amendment." They had moved *Lady Chatterley's Lover* from the censorship of immorality arena into a heresy fight. And, as Rembar notes, heresy has never been countenanced under the U.S. Constitution.

Still, Kingsley and London lost both rounds in the New York courts. When the Supreme Court finally heard the case in 1959, no one knew what would happen. The decision was unanimous against the New York censors, but this time there was no per curiam decision; in fact, quite the opposite. The decision came with five separate opinions. Potter Stewart, writing for the majority, found New York's statute banning films that presented "immoral" ideas flatly unconstitutional. Tom Clark reminded New York of what he had written seven years earlier in the *Miracle* decision — that it should be banning films only in exceptional circumstances. Felix Frankfurter, John Marshall Harlan, and Charles Whittaker found the statute constitutional but incorrectly applied to *Lady Chatterley's Lover*. (Frankfurter noted that only the "stuffiest of Victorian sensibilities" could find this film offensive.) All New York's attempts to define immorality had failed. All that was left now was obscenity.

Censorship was severely weakened. By 1960, court challenges at all levels had lopped off every censoring standard but obscenity. Still New York, Maryland, Virginia, Kansas, and cities such as Chicago and Memphis went on censoring. No one knew if the Supreme Court would someday invalidate even censoring for the obscene.

So, emboldened by *Burstyn* and its progeny and by a six-case winning streak, distributors kept challenging in state courts, hoping for a definitive blow from the Supreme Court. In 1960–1961, another film distributor decided to try for a clear-cut case: to test the constitutionality of a censor law without muddying the issue with facts. That company was Times Film Corporation, the same distributor who had challenged Chicago censors a few years earlier. It had won that case, but only with a per curiam decision. Now, the company's objective was to force a constitutional showdown by bringing a censorship case to the court without submitting a film for review. Its attorneys attacked the fact that they had to submit a film at all. This way, they reasoned, the Court would have to reach the constitutionality question. They were moving in the right direction, but the decision did not go the way Times Film had hoped. In a five-to-four decision, the majority held that it was not up to the Supreme Court to decide what methods state and local governments should take to protect their citizens. Moreover, Times Film had used the wrong strategy: during oral argument Frankfurter and Clark advised its lawyers that their case would have been stronger had they exhibited the nonlicensed film and then challenged the arrest.

Times Film had lost this bold challenge – it was clear that the Court was not ready to release all movies from prior restraint – but four justices dissented vehemently: Chief Justice Earl Warren and Associate Justices Hugo Black, William O. Douglas, and William Brennan. Warren wrote a polemic against censorship, arguing that if newspapers were freed from prior restraint, so should be movies. What really concerned him, though, was the delay inherent in the system. It had taken Edward Kingsley three and a half years to get before the Supreme Court. It had taken Times Film three years. "This," Warren warned, was the real problem — "the injury done to the free communication of ideas."

Times Film v. Chicago (1961) was a true setback: the first time the Court had ruled in favor of the censors since *Mutual* in 1915. But Warren had pinpointed the real issue: the amount of time it took to get into a courtroom when a movie had been banned. For decades the censors could point to judicial review of their decisions as proof that the censoring process was fair. But at the start of the 1960s, it was becoming obvious that recourse to the courts was not the guarantee of fairness it had appeared. It simply took too long. This was the issue that would bring governmental censorship down.

The Pivot Point

The first major shift in movie freedom had come in 1948 with the *Paramount* decision's implication that movies deserved First Amendment protection. The second major shift came with *Burstyn* four years later. Although it did not seem so at the time, with all the confusion from Clark's rather ambiguous prose, it is now clear that *Burstyn* was the major dividing line between a legal culture that accepted the harmful potential of movies, which justified their prior restraint, and an evolving legal culture receptive to the communication rights of individuals.

Indeed, most historians and political scientists have seen *Burstyn* this way. Writing in 1968, Richard Randall attributed to *Burstyn* the turnabout in governmental receptiveness to pressure groups. Two years later, Ira Carmen used *Burstyn* as his breakpoint between acceptance of censorship and what he called the "modern period" when courts were willing to act as umpires in censorship squabbles. In 1982, Roger Newman and Edward de Grazia called the case a "radical" change in the course of "freedom of the screen." And in 1997 Gregory Black called it a "stunning decision for freedom of the screen."

The question of individual speech rights versus the communal good had been settled in the Progressive Era in favor of the commonweal. That position was sustained through the 1930s and World War II. But both the legal culture and popular taste were shifting toward the right of the individual to speak, see, read, and hear. The case brought by Burstyn was, in hindsight, clearly the pivot point in the creation of a new discussion of individual speech rights versus the communal good in matters of art and entertainment.

The man who had set it all in motion, Joseph Burstyn, would not be around to see the plot twists that were coming. Just one year after his name had become synonymous with film freedom, Burstyn set off on a European buying trip for the next season's films. As he left New York on a TWA flight bound for Paris, the fifty-three-year-old Burstyn was undoubtedly thinking about finding his next big film. But he would never get to any film festivals that year. He suffered a coronary thrombosis while in the air, and by the time the plane could be landed at Shannon Airport, Burstyn was dead.

Two weeks later, Burstyn's friend and anticensorship ally, Bosley Crowther, used his weekly column to combine news about three new lower court cases with a eulogy for his friend, the "indomitable champion of the screen's freedom." Titled, "The Case of Burstyn: The Fight on Film Censorship Goes On, in an Honorable Name," Crowther drew attention to Burstyn's "sadly unremarked" passing, finding it strangely fitting that the man who had been ignored by the U.S. film industry should still be ignored in death; yet his name, a precedent now for all time, was still being used in the fight against film censorship. Two of the cases Crowther was writing about concerned *The Moon Is Blue*, one in Jersey City, New Jersey, another in Maryland. Both overturned censor determinations using *Burstyn* as precedent. The third case, concerning a social commentary film called *Teenage Menace* that had been banned by the New York censors, provoked a comment from Judge Milton Halpern of the New York Supreme Court Appellate Division that would have made Burstyn proud: "Freedom of expression is freedom alike for 'propaganda,' which we deplore, and for 'education,' of which we approve." In making that final statement, Halpern had cited as his authority *Burstyn v. Wilson*.

Burstyn had tackled the monoliths of the PCA, the Catholic Church, the City of New York, the State of New York, and the potent idea that people needed protection from what they might see on a movie screen. The litigation alone had cost him somewhere between

$60,000 and $75,000 — equivalent to more than $5 million today. With his considerable experience in the film importation business, it is not likely he thought he could ever recoup the investment with profits from *The Miracle*. But, as he reported, the fight had been worth it to him. He was proud that he had defended the right to show *The Miracle* by himself. He spurned several offers of aid because the sources insisted on remaining anonymous. "I could use their money," Burstyn told an interviewer, "but if they would not stand up with me, I would rather be without it."

That Burstyn and London challenged New York State, with meaningful help only from the ACLU and at the height of the McCarthy era, makes their effort even more astonishing. Burstyn took action at a time when many others in the film industry were keeping their heads down, surrendering to the demands of the more strident voices. At the time, to those who favored lifting restrictions on filmmakers, it surely seemed a grand turn of events. Whether those who fought to end film censorship would still think so twenty years later is a different matter.

CHAPTER 6

The Legion of Decency
after *Burstyn*

Even though *Burstyn* failed to eradicate prior censorship, and the case did not make many people less suspicious of movie content, the controversy did change the balance of power in the debate over movies. It put censors and their supporters on the defensive for good. The *Burstyn* decision had symbolic significance by becoming the new touchstone in debates over freedom for movies. No longer would conservatives dictate how movies and their audiences would be treated. Instead, an emerging liberal consensus pushed a two-part approach: first, a movie deserved a chance to be seen before it was judged and second, the standards by which that movie was judged should not be controlled by a religious institution.

Of course, the effect of the *Miracle* decision on the Catholic Church and its Legion of Decency illustrated this point most clearly. As critic Richard Corliss noted a few years later, the *Miracle* case marked the beginning of the end of Catholic control over movie culture. Catholic officials understood that their power in Hollywood rested on the church's ability to call on its faithful to boycott not only certain movies but also the theaters that showed them and the studios that made them. Such economic leverage had persuaded film moguls to give Catholics a seat in the collective editing room; as head of the Production Code Administration (PCA) and chief enforcer of its code, Joe Breen had so much say over movie content that he could have been credited as a producer on hundreds of films. And as historian Gregory Black's research shows conclusively, the Legion of Decency was involved not only in reviewing movies for its coreligionists but also in backroom negotiations before and during filming. This power began to fade when Catholic action over *The Miracle* failed. Black concludes, "The vicious nature of the Catholic action—the boycotts, the pickets, the accusation that anyone who saw [*The Miracle*] was not only committing a sin but was also supporting communism—repelled many thoughtful Catholics as well as Protestants."

Yet many conservative Catholics thought a great deal more than a single movie was at stake in this controversy. The editors of *Ave Maria* viewed support for *The Miracle* as part of a general conspiracy against Catholics and other religious Americans. They approvingly reprinted Cardinal Spellman's remark that "Satan alone would dare such perversion." The editors asked, "If the Paris Theatre exhibited a picture in which a crazy woman imagined a like situation as the result of an imagined illicit relationship with, say, Washington or Lincoln, would *The Miracle* be permitted to be exhibited in a New York theatre?" Accordingly, the journal claimed that Catholics were attempting only to combat antireligious bigotry. Moreover, the Legion saw itself as nothing less than the most constant bulwark against all forces threatening U.S. moral health. It stood for religious freedom and against the defilement of religious truth. It protected young people from the corrosive effects of consumer culture. And it spoke *to* all Americans, rather than *for* all Americans.

Historian Una Cadegan explains this seeming paradox of midcentury American Catholicism. Although "Catholics were often accused of stepping over an implicit boundary demarcating the sphere of influence acceptable for a partisan group . . . [they] were also gaining allies in their efforts from among the very Americans whose boundaries they were supposedly transgressing." Many non-Catholics saw the church as an advocate for tradition in the fight against the "acids of modernity." It was one of the few institutions that continued to proclaim a mission of protecting society and its most vulnerable members—children—from the trappings of mass culture. Thus, even though Catholics faced charges of being fascist or at least antidemocratic, those who defended the church shot back that they, as good Americans, had an obligation to combat the evils of the modern world. Church leaders repeatedly claimed in print and in principle that they were not censors and did not support censorship.

"For a Free Screen?"

Catholics were not alone in taking action against films they found offensive. At the same time as many Catholic New Yorkers condemned Rossellini's film, Jewish New Yorkers awaited the release of David Lean's *Oliver Twist*. The responses to the two movies offer striking parallels. The filmed version of this Charles Dickens classic had premiered in London in the summer of 1948 to mixed reviews. The most notorious aspect of the film—and the one that threatened its marketability—was the depiction of the character Fagin, played by a young Alec Guiness with makeup that included a large putty nose. Fagin's exaggerated appearance reflected the way the character first appeared in a nineteenth-century illustrated version of Dickens's novel. Lean told film historian Kevin Brownlow that he was "mystified" by the flap caused by Fagin's appearance. He said he didn't intend his caricature to be taken as a political statement—and certainly not an offensive one at that. He had intended it to be authentic to the original publication's illustrations.

Producer J. Arthur Rank had invested more than $1.5 million in the film and expected to sell the U.S. distribution rights to make back some of that money. Rank had a reputation within the U.S. art film market as a producer of quality British films. And so in the late summer of 1948, as he made preparations for its premiere in the United States, he decided to screen *Oliver Twist* for U.S. representatives of Jewish organizations. This audience found Fagin a deplorable caricature and called the film anti-Semitic. The Anti-Defamation League and the New York Board of Rabbis issued statements in opposition to its impending U.S. release; the latter also petitioned the MPAA to ban it from U.S. screens. So far, the situation was similar to the requests of Catholics regarding *The Miracle*. The main difference, aside from the different religious group offended by the movie, was the action requested. The New York Board of Rabbis asked the Motion Picture Association of America (MPAA), a private group, for assistance in keeping the movie off the screen. The Catholics, however, had asked the state government to keep *The Miracle* off the screen.

Rank received another setback when the film premiered in Allied-occupied Berlin in February 1949. In successive incidents, demonstrators disrupted screenings of the movie so severely that the theater's management had to pledge to remove the picture from exhibition. These incidents made the front page of the *New York Times*, complete with photographs of German police turning fire hoses on demonstrating Jews in the city's streets. Additionally, in November 1950, as the Inter-State Circuit of Texas made plans to book *Oliver Twist*, Joseph Breen refused to grant a PCA seal based on its potential to insult and offend a religious group. The U.S. distributor, Eagle-Lion Classics, appealed that decision to the MPAA. Not surprisingly Breen won, and the film was cut to be less offensive.

Like the controversy involving *The Miracle*, Lean's film caused a split in movie culture as well. In 1950, the New York censors approved the film without cuts, and the National Board of Review, the American Civil Liberties Union (ACLU), and the American Council for Judaism lined up against the attempts to suppress and censor the film. The latter group issued a statement: "We condemn such pressure to prevent the exhibition of the film *Oliver Twist*. . . . Opinions formed or opposition voiced after the event constitute the proper exercise of public opinion to precensorship, as opposed to precensorship or suppression." Formed in 1942 by a group of dissident Reform rabbis, the American Council for Judaism grew out of a Jewish critique of Zionism and the establishment of a Jewish state. The participation of the group in this controversy was similar to the role played by *Commonweal* and different Protestant churches in the controversy over *The Miracle*. Debates over both movies illustrated not only that the idea of film censorship was under fire but that support for greater religious pluralism was informing that fight.

New York Times film critic Bosley Crowther took up the commingling of the issues involved in *The Miracle* and *Oliver Twist* in an article titled "For a Free Screen?" In what was perhaps his strongest statement against censorship, Crowther suggested that the controversies over *The Miracle* and *Oliver Twist* "should be compelling occasion for people to give most solemn thought to the question of whether they are in favor of freedom of the screen—and how much." He was careful to characterize the issue of screen offense as something to take seriously and something to parse out in terms of the law and the understanding of democratic culture. "But the basic consideration . . . in the case of any picture which some element or groups may oppose . . . is whether real freedom of expression on the screen is sincerely desired and whether the cause of this freedom is worth enduring offense to maintain. For it goes without too much saying that freedom is restricted and imperiled by every successful endeavor to suppress or willfully expurgate a film for any cause whatsoever, except patent and gross obscenity." Perhaps a bit naively, Crowther posited a faith that the public and the open market for films would ultimately guard against films that simply went too far. "After all if a certain type of picture is not to the general public's taste it is not—and will not be—expedient for theatres to show that type of film." In other words, if you don't like a movie, don't see it, but don't prevent others from seeing it, and please do not prevent someone from making it.

The *New York Times* printed six of the dozens of letters Crowther's article provoked. Five of the six were negative and took issue with Crowther's idea that offensive films deserved a chance for public exhibition. Typical of the letters was one from Myrtle Ilsley Passantino of Forest Hills, an upscale neighborhood in Queens, New York, who asked, "Is freedom *really* restricted when blasphemy . . . is not permitted? What kind of freedom is it, Mr. Crowther? Surely not *religious* freedom?"

The Religious Issue

"Sometimes it seems as if we American Catholics reduce the struggle for the hearts and minds of men to a contest between picket lines and pressure groups and in doing so slight the emphasis Catholic doctrine puts on free consent and reasoned morality," the editors of *Commonweal* wrote in response to the official Catholic reaction to *The Miracle*. "Too often our fellow citizens are rather inclined to look upon us as threatening liberty rather than enlarging it, as powerful nuisances who put an undue strain on their democratic toleration. . . . We may have merely made them feel as if they were being treated like children by an alien force that didn't give two cents for their personal liberty." Historian John McGreevy notes that the most popular, if notorious, indictment of Catholic attitudes appeared in Paul Blanchard's book *American Freedom and Catholic Power*. The book began as a series of essays for the *Nation* and went on to become a huge best-seller and a Book of the Month Club offering. The basic thesis was that Catholic thought differed little in regard to individual liberty from fascism and Soviet communism and therefore Catholicism was, like totalitarianism, a threat to U.S. democracy. Many leading public intellectuals in the United States apparently agreed with Blanchard's assessment. McGreevy suggests that the positive response to the book "helped define the terms of postwar American liberalism. These terms included the insistence that religion, as an entirely private matter, must be separated from the state, and that religious loyalties must not threaten intellectual autonomy or national unity." In short, many liberals argued that "pervasive Catholic separatism — on philosophical matters and in schools, hospitals, and social organizations [such as the Legion of Decency] — posed an 'integration' problem."

Catholics had to respond to such broad-based condemnation. One way was to link Catholic social thought to the basic assumptions of democracy and religious freedom through the idea of pluralism. During the controversy over *The Miracle*, liberal Catholics snapped into action.

One such Catholic was Otto Spaeth, a prominent lay Catholic and founder of the Dayton Tool and Die Company and Metamold Aluminum of Cedarburg, Wisconsin. He and his wife were also art collectors and therefore members of the country's cultural elite. For example, Spaeth was, at different times, the director of the American Federation of the Arts, president of the Liturgical Arts Society, and vice president of the Whitney Museum. And he disagreed with the church's reaction to *The Miracle:* "At the outbreak of the controversy, I immediately arranged for a private showing of the film. I invited a group of Catholics, competent and respected for their writings on both religious and cultural subjects. The essential approval of the film was unanimous," he related in an article for the *Magazine of Art*. His point was that Catholics were not a monolith and that he, at least, had been embarrassed by the tactics used by certain Catholic groups. In this context, he recounted with great displeasure the protest by the Catholic War Veterans directed at WPIX, the New

York television station, that led to the cancellation of a series of Chaplin films. "Thus one more skirmish in the ancient battle for the fundamental liberty of the arts was lost, and with hardly a peep of public protest."

Here was the larger significance of Spaeth's essay – he wanted people to protest the suppression of speech. The liberal, centrist political organization Americans for Democratic Action reprinted Spaeth's entire editorial in *ADA World* in February 1951. And opinions of similar tone resounded in the pages of *Commonweal*.

The most provocative of the statements in *Commonweal* came from William P. Clancy, at that time a lecturer at the University of Notre Dame. He thought Catholics had acted like philistines. In an essay that captured the pivotal nature of the *Miracle* case, Clancy accused Catholic officials of "semi-ecclesiastical McCarthyism." Catholics had established a pattern of behavior that reflected poorly on the church's role as member of a pluralistic, democratic society. To Clancy the church had a great deal to lose by reacting in a way that was disproportionate to what was at stake in the case. He called on Catholics to cease using economic pressure against the ability of artists to work freely, and for people to see art freely. "It is a spectacle which many of us, as Catholics, can view only with shame and repulsion, for we know that neither art nor prudence, religion nor country, intelligence nor morality can be served by such means." He pointed out that positive critical response to *The Miracle* suggested that it had some merit as art. As such, the lively debate illustrated that there was more than one way to view the film. Reflecting on the work of Catholic philosopher Jacques Maritain, Clancy explained that there is never "such a thing as a theme which is denied to the artist because it is immoral *in itself*. Its ultimate morality and immorality will depend upon its treatment at the hands of the artist. . . . The real danger to public morality would seem to lie not in the cause but in the proposed cure. Vulgarity, like bad philosophy, can never bear good fruit." Clancy rejected the notion that pickets could establish a highly complex idea such as blasphemy. Moreover, to resort to such pressure created a dangerous alliance between religious doctrine and secular power. Clancy concluded that the rash reaction of church leaders led to a profoundly un-Catholic attack on art, freedom, and the construction of morality.

But to whom or for whom was Clancy speaking? Clancy was part of a larger movement within Catholic intellectual circles that wanted to lead the church away from its image as a medieval institution locked in battle against modernity and toward a position in civil society that accepted religious pluralism. Catholics for Cultural Action, the breakaway lobbying group that London had so desperately wanted as an amicus participant, is another example of Catholics who thought as Clancy did.

However, for more traditional Catholics, the Supreme Court's decision in *Burstyn* and its aftermath were a travesty. *Ave Maria* titled its editorial on the decision "God Loses Again." In a play on the language used by Justice Clark, the *Sign* believed that it showed the Court "adrift without charts" and that the decision was bound to lead to a "holiday for the merchants of pictorial hate and smut." Its editors scowled that Catholic Americans must be "sad and disturbed by the implications of such a decision as one more example of the creeping secularism threatening this country, its government, and its mores." The ideologically moderate Catholic magazine *America* asked: "Doesn't the United States stand for *anything* in a religious sense? Doesn't American law recognize, in any way at all, the religious meaning of American democracy?"

Commonweal, not surprisingly, went the opposite direction. Relying on interpretation of constitutional thought by a leading liberal Catholic priest, John Courtney Murray, its editors argued that the Court's decision had not harmed but had saved civil society. "The civil power," they wrote, "was in danger of playing the role of theologian by attempting to determine a properly religious concept." *Commonweal* reiterated a notion much discussed in this period, that American Catholics had to learn to participate in a pluralistic society, one in which a Catholic voice could be strong but not tyrannical. "Catholics might well make it clear that they accept the modern 'lay' state, with its division of civil and religious power, as something to be grateful for, and resist any such attempts to vitiate or alter the character of this state as were present in the New York censorship of a film which many found distasteful."

Like other liberal critics, the writers at *Commonweal* felt acutely this crisis over cultural freedom. The *Miracle* case gave liberal Catholics an opportunity to call on all believers to give up the overwrought denunciation of modernism and the "secularist basis of modern liberalism" in favor of more direct and intelligent involvement in shaping the modern world. In order to "baptize" the modern world, the editors wrote, Catholics needed to come to grips with the fact that "living in it involves certain hazards which are absent from a sacral order, but that the acceptance of these hazards and their related discomforts is an easy price to pay for the great advantages which this world offers."

A few months later, *Commonweal* ran a special issue devoted to Hollywood. The essays commissioned by the journal illustrate that after the Supreme Court's decision, doors were opening for a general reassessment of Catholic views on movies. In short, the dispute over *The Miracle* signaled the demise of the extralegal censorship practiced by the Legion and enforced through Hollywood's PCA, and instead pushed a debate on Catholics and popular culture and the state. Walter Kerr, a Catholic and a well-respected drama critic for the New York *Herald-Tribune*, edited the issue and wrote its most provocative feature. His piece was a general critique of the drift of Catholic movie criticism toward irrelevance, arguing that the standards by which Catholics seemed to judge motion pictures had little to do with aesthetics or intelligence and much to do with how simplistic, pro-Catholic messages were projected. As a consequence, Kerr explained, "The identification of good will with good work is commonplace in the Catholic press. Unfortunately, the sort of art which Catholics are urged to admire is commonplace, too — and the power which Catholic spokesmen have come to wield over the motion picture has helped make the motion picture even more commonplace than it need have been."

What the Legion in particular had done to Catholic opinion was, Kerr believed, truly disheartening. The Legion had engendered a "petrifaction of taste" that "discredits the entire Catholic intellectual tradition." The association of bad taste with Catholic opinion led to the conclusion on both sides of the issue that Catholic pressure groups such as the Legion had only one tool to use against the movies — the threat of economic boycott. "The only persuasiveness we have been able to whip up is the persuasiveness of the dollar," Kerr argued. Thus, rather than join in the debate over the complexity of art, Catholic officials, especially the Legion, had diminished the respect others had for Catholic opinion and harmed the quality of motion pictures in general by dictating the Production Code. "What is both wrong and foolish about the present production code is that it insists that God write straight with straight lines, that He attend strictly to business as the business is conceived by an either-or, black-and-white, pay-as-you-go mentality. Art without crooked lines is un-natural art—inevitably inferior art."

Historian Frank Walsh points out that "for the first time, a few Catholic publications criticized the church's strong-arm tactics of picketing and raised questions about its right to dictate what non-Catholics could and could not see." The Legion's power rested on the assumption that such tactics were right not merely for Catholics but also for the betterment of society. That was why Kerr attacked both the Legion and the Production Code. Jack Vizzard, one of Joe Breen's assistants at the PCA, was not about to let Kerr's challenge go unan-swered. He responded, "The code is not sponsored or financed by the Church. It is an instrumentality of the movie industry." Although this claim was technically correct, it did not reflect reality. Vizzard argued that the code had not prevented reality from being shown on the screen by pointing to films like *Scarlet Street*, *Madame Bovary*, and *A Streetcar Named Desire*. Readers ignorant of Breen's role as the church's strongman in Hollywood understandably would not have known that every one of those films, and hundreds more, were the bastard products of haggling with the church. If anything, Vizzard was using the wrong argument—the production histories behind these three films had actually confirmed Kerr's point. Each had gone through substantial revisions to placate the Legion. Yet Vizzard felt compelled to respond to Kerr, and his response betrayed the cracks growing within the system.

As we have seen, both the code and the Legion's power operated on economic assumptions—Hollywood's concern for profit and fear of Catholic boycotts threatening that profit had cemented the rela-tionship between the PCA and the church for two decades. Although *Burstyn* did not alter this fundamental relationship, the debate about the case and the intellectual fallout from the decision eroded the rationale for Hollywood-Catholic collusion.

No legal decision could have ended Hollywood's self-censorship, for it operated as a supposedly voluntary system. Control over movies was as much a cultural situation (in Hollywood) as it was a legal arrangement (through state and local censors). However, when Joseph Burstyn attacked statutory censorship in his case against New York State, the controversy that grew around *The Miracle* also encouraged a full frontal assault on extralegal censorship. It was impossible for any one case to change the practice of censorship, but the debate over the legitimacy of censorship that raged following the *Miracle* case illustrated just how significant *Burstyn v. Wilson* was. Ultimately the case stood as a victory against the regimes of censorship and the sensibility that supported them.

The Crisis of the Code

The clearest illustration that this controversy inaugurated a new era was a series of nonlegal confrontations over the Production Code that followed the Supreme Court's decision. Now Hollywood's liberals went on the attack. At the front was Otto Preminger, perhaps the most defiant of all Hollywood directors. And the film that punctuated the new era was his saucy, humorous *The Moon Is Blue* (1953). The film was billed as an adult picture, in the days when that label suggested a sophisticated script rather than heavy breathing. A verbose movie with little action, *The Moon Is Blue* was made from a popular play about a "professional virgin" who flirts with two eligible bachelors, pitting one against the other, to wind up with the more marriageable man. There is no sex in the movie, just lots of talk about seduction. Nevertheless, Breen rejected it for its "cavalier approach toward seduction and illicit sex," write Leff and Simmons. Preminger fought Breen's decision, and rather than slink back into the editing room as so many before him had done, he arranged to release the film without the PCA seal.

One of the reasons Preminger wanted to make the movie was to challenge the PCA, which he saw as outmoded and harmful to the industry. Preminger could take such seemingly radical action because he made the film for United Artists, which was not an MPAA member studio. After the *Paramount* decision had ordered MPAA studios to divest themselves of movie theater holdings starting in 1948, more independent screens were slowly opening up to moviemakers like

Preminger. Lack of a code seal was no longer the box office disaster it had been before *Paramount* and *Burstyn*. He trusted that the audience, despite any bad press whipped up by the Legion (or perhaps because of it), would find the film enjoyable enough to recoup its modest $500,000 budget. When the Legion of Decency condemned *The Moon Is Blue*, the film earned immediate appeal as controversial. The film earned more publicity as it became embroiled with the state censors of Kansas, who, as we have seen, lost a legal challenge brought by its distributor and were forced to allow it to play. It went on to be one of the top grossing films of 1953.

The Legion depended on the PCA's ability to coerce recalcitrant filmmakers, and Preminger had successfully bucked that system. The *Miracle* case had made sure that the church could no longer influence government censors; *The Moon Is Blue* illustrated that questions raised during the debacle over *The Miracle* had weakened the church's ability to control Hollywood, too.

Throughout the 1950s, Hollywood and the Catholic Church constantly adjusted how each addressed controversial movies. The symbiotic relationship between the industry and the church meant that every little wrinkle in movie culture forced both institutions to reevaluate the rules that governed moviegoing. They were codependents.

They shared another commonality. Unlike state censors, the PCA and the Legion needed their constituencies to follow the rules. And here they were most vulnerable. Both groups would become powerless if their respective constituencies chose to disregard them. *Burstyn* made such disregard imaginable.

In late 1953 and early 1954, the Production Code came under attack from within the industry itself. Samuel Goldwyn, a veteran Hollywood producer and a new ally in the fight to liberalize the code, wrote a letter to Eric Johnston contending that the code was heading for general irrelevance unless it was "brought reasonably up to date. . . . Audiences today realize what creative people have always known — that drama is worthless unless it has integrity and resembles life. To portray life honestly on the screen requires a greater degree of latitude, within the bounds of decency, than exists under the code. The time has come to recognize this fact." Goldwyn's argument certainly echoed the opinions of many moviegoers — clearly foreign films were doing well in urban markets because they appealed to the urge for harder-hitting, more mature themes.

But Goldwyn's argument was not just a simple plea for greater artistic freedom. Underneath issues of film content was a strong subtext to be addressed: who should have the power to control movies? And by what process should the movies be controlled? Producers and theater owners wanted the flexibility to react to audience preferences and build new markets for pictures. Few of those involved in the business of movies actually cared about the "reality" or "honesty" of film content unless it affected their bottom line. Thus it was not surprising that Johnston responded to Goldwyn's challenge by rallying industry executives ostensibly in defense of the Production Code. A better indication of the effect Goldwyn's challenge had on movie culture was the buzz it started among Catholics. The Production Code was a product of Catholic pressure, and as such, was the most useful tool for Catholics to control the industry.

On this point, no better barometer existed than Martin Quigley. Quigley accused Goldwyn of unwittingly associating himself with "that cabal of clamor against the Code by those who seek the destruction of all restraints and standards in motion picture entertainment." To revise the code, Quigley thundered, was "tantamount to calling for a revision of the Ten Commandments." The editors at *Commonweal* issued perhaps the most effective kind of attack on Quigley's hyperbole—they pointed out (rather slyly) that unlike the author of the Ten Commandments, Quigley and Father Lord had drafted the original production code in 1930. It followed, the editors suggested, that "neither Mr. Quigley nor Father Lord would claim infallibility in drawing up a specific moral code, especially a code which, by the nature of things, can never be frozen as absolutely binding, good for all people in all places at all times."

Quigley had always been the most vocal defender of the code. Again and again, he railed against calls for change. In *Commonweal* he argued that the code "was intended to provide a reasonable, prudent standard for theatrical motion pictures, patronized by persons of all ages and social groups." Nonetheless, Quigley argued, "The attainment of artistic effects [did] not justify a defiance of any applicable moral standard." Although in the abstract one can sympathize with the need for a check on what passes for public culture, Quigley's explanation belied the more important implications behind changing the code — the loss of power over who got to determine what "artistic effects" looked like and who established the "applicable moral standards" by which those "effects" were measured.

The code continued to hold in the mid-1950s, but the intellectual edifice that supported it was beginning to give way. As state censorship cases reached the Supreme Court and the justices overturned one government ban after another, the notion of state censorship lost ground. This explains why Quigley became more publicly vocal in his support of the code, and why conservative Catholic journals and officials grew more frantic in their denunciation of movies and attacks against censorship. A tipping point was fast approaching — a point beyond which support for the code and the Legion would no longer make sense.

The journal *Catholic World* ran a long editorial in March 1954 following the Supreme Court decisions in the *La Ronde* and *M* cases. Here the Court had struck down two more censoring standards: "harmful" from Ohio's statute and "immoral" from New York's. The editors of *Catholic World* reminded Catholics that these decisions meant "that they will have to be more vigilant than ever in guarding against immoral films. The sad prospect is that Catholics will have to be critical and censorious for the moral future of the movies is not bright." The editors returned to the most common argument against the movies: that they were made for a broad public audience. "It seems to me," wrote one, "that the Court, by relaxing censorship, is clearing the way for films that appeal to the most vulgar tastes of the mass audience. One never raises the standard of art by stooping to satisfaction of animal instinct." In the end, what *Catholic World* wanted was "to see films made according to the best traditions of art and the eternal laws of God." Colorado Senator Edwin Johnson agreed: on the floor of the U.S. Senate, he called for the Legion of Decency to be more vigilant in protecting Americans from immoral movies because the state censors were seeing their authority stripped by the Court. Denunciations came from pulpits as well. Archbishop John Francis O'Hara of Philadelphia issued a pastoral letter warning all Catholic parents that "the Supreme Court has underscored your duty of conscience. . . . In effect, the Supreme Court has ruled that the States may label as poison only what affects the body, not that which can destroy the soul." And Auxiliary Bishop Joseph F. Flanelly of St. Patrick's Cathedral wondered whether the Supreme Court had "exploded a moral atomic bomb."

But, as before, not all Catholics agreed. William Clancy once again seized on the opportunity presented in these two post-*Burstyn* cases to affirm the "freedom of the screen." By this time he had been fired from his position at Notre Dame (probably because of his essay on *The Miracle*) and had moved to New York to become an editor at *Commonweal*. In another strong essay for that journal, he argued, "The question of whether or not the present Hollywood Code should be revised is obviously not world-making, but the attempt to commit Catholic opinion, *en bloc*, against even the possibility of revising it has interesting historical parallels. It is symptomatic of a tendency among us which is 'reactionary' in an almost classical sense." Clancy believed the fights engaged in by Catholics were dangerously disproportionate to the issues involved.

> The dire predictions of moral ruin for the nation should all official censorship of motion pictures be ended, leads one, inevitably, to a certain conclusion: that a rather shocking misunderstanding of the metaphysics of a democratic society (which include, by definition, the notion of limitation and hazard) still exists within a large body of American Catholic opinion, and that this misunderstanding is joined to an estimate of human nature that is more Calvinist than Catholic in its pessimism. To believe, for example, that if the Supreme Court rules out prior censorship it has, in effect, ruled the concept of immorality out of our national life is to reveal an attitude that would make democracy itself impossible.

Clancy declared that the Court, far from harming the public, was "protecting this medium from the exercise of arbitrary power by limiting, further and further, the area in which such power can operate." And although he recognized that "due process" and "freedom . . . involve certain risks," it seemed to him "time to recognize that without risks there can be no freedom. Democracy can never be made completely 'safe.'" He concluded with a ringing endorsement of democratic principles: he was not against laws protecting the public from obscenity and incitement to crime, but he could not support arbitrary action before any act was committed. The censor who cut films or prevented them from being shown had, "in the name of virtue," violated a basic tenet of the democratic process. "Democracy must, sometimes, be saved from the righteous as well as protected against the wicked," he counseled. "The country has survived with freedom of speech and of the press; it will probably survive with this new freedom. The unfortunate thing is that too frequently it is Catholic voices which are raised most violently in protest and fear whenever a freedom is born."

The issue finally came down to process: how does a democratic society best protect culture that might offend the majority or a large minority? When the Supreme Court protected *The Miracle*, it gave official approval to the idea that popular culture could be considered in the abstract — rather than as merely an industrial product. In other words, if one accepted films as an expression of art and speech, as Burstyn and his defenders had argued, then one could no longer consider films in merely commercial terms. And yet, although legal protection for films was undoubtedly deserved, extending the First Amendment to movies was not an end in itself. Rather, the question of free speech generated a broader debate about how to set limits in a culture that no longer belonged to censors. Catholics and the PCA both stood as examples of the power to censor without needing to address free speech in any form. What neither could dismiss ultimately, though, was that movies deserved better treatment than either institution had offered. Treating the movies arbitrarily reflected badly on how both Hollywood and the Legion of Decency viewed the moviegoing public. The audience for movies expected more out of an art that belonged to it.

By 1956, the forces unleashed by *Burstyn* were producing a seismic shift in U.S. movie culture. That year, Hollywood revised its Production Code for the first time since 1934, and the Legion unleashed what would turn out to be its last great boycott against a Hollywood film. Both situations established new paradigms in movie culture. Hollywood's code revisions illustrated that the industry was willing (as it always had been) to mold its artistic standard to fit audience taste. Pushed by the new legal foundation of movie freedom and by producers eager to incorporate daring content, the revised code allowed some treatment (if tastefully done) of previously banned topics such as drug trafficking, prostitution, abortion, kidnapping, child-birth, and miscegenation. Previously forbidden words like "hell" and "damn" were also permitted if not used excessively.

The code revision was done despite Catholic objections, thus signaling the church that it could no longer dominate internal Hollywood operations. Denied its traditional conduit for control, the Legion inaugurated a tactic that had come to define opposition to movies in a postcensor world — creating spectacle disproportionate to the intellectual stakes actually involved in the release of a movie. The church had used the threat of boycotts to shock movie industry executives into controlling content. In a postcensor world, this last-resort tactic became the default position — boycotts became the only way to influence movie culture. In broader terms, controversial films were handled as public spectacles rather than through backroom negotiations.

———

Baby Doll

In late 1956, Bosley Crowther used the ousting of Dore Schary as head of production at MGM and the Legion's condemnation of Elia Kazan's *Baby Doll* (1956) to discuss the new imperatives affecting movie culture. Schary, an industry friend of Crowther's, held a position that no longer made much sense in a world of growing independents. "With a few exceptions," Crowther explained, "the administrators of the big outfits [studios] are pretty much businessmen. They make deals with the independents, usually in close association with the heads of their companies in New York, and sit in judgment on the films of their own studio units." The collusion between studios that made the PCA function effectively was vanishing. In its place came a more fluid business model that allowed more freedom for the filmmakers because there was almost no way to control picture content in any comprehensive way. Crowther observed: "This is why the Legion's recent blast not only at *Baby Doll* but also at the industry's own Production Code administrators, who have already approved the film, is unusually ticklish." At issue was not the harm the movie would do or the ineffectiveness of the code, but the ability of the Legion to continue to flex its strength. Government censors' hands were becoming increasingly more tied as the Supreme Court continued to hand down restrictive decisions and the PCA approved more daring films like *Baby Doll*.

As an unabashedly liberal provocateur, Kazan relished a chance to stick his fingers in the eyes of the Legion. Like his controversial *Streetcar Named Desire*, this film also was based on a play by Tennessee Williams. It is the story of a twisted love triangle. At the center is "Baby Doll" Meighan, a nineteen-year-old virgin married for two years to Archie Lee, owner of a run-down cotton gin. Archie is deliriously happy as Baby Doll's twentieth birthday approaches because that is when they will, by prearrangement, consummate their wedding. The movie is an unpleasant view into a dysfunctional relationship punctuated by scenes of a scantily clad Baby Doll sleeping in a crib and sucking her thumb with Archie leering and lurking about, counting the days until he can take his wife. When Archie burns down a rival's cotton gin, the rival decides to take vengeance by seducing the still virginal Baby Doll. Despite its air of desperation and its sexual theme, it was passed by the PCA because sexual activity is never shown. Would a prerelease C rating for *Baby Doll* have the power to affect not merely the audience for *Baby Doll* but the ability of the Legion to command respect as a cultural arbiter? The answer was revealing.

At a mass at St. Patrick's Cathedral on December 16, 1956, Cardinal Spellman publicly condemned *Baby Doll* from the pulpit. He told an estimated 2,000 people gathered in the hallowed cathedral that he was "shocked" to see the release of "another motion picture [that] has been responsibly judged to be evil in concept and which is certain to exert an immoral and corrupting influence upon those who see it." He further found it "astonishing and deplorable" that Hollywood's leading authorities approved *Baby Doll* for general viewing. "It is," the cardinal thundered, "the moral and patriotic duty of every loyal citizen to defend America not only from dangers which threaten our beloved country from beyond our boundaries, but also the dangers which confront us at home." The cardinal had personally spoken like this only two other times: to attack communism and to discuss the imprisonment of Josef Cardinal Mindszenty in communist-controlled Hungary. "It has been suggested," he sneered, "that this action on my part will induce many people to view this picture and thus make it a material success. If this be the case, it will be an indictment," he declared, "of those who defy God's laws and contribute to corruption in America."

Spellman's sermon was unusually harsh and public. His indictment both of a movie and anyone – Catholic or non-Catholic – who dared to see *Baby Doll* was unprecedented. His call to action over *The Miracle*, intemperate as it seemed at the time, describing the movie as a "perversion," "diabolical," and "art at its lowest," had only asked all "right-thinking Americans" to join the attempt to change New York's law. The fury with which Spellman attacked *Baby Doll* revealed that something more serious was afoot within the Catholic Church. During the period between *The Miracle* and *Baby Doll*, the church's authority on matters such as movies had grown increasingly tenuous. The Supreme Court's decision in *Burstyn* weakened the church's power to exercise Catholic influence through state censors. And the kind of movie culture that took shape in its wake illustrated a predilection among moviegoers – many of whom were Catholic – for more mature and, therefore, potentially controversial subject matter. The church watched worriedly as Hollywood responded to the new tastes emerging among a better-educated and perhaps more daring audience. Thus, underlying the crisis for Catholic cultural authority was an uneasy sense that culture belonged to the people who made it important. Moviegoers grew increasingly less tolerant of Catholic denunciations; protests like Spellman's simply struck many people as sanctimonious at best and authoritarian at worst.

Commonweal's John Cogley tried to make sense of this moment. Like Clancy, Cogley also worked as a writer for the Fund of the Republic, a quixotic but significant intellectual project that championed U.S. civil liberties. He observed that the controversy over *Baby Doll* played out like a "classic dance . . . the 'rational debate' one might have hoped for was doomed almost from the beginning." Once again, he noted, "Catholics speaking against *Baby Doll* occasionally sounded as if they were finally in grips with a really big evil in an age of totalitarian horrors; some liberals rushed off to the barricades as if they were saving the Republic from Torquemada." Lost in the debate were questions involving aesthetics, art, and the nature of disagreement in a democracy. And although Cogley acknowledged that Spellman had a responsibility as a religious leader to speak out against that which offended him and his flock, the church also had resorted to means that had little to do with morality and intellectual discourse. Did this case reveal to the church that it had lost its power? Cogley offered, "The church has to rely on moving the hearts and minds of men. It must persuade. It cannot use force and coercion without hopelessly clouding and distorting its own image. The world has changed radically since spiritual authority was wont to turn to the 'secular arm' for support. In our society economic strength is the rough equivalent of the Inquisitional power." He noted that by using economic leverage the church left itself open to criticism not merely from those outside but also from its own people, who expected it to rise above such tactics. "A democratic society needs the Church too, and the Church loses in meaningful influence to the degree that it hides its own . . . identity behind swagger and cockiness."

The Catholic boycott was both successful and disastrous. There was evidence that the controversy generated by Spellman's reaction kept *Baby Doll* out of hundreds of theaters, though the film still opened and played in hundreds of other theaters and was in the box office top ten for two months. For Spellman, the Legion, and those who hoped Catholics would continue to exert control over motion pictures, the boycott proved to be their last stand. In 1957, American Catholic bishops met and decided to add new categories to the Legion's rating system, thereby expanding what adults could see without imperiling their souls. This was a clear indication that the church was drifting away from the conservative tactics that had inspired the boycott against *Baby Doll* and toward a stance that recognized the church's role within — rather than in domination of — U.S. culture. The church would continue to be critical of movies, but would no longer act as a proud censor. Such a development was indeed a kind of miracle.

CHAPTER 7

Film Freedom and Sexual Content

While the Motion Picture Association of America (MPAA) was loosening its restrictive code and Catholic bishops were liberalizing the Legion's ratings, the Supreme Court began relaxing the definition of obscenity. Before 1957, obscenity controversies remained local, decided at the state and lower court levels. As obscenity prosecutions came before the lower courts in the 1930s, judges were called upon to uphold the old ideas or look for new answers about what was legally obscene and therefore nonprotected speech. Discarding the ancient *Hicklin* rule and the idea that protection of children justified suppression for all, the courts moved forward, struggling with the difficult concept of how to protect society without unconstitutionally restricting content.

In 1956 and 1957, the Supreme Court abruptly jumped in, hearing three cases: one involving a Michigan book censorship statute, a second asking what could be prohibited from the U.S. mail, and another challenging a California penal statute's application to obscene content. In its decisions in these cases, the Court laid down some ground rules: if obscenity were to remain outside the protection of the First Amendment, then it needed to be defined. These early cases found the justices trying to define what Potter Stewart would later so famously say was indefinable (in *Jacobellis v. Ohio* in 1964, Stewart said that he did not think he could define hard-core pornography, "but I know it when I see it"). In the first case, *Butler v. Michigan*, the Court agreed that a state statute could not use protection of children as a rationale for keeping a book from adults. That would be tantamount, wrote Justice Frankfurter, to "burn[ing] the house to roast the pig."

In the second and third cases (decided jointly under the name of *United States v. Roth*), the Court attempted to define the elusive word *obscene* by setting up a five-part test: whether the "*average person*" using "*contemporary community standards*," would find that the "*dominant theme*" of the work *as a whole* appeals to the "*prurient interest* in sex" (it had to appeal to an abnormal or unusual interest in sex, not a healthy one, to be called obscene). Significantly, the Court used this case to say that matter dealing with sex was not necessarily obscene. "Sex and obscenity are not synonymous," the Court wrote. But that which stimulates a "prurient interest in sex" could be obscene. Although not entirely satisfactory, the five-part test—the average person, community standards, dominant theme, the entire work, appealing to an abnormal interest in sex—was a reasonable attempt to provide some sort of clarification regarding what could be kept from the public. However, the ruling applied to books and mailed material, and made no mention of movies.

Over the next decade, as it continued to allow prior restraint of obscene movies, the Court continued to work on defining the term, trying to get wording that would be more clear, yet still protective of First Amendment rights. In 1962, trying to clarify the five-part *Roth* test, the Court further defined "prurient" as something "patently offensive," and two years later, it specified that only "worthless" matter "utterly without social importance" could be banned. So, by the early 1960s, the only matter that could be deemed legally obscene and thus not protected by the First Amendment was material that in its entirety was clearly offensive and totally without social, political, or cultural importance.

But this standard applied to adult reading material. Although it liberalized obscenity law for books that adults might read, the Court also recognized that it was not an unreasonable use of a state's police power to keep harmful material away from minors. In 1968, the Court set out what came to be seen as a clear double standard of obscenity: governments could constitutionally keep material deemed harmful from minors but could not keep such material from adults unless, of course, it was "utterly without" social value and the work as a whole was "patently offensive" as defined by contemporary community standards. Two different layers of protections henceforth existed—one for children, a different one for adults.

After the U.S. Postal Service failed in its attempt to keep *Esquire* from the mail in 1946, various postmasters general continued to try to keep allegedly obscene magazines from the mail in the 1960s. In 1962, the post office tried to ban several homosexual-themed magazines but the Supreme Court intervened, saying that material could only be restricted if it was so "patently offensive" that it affronted contemporary standards of decency. The next year, the postmaster general tried to keep an issue of *Playboy* out of U.S. mailboxes, but a New York City jury deadlocked on whether it was truly obscene. In both cases the magazines went out.

Freedman v. Maryland (1965)

In November 1962, as judges were loosening obscenity restrictions and as the Legion's and the code's grips were weakening, an exhibitor joined the list of litigating film distributors. Baltimore theater owner Ronald Freedman was showing a film he had refused to submit to the Maryland censor board and had promptly been arrested. This was the case that the justices had hinted was necessary during oral arguments the year before in the Chicago *Times Film* case.

After years of reluctantly bowing to the whims of the state's censors, Freedman had decided to fight back with the help and encouragement of that brazenly anticensorship film distributor, Times Film Corporation. This round with Freedman was to be Times Film's third major legal challenge. The company had already met the Chicago censors twice at the U.S. Supreme Court (winning in 1958 and losing in 1961). Spoiling for another fight, Times and Freedman had picked *Revenge at Daybreak*, a totally unobjectionable ten-year-old film about the Irish revolt of 1916. Other than its selection by Freedman and Times Film as their celluloid line in the sand, this movie should have no place in a book about censorship. Not even the most stringent censor could have found fault with *Revenge at Daybreak*.

But Freedman was dedicated to bringing down the Maryland censor board and *Revenge* would be his vehicle, specifically chosen because it was so unobjectionable. Full of "pep and vinegar," in his own words, he relished the fight. As he was led away from the Rex Theatre in handcuffs after showing *Revenge* without the necessary license, he instructed his employees to reletter the marquee to read "Fight for Freedom of the Screen."

Freedman and Times Film had reason to think that the time was right for this kind of challenge: two Supreme Court justices had recently retired, replaced by the more reliably speech-friendly Arthur Goldberg and Byron White. Both were viewed as likely to join the usually anticensorship bloc of four — Warren, Black, Douglas, and Brennan — the ones who were probably keeping the string of per curiam opinions going. This meant six votes Freedman could count on. As another promising sign, this Court had just invalidated a Rhode Island book censorship commission. In 1956, that state's legislature had created a nine-person advisory board empowered to review books, bring pressure on book wholesalers, and recommend prosecution for the sale of books the board considered unwholesome. Although its pressure tactics were more like extortion than statutory censorship, this board held exciting potential for those who wanted to challenge movie censorship. When four book publishers brought suit in 1963, the Court found the commission's activities tantamount to "governmental censorship," necessarily suspect. "Any system of prior restraints of expression comes to this Court bearing a heavy presumption against its constitutional validity," wrote Justice Brennan for the eight-judge majority. Noting that the Court had allowed prior restraint only when it operated under "judicial superintendence" and with "almost immediate judicial determination of its validity," Brennan held that the Rhode Island commission allowed nothing of the kind. Those last words — "almost immediate judicial determination" — contained the germ of what would bring down almost all governmental film censorship: the inevitable delay in systems of prior restraint. And it was this issue of delay on which Freedman and Times Film would build their case.

It was a good thing that the Court was looking more promising, because in this fight Freedman and Times Film had little help. The MPAA had helped Freedman in the state court rounds but decided to abandon him if the case went to the Supreme Court. Apparently, it was now willing to help a foreign film, but only in dealing with an internal Maryland situation (Maryland's was considered one of the more stringent censor boards). When the case became a national concern at the Supreme Court, the MPAA bailed out. The ACLU, which ignored Freedman's case in the lower courts, did file an amicus brief when the case was accepted by the Supreme Court but, according to Freedman, did little else.

As it turned out, Freedman and Times Film did not need much help. By unanimous decision, the U.S. Supreme Court agreed that the delay in prior restraint was problematic, and declared that most of the methods used to exercise such restraint on films were unconstitutional. In *Freedman v. Maryland* (1965), all nine justices agreed that it was time to make *Burstyn* stick: the requirement the Court had handed down in 1952 that the censors, not the distributors, should bear the "heavy burden" of proof that a motion picture was dangerous and should be kept from the public. It had taken thirteen years for the Court to put teeth into its own pronouncement and end the reverse burden of proof that had kept one industry—motion pictures—in second-class legal status since the Progressive Era.

Freedman's case turned out to be the final blow to the statutory censors. From 1965 forward, if a government wished to censor movies prior to exhibition, it was required to do so quickly. If it did not promptly issue a license, the censor board was required to institute legal proceedings against the distributor to prove to a judge that the movie was not protected expression and could be banned. No longer was it the distributor's burden, as it had been for more than five decades, to prove that a film was not dangerous. Even though censors were allowed to ban movies only for obscenity by the early 1960s, every movie, no matter how innocent, was required to be examined. The Court found this an undue restraint on both protected and unprotected communication. Because so much protected speech had been forced to run through the sieve of prior restraint, the Court took steps to ensure that only unprotected speech be halted. So, with the new procedures, the censors would have to prove to a judge that a movie contained unprotected speech (at this point limited to obscenity) before the censors could keep a movie from the public. And it had to be done quickly. The delay inherent in motion picture censorship, especially for those films not licensed, had a chilling effect on all speech, Justice Brennan wrote for the Court. But the idea that movies were different, that they had a "special capacity for evil," lived on. Although the Court expected judicial review of allegedly obscene books within two days, all Brennan said about judicial review for movies was that it had to occur "considerably more prompt[ly] than has been the case under the Maryland statute." He refused to "lay down rigid time limits or procedures," but did encourage the censoring states "to avoid the potentially chilling effect of the Maryland statute on protected expression." So, the burden of proof had shifted to the state, but Maryland, Virginia, Kansas, and New York faced no definitive guidelines about how "prompt" their action against objectionable movies had to be.

The decision was, as Bosley Crowther crowed, a "left hook and right upper cut," but it was no knockout. Film censorship could still stand but state and local statutes needed serious revision if governments were going to continue to censor movies. *Freedman* had not succeeded in getting censorship declared unconstitutional, but the decades-long presumption that constitutionality existed so long as the banned film had recourse to judicial review — no matter how long that review took — had been recognized as innately unfair.

And so Maryland, New York, Virginia, Kansas, and a few cities like Chicago and Detroit all had their censorship statutes overturned. Maryland's attorney general did not take it well: he called the case "the Armageddon of motion picture censorship." Of the states, New York and Kansas attempted to conform to Freedman's procedural requirements by adopting new rules, but both efforts were ruled unconstitutional by their state supreme courts, and both were out of business by 1966. Only Maryland redrew its entire statute — and did it so well that it survived further constitutional challenges, allowing the state to continue censoring for another sixteen years, giving up its solitary pursuit only in 1981.

The decision in *Burstyn v. Wilson* had been a true watershed, a dividing line between thirty-seven years of jurisprudence that endorsed censor supremacy and a thirteen-year period of continual censor questioning. By volunteering to oversee censor decisions, the *Burstyn* justices empowered strict scrutiny of censor actions. Eventually, that scrutiny led the justices to decide that the reverse burden of proof inherent in prior restraint was no longer justified by societal concerns over "vulnerable viewers," to use Frank Couvares's succinct term. Those innocents had been the historical justification for censor legislation, according to historian Andrea Friedman. But by the mid-1960s, as concern over vulnerable viewers diminished, and as the Court ramped up its speech-protective jurisprudence, the film censorship statutes became vulnerable when attacked on constitutional grounds.

But vulnerable viewers never completely left the legal stage; indeed they are still present in broadcast and movie debates. In the late 1960s, as the areas protected by the Free Speech Clause of the First Amendment were expanding, the courts were also making clear that they had no problem with the double standard set out: whether speech would be experienced by adults or by children would make the difference in its constitutionality. *Ginsberg v. New York* (1968) showed that the Court would not strike down carefully drawn anti-obscenity laws designed to protect children. The notion that harm could be done to children by movies — a powerful underpinning of the entire censorship regime — was still prevalent in judicial thought. The legal tension between the First Amendment's seemingly absolute language and concern over children's viewing began in earnest with the *Burstyn* decision and still plagues thoughtful social critics and parents today.

Burstyn had set in motion state-level attacks on censorship statutes, some successful in the 1950s (Ohio, Pennsylvania, and Massachusetts), others not until the 1960s (New York, Virginia, and Kansas). *Burstyn* proved to be, as Lillian Gerard claimed, a sort of "Emancipation Proclamation of film." It marked the dividing line between the early era of film when most people were willing to acquiesce to censors and the modern period when censors and film freedom conflicted repeatedly, when censors' work was questioned, and film producers began to question their own content management system in the Production Code. Yet, like the Emancipation Proclamation, which had little immediate effect beyond signaling a new direction, the *Burstyn* decision had also taken time and more work before motion pictures would be freed from prior restraint.

———

A Change in Attitude

By the mid-1960s, U.S. movie culture had grown up, and the old authorities had to shift their practices to contend with its new directions. Thus, it was no coincidence that in 1965, the same year state censorship effectively ended, the Legion changed its name, and, a year later, the PCA dropped its code. As the courts responded to mounting legal challenges, Hollywood and the Legion had to learn how to respond to the implications of those cases. In other words, as the courts acknowledged that movies were a legitimate form of speech that deserved protection from prior censorship, Hollywood and the Legion had to acknowledge that audiences expected different kinds of movies. The emergence of a pluralistic movie culture was a clear legacy of *The Miracle*, resulting from both the legal outcome of the case and the cultural battle over the movie.

Changes to the Production Code and the Legion marked the culmination of almost a decade of controversies and minor shifts. And as had happened from the beginning of their histories, the PCA and the Legion changed together. By the mid-1950s, the conservative authorities who dictated both the PCA and the Legion had retired, and younger, more liberal successors had taken up the task of responding to a more fluid movie culture. In 1956, the Production Code had been revised; in 1957, the Legion adopted an A-III rating for movies that were acceptable for "adults." These new regimes with their new rules tacitly approved a new movie culture but, unlike in the past, when the Legion of Decency and the code administrators held sway, now they had little control. The PCA had to contend with producers who openly flouted the need for a code seal if their demands were not met. Similarly, the Legion had to learn to deal with a constituency — the Catholic laity — that simply disregarded its ratings. The series of legal decisions set off by *Burstyn* had created an era of rising expectations among moviegoers and some filmmakers that Hollywood and the Catholic Church either had to accept or risk being passed over as irrelevant.

The Legion changed its name and its goals after the *Burstyn* concept matured into the *Freedman* requirements. Six months after Freedman, in December 1965, the Legion became the National Catholic Office for Motion Pictures (NCOMP). Along with a new name, the organization had a new mission. "Its work once limited to the moral classification of film, [NCOMP] now also embraces the positive endorsement of outstanding films and concentrates more and more upon the promotion of film education. . . . In our free society, appreciation and support of good films on the part of all mem-

bers of the community are essential to the future of the motion picture industry." This name change intentionally and significantly
coincided with the Sunday in December that the annual pledge was
taken. In her study of the NCOMP, Mary McLaughlin explains,
"The Legion of Decency was considered too militaristic and too
closely associated with theatre picketing and boycotts, all of which
were considered by the Legion to be out of harmony with a post–
Vatican II approach to a pluralistic society." Even the director of the
old Legion, Monsignor Thomas Little, had to admit that it had
become to many a "stubborn, antiquarian, unrealistic defender of
Catholic moviegoers against moral corruption."

By 1965, the NCOMP was also changing the way it reviewed
movies. In the old Legion of Decency days, a group of lay Catholic
women had done most of the reviewing, buttressed by some of the
priesthood. The International Federation of Catholic Alumnae had
been the backbone of the reviewing cadre. But in the 1960s, the
Legion began to use consultants to help review and categorize films.
By a slight majority, laypeople outnumbered clergy among the eighty-
four consultants. Almost all were college graduates, many had
advanced degrees, most were men, and there were more in the twenty-five to thirty-five age group than those over fifty. Ironically, the
film critic most of these consultants favored by a large majority was
the Legion of Decency's old nemesis, Bosley Crowther.

This change in attitude has often been associated with the arrival
of Father Patrick Sullivan in 1957 as the Legion's assistant executive
secretary. Sullivan was a Jesuit, and thus belonged to an order that
had criticized Legion decisions in the past. His appointment was
meant to appease educated Catholics and, as McLaughlin notes, "to
channel Jesuit scholarship, reputation, and energy to improving the
image of the Legion."

One example of this new approach was the controversy that
swirled around *The Pawnbroker*, a 1965 film that contained a brief
scene of nongratuitous female nudity encased within a serious story.
The film did receive the Production Code seal after a fight within the
PCA, but the Legion issued a condemned (C) rating. Even at this late
date, dissension between the PCA and the Legion of Decency was a
rare occurrence. But the Legion may have overreacted: Monsignor
Little told the newly arrived Sullivan that the Legion had received

"many well-written letters of criticism" in response to the rating. He also told him that it was a "well-known fact that many Catholics, including the clergy, patronized the film."

The NCOMP was trying to change with the times. That same year, the NCOMP began handing out awards for best films of the year in their various categories, including "best for mature audiences." By 1966, Catholics gave these awards in conjunction with the Broadcasting and Film Commission of the National Council of Churches, an organization that included Protestant and orthodox Christian churches. In 1967 the award for best film for mature audiences went to the critically acclaimed but violent *Bonnie and Clyde*. By way of explanation, the NCOMP declared that the film was "a genuine folk epic challenging the individual viewer to recognize within himself the needs of meaningless violence which are just below the surface of an easy conscience." This choice was not lost on the Catholic press. This was a film that even a few years earlier would have been considered morally objectionable for any Catholic. The other films running against *Bonnie and Clyde* that year included *In Cold Blood*, *In the Heat of the Night*, and *The Graduate* – all mature and, to varying degrees, controversial films that a few years earlier would have earned the Legion's wrath.

The one category that remained a problem, though, was sex. Monsignor Little feared that because pornography had become commonplace on newsstands, it would transfer to the screens. Despite such foreboding, Catholic journals such as *America* were arguing for the NCOMP to loosen its rules against nudity and sexuality. Films such as the import *Blow-Up* (1966) had won critical acclaim and had box office success despite being released without a PCA seal and with a C rating. In an interview with the *St. Louis Review*, Little revealed just how much the church's position had changed since the time when it could condemn Mae West and destroy her career. Now he admitted that "Catholic people should know that they can go see a serious work like *Blow-Up* without any scandal to themselves or others so long as they are serious about their purpose. The C does not prohibit the exhibition of these films, but the C is still there and it is a problem."

That C was no longer a problem for Hollywood, though. The power of the condemned rating, which twenty years earlier would have been seen by the PCA as a slap in the face, by 1966 had been eroded. The code was also enfeebled. That same year, fully 41 percent of all films released in the United States hit theaters without the benefit of a code seal. To avoid having to outlaw the new mature themes of movies, the MPAA recognized the trend and revised its tottering code for the final time by including a new category: "Suggested for Mature Audiences." It was a label created to avoid further embarrassment about the number of well-received and lucrative films being released in direct opposition to the PCA.

Although the code still existed in name, in practice it was completely ineffective. An editorial in Martin Quigley's magazine, the *Motion Picture Herald*, summed up the situation: "Everything expressly prohibited in the Production Code apparently is to be approved, one way or other." The industry had effectively taken itself out of censoring movies.

The code's impotence was apparent to everyone associated with the movie industry, especially the new head of the MPAA, Jack Valenti. Much like Will Hays, his distant predecessor, Valenti needed to find something to placate industry critics now that a vacuum had opened with the demise of the code. Without faith in the industry's ability to regulate itself, and without government censor boards to manage screens, communities across the United States had begun to establish independent rating boards to regulate films. In 1968, one such board in Dallas found itself sued by the Interstate Theatre Circuit over its classification of Louis Malle's *Viva Maria* (1965) as "not suitable for children under 16." The Supreme Court overturned the Dallas ordinance as overly vague, which seemed a victory for those such as the MPAA who did not want to see classification boards springing up around the country. However, Justice Thurgood Marshall, writing for the eight-to-one Court, clearly indicated that although Dallas' statute was flawed, and the classification of *Viva Maria* was therefore unconstitutional, the Court would not look unfavorably on other classification schemes if narrowly drawn. It was not classification the Court found unconstitutional, just the version of classification in Dallas.

Here, the Court was undertaking a firm stance regarding smut and children. As it had found in other areas — books and magazines — there was no absolute right to speech, and the Court had no problem creating a double standard of free speech rights: a more nearly absolute one for speech that would reach adults and another that recognized the states' interest in keeping obscene or indecent speech from minors.

When the U.S. Senate, under the prodding of Senator Margaret Chase Smith, began hearings on mandatory film classification, Valenti announced that the MPAA was working on its own voluntary rating system. Faced with the threat of federal censorship, once again, the motion picture industry responded as it had more than thirty years before—by insisting it could clean its own house.

And so the movie industry created its own comprehensive rating system. Stephen Vaughn explains that when Valenti unveiled the system in 1968, "filmmakers gained the freedom to show almost anything." Gone were the preproduction and postproduction bargaining that constituted the earlier censorship of the code administrators. The rating board would not interfere, it claimed, with what those over seventeen could see. Instead, it would classify finished movies G through X as a guide for parents. Although the content of films was still contested, the industry no longer had the leverage to prevent the release of a film. In the future, debates over content focused on the kind of rating that might determine a film's financial viability. However, a director or a distributor no longer had to convince Catholics and code officials that his or her film was inoffensive. And unlike its predecessor, the Code and Ratings Administration (CARA) depended solely on voluntary compliance. Thus, since 1968 only a fraction of the films released in the United States have actually been reviewed and rated by CARA—an average of about 500 movies per year from 1969 through 1999.

Hollywood had concluded by 1968 that its audience wanted mature pictures, and the industry had to find a way to deliver them but still look respectable and responsible. Film historian Jon Lewis explains, "American movies after the fall of 1968 look and sound different from those produced before then. Valenti's rating system also promised to better insulate the studios against local efforts to interfere with the production, distribution, and exhibition of their product." Although Valenti was somewhat dismissive of foreign directors who were the darlings of film critics, he also understood that a new generation of Hollywood directors would have to create films similar to the imports if the U.S. industry was to regain its footing. In 1967 alone, the number of films that earned the designation for "mature audiences" rose from six to forty-four.

This relative surge in such movies did not, however, solve Hollywood's box office problems. In 1969, the two most talked-about movies were the soft-core Swedish import *I Am Curious, Yellow* and the defiantly independent *Easy Rider*. By 1970, even though there was a general ad ban on X-rated movies, box office performance for sex films was brisk. The Danish film *Without a Stitch* (1968), with nudity and simulated sex, grossed $30,000 a week for five weeks at the Loew's Theater on Broadway. Lewis concludes: "The message was clear: even the biggest and best theaters were willing to book soft-core titles so long as they made money."

Valenti and Hollywood's new rating system had helped create that dilemma. CARA could give an X rating, but to avoid an X rating, about a third of the movies submitted in 1969 and 1970 were edited. Exploitation filmmakers and their distributors were thrilled with the new distinction, though, because it helped them market their movies as both legitimate and salacious — exactly the combination that the old Production Code had been created to prevent.

With the demise of the Production Code, the Legion of Decency, and state censorship, U.S. movie culture fractured. For many in film communities that existed outside the Hollywood universe, the period that began around 1968 was a heroic time. Limits on the screen had fallen, ushering in a generation of filmmakers and moviegoers no longer beholden to arcane cultural assumptions. By the late 1960s, it was possible to explore what a free screen actually meant.

After New York's censorship regime received its fatal blow in 1965, Bosley Crowther noted that the legal designation of "obscenity" was the last frontier movies still could not enter. And if movies did, he said approvingly, "the charges of offense must be aired in open court with the public given some inkling of what it is being protected from." Although Crowther had championed (one might even say pushed) greater freedom for movie culture, he also began to grow concerned about the consequences of such freedom without any checks. In a 1965 column titled "The Heat Is on Films," he worried that the "flow of films of a cheap and sordid nature" threatened gains made against censorship and encouraged the rise of a new repressive regime of control. Crowther put the responsibility directly on the producers. "The moral integrity of a picture, like its artistic quality, is inevitably controlled by the people who make it. And it is up to them to assume responsibility." He advocated "active education and elevation of public taste," calling for "more solid critical guidance." And, he argued, "It is absurd that this mature and mighty medium should be entirely downgraded and exposed to public scorn because of a run of cheap, stupid, and easily avoidable mistakes." However, the problem was not that the moviemakers had made mistakes. It was that Crowther had grown unwilling to come to terms with a movie culture that had been freed as much from liberal notions of taste and style as from the codes of moralists.

By 1967, Crowther's ire toward new film styles made some of his reviews sound like sermons. Moreover, he wrote with an earnestness that grated against the revolution in values that had energized both filmmakers and the moviegoers who followed them, rather than Crowther, as the new high priests of art. "So rapid has been the exorcising of moral taboos in our society in recent years and so commonplace has permissiveness of expression in all the arts become that anyone who got engrossed by movies as they were 30 years ago might well be confused beyond adjustment by what he sees and hears on the screen these days." Crowther took pains to explain that he was not condemning the exploration of sexual themes, for "it is proper and inevitable that many aspects of human behavior and many conflicts of a dark and ugly sort should be broached and explored by filmmakers — maturely and significantly, one might hope." Of course, therein lay the problem: Crowther often failed to distinguish filmmakers who pushed the limits of public tolerance for controversial art from those who merely exploited those limits for commercial gain. "The responsibility for determining and demanding responsible entertainment on the screen falls as much upon the critics and the patrons as it does upon the people who make the films. It is up to the critics and the patrons — but mostly the critics who can make themselves heard — to resolve and defend the major issue. That is responsibility."

Yet what did responsibility mean in a culture of freedom? In the past, the word had been code for staid and even oppressive mores forced on a diverse population as if one taste in movies had to fit all. But a new generation and the new freedom unleashed by *Burstyn* and its progeny required a new sensibility. Critic Susan Sontag captured the essence of this cultural revolt in her groundbreaking collection of essays called *Against Interpretation* (1966). Sontag argued, "The purpose of art is always, ultimately, to give pleasure. The new sensibility demands less 'content' in art and is more open to the pleasures of 'form' and style; it is also less snobbish, less moralistic—in that it does not demand that pleasure in art necessarily be associated with edification." Sontag's thought represented a frontal assault on all that censors symbolized. Censorship had been the most extreme form of repressive criticism; Sontag wanted to release criticism and art from the grip of moralists. Here was an inverse of the censor's logic in pursuit of what sounded like common ends. Historian David Steigerwald explains: "In Sontag's view, a culture built on such aesthetics held out hope for vast improvements in the formal arts and, most important, in society at large. Freed from the tyranny of interpretation, artists would not presume to judge and, therefore, would never see formal art as superior to popular culture. The new culture was therefore pluralistic and egalitarian." The kind of cultural authority that had banished movies to a world beneath the rest of culture—a place where censors could exercise control—was fast becoming obsolete.

New York City, the source of much of this new culture, was a case in point. By the late 1960s, the city had become an inversion of its former self. Once a place strongly influenced by Catholic culture and controlled by censors, the city's movie culture had become like a house of mirrors, with different kinds of theaters showing everything from musical comedies to blue movies. And all of it coexisted in an atmosphere of legal ambiguity and cultural triumphalism. In 1963, *New York Times* legal affairs reporter Anthony Lewis saw what was to come: "Today the voice of the sophisticated critic is dominant, and the Philistines are on the run." Indeed, it was a heady time to feel oneself part of the artistic vanguard breaking through cultural barriers that had existed since the nineteenth century.

Sex

Of course, sex became the symbol of this liberated culture. In movies, sex was the cultural barometer, testing just how much freedom a society and its courts could tolerate. New York, the nation's largest and most diverse movie market, exercised a profound influence over the shape of movie culture across the nation. Unlike other locales that were dominated by much more traditional notions of moral authority, New York was a community in which determining a single standard was frankly impossible. After all, the welter of communities that make up New York had given birth to *The Miracle* controversy and the *Burstyn* case. The *Burstyn* decision had made clear that one person's sacrilege was another's orthodoxy and that one person's art was another's trash. The new wave of controversial films that resulted had pushed the boundaries of public culture even further.

In 1968, U.S. customs officials in New York City seized the soft-core Swedish film *I Am Curious, Yellow.* Barney Rossett of Grove Press sued to release the film for theatrical exhibition, and Grove Press had its day in court. As a publishing house that had become notorious for distributing sexualized novels and magazines, Grove came into the trial seemingly poised to play the bad guy — the purveyor of smut. However, this was the late 1960s, and the federal government represented traditional authority that was suffering from revolutionary levels of scrutiny. This case also benefited from a decade of legal rulings that made defending such a film a much more legitimate prospect.

As a serious film, *Curious* presented an intriguing situation, for it seemed a timely work of art with a story about contemporary youth challenging social, political, and sexual conventions. The film masqueraded as a documentary about a young girl exploring the realms of sexual relationships and the leftist politics of the time. And although it contained unusually frank nudity (the first serious film to show fully nude actors) and a few simulated sex scenes, it was also well received by film critics. Among its supporters was John Simon, who characterized the story as "a young girl's search for identity in contemporary Sweden, in the course of which she rummages around in all accepted values: political, social, and sexual." Another critic and expert witness, Stanley Kauffmann, put it succinctly: "What used to be thought of as a clear dividing line, an iron barrier between art and life, should go or can go or has gone, and we are not really aware of it yet."

The jury thought differently. It found that the film met the test for obscenity, and so upheld the ban on distribution. A little less than a year later, though, justices on the U.S. Court of Appeals for the Second Circuit overturned the jury decision, writing an opinion full of conflicted opinions. Although the three judges believed that *Curious* was offensive, two of the three determined that the film was not legally obscene according to the standard established by the U.S. Supreme Court in *Jacobellis v. Ohio* (1964) and *Memoirs of a Woman of Pleasure* (1966). *Jacobellis* had applied the five-part *Roth* obscenity test specifically to movies, adding that only "worthless" matter "utterly without social importance" based on national standards of decency could be censored. One of the judges frankly acknowledged that the film's sex scenes and sexual themes were presented "with greater explicitness than has been seen in any other film produced for general viewing." Yet based on his reading of the Supreme Court's obscenity definition, and citing *Burstyn*, he concluded that "whatever the differences there may be in the application of obscenity standards, a motion picture, like a book, is clearly entitled to the protection of the First Amendment." Barney Rossett could release *Curious* for public consumption. Even cultural expression that carried the clear potential to offend could not be circumvented before it was given a chance to be seen and even then could only be kept from public exhibition if patently offensive with no redeeming artistic or social value – a high standard of proof for moral guardians to meet. The days of prior restraint in New York, Virginia, Massachusetts, Kansas, Ohio, and Pennsylvania were gone. Ultimately, the U.S. Supreme Court would have to decide when an offended community – represented by a jury – trumped the artistic value of the offending film.

The Court of Appeals decision was the green light Rossett was waiting for. A specialist in ruffling propriety feathers, he intended to bring *Curious* to as many states as possible. In that pursuit he ran into the only state censors left, the Maryland state board, which balked and ruled the film obscene in 1969. The state court, after hearing from a rash of experts who claimed alternatively that the movie was obscene and was not obscene, decided that it was time to draw the line against "pornography." Although Judge Joseph L. Carter said he did not wish a return to Puritanism, he did hope to see "a return to sense and decency." He was not about to release *Curious* to Marylanders despite the slew of experts put up by Rossett who claimed that the film had some redeeming social value.

A year later, the Supreme Court got the chance to rule on *Curious*. Rossett, who liked to call himself a "combat publisher," was itching to get the case before the High Court. His case was buttressed by amicus briefs from the Independent Film Importers and Distributors Association, the National Association of Theater Owners, the Adult Film Association of America, and the MPAA (which had decided it was time to fight for film freedom against Maryland). Rossett's attorney, Edward de Grazia, showed that the movie had been seen in 180 cities, in 40 states, to more than 5 million people. Those numbers alone were clear evidence, he said, that the film was not pornographic. Maryland's attorney general argued that if a movie as offensive as *Curious* could be shown, then the censorship board was completely irrelevant. (To which we can imagine Rossett's response.)

Again, as they had so many times since 1952, anti- and procensorites hoped for a definitive statement from the Supreme Court. But on March 6, 1970, in *Grove Press v. Maryland State Board of Censors*, the Court divided equally (Justice Douglas had recused himself because he had recently published an article in a Grove Press publication). The four-to-four decision necessarily left the Second Circuit's ruling standing. And so the issue of whether films were constitutionally protected speech had been avoided by the Supreme Court yet again. However, because the Second Circuit's ruling had been in favor of exhibiting *Curious* and that decision now stood, Rossett and others like him could argue that sex films had reached a platform of legal legitimacy.

In spring 1969, *Newsweek* ran a long article titled "Sex and the Arts" that attempted to catalog, and thereby make sense of, the convergence of the sexual revolution with the artistic world. The writers prefaced their article with a reference to a similar essay that had run two years earlier (in November 1967) titled "Anything Goes: Taboos in Twilight." That piece had highlighted the ways in which movies like *Bonnie and Clyde* had come to reflect and promote a broad generational divide within U.S. society. Just two years later, according to *Newsweek*, sexual themes in the arts had "become a matter of national concern." Whereas the text provided evidence that sex and erotica had artistic integrity and therefore a legitimate place in U.S. culture, photos of nude dancers and movie stars that accompanied the piece illustrated that the sexual revolution was also about feeding the public's salacious expectations.

Thus the court cases involving *Curious* showed two sides of a thorny issue. The film deserved to be protected from prior censorship and from a general ban on its distribution, but the fanfare surrounding these cases also bestowed societal endorsement on cultural expression that was popular mostly because of its sex scenes. In the *Newsweek* essay, the writers cited the public reception of *Curious* as evidence of the paradox at the heart of the new culture — sex in culture could be both good art and good money.

After *Curious* had been cleared for release by the Second Circuit, it opened at Cinema 57 Rendezvous on Fifty-Seventh Street in Manhattan, close to Carnegie Hall. Moviegoers described as "well-dressed, healthy-looking people" formed a line at 10 o'clock in the morning to pay $3 a ticket to see the sexiest art film in the city. In its first week it broke all records for art films — if in fact it could be categorized as one — by grossing $79,101. It outgrossed a film playing at Radio City Music Hall for two days in a row, even though Cinema 57 Rendezvous had less than 10 percent of the seats Radio City had. One film distributor told *Newsweek* he wanted the film because he was sure he could make $2 million dollars in Texas alone. "This can no longer be called a film — it's a social phenomenon," said another distributor.

Indeed, *Newsweek* continued, "The floodgates have opened one by one, and the inundation is now a matter of fact, in the hinterlands as well as the big cities." Examples abounded: books like Philip Roth's *Portnoy's Complaint* and magazines like *Screw* and the *New York Review of Sex*; films such as *Curious* and exploitation films from Russ Meyer and Radley Metzger; sexual innuendos on Rowan and Martin's *Laugh-In*; and sexy lingerie in magazines and on fashion runways all confirmed that nudity was in and sex sold. To many Americans, this explosion was all of one piece, and the courts were to blame.

Newsweek explained, "It is a fact of recent cultural history that both the legal definitions of and the accepted standards for obscenity, pornography, and their like are in a state of total confusion."

Porn

Although some observers mourned the loss of an older moral system, Richard Gilman, a contentious drama critic and the literary editor at the *New Republic*, argued that as legal restrictions receded, finally an opportunity had come to separate artistic sexuality from crass porn. "The first distinction it's necessary to make is between the legal and the moral and psychological aspects of the subject," he wrote. "The second is between what is merely sexual and what is wholly sexual, sex as a part of life and as a replacement for everything else." His argument echoed a view held by many intellectuals, especially Susan Sontag, contending that sex and the arts was a variegated situation — it was wrong to dump all sexual expressions into the categories of obscenity and pornography. Gilman suggested that, for the most part, the majority of "hard-core" stuff was available only in restricted areas, such as Times Square. Opposition to pornography, he observed, tended to be so broad that it threatened to return U.S. culture to its arcane past. "What remains, as always after the Law has finished speaking, are all the important questions: What *is* pornography? Obscenity? How do we distinguish them, if they be isolated, from sexual expression in general? Why . . . do men produce such problematic dispositions of sexual experience and possibility and other men consume them?"

Gilman believed that pornography was a genre and that its status as an outlaw social phenomenon came from the repression of basic human nature. In other words, the illegality of obscenity was a product of illegitimate cultural standards. Unduly repressive standards made it "wrong" to produce and consume pornography; but pornography in and of itself was not inherently and absolutely "bad." As long as people spoke about culture in moral terms — what is good and what is bad — pornography would always be seen as a rebellion against moral absolutes. But if culture was understood in aesthetic terms, then pornography could be part of a spectrum of cultural expressions. "We have to be permitted our consciousness, wherever it takes us," he declared.

Gilman's analysis was the exact opposite of the sensibility of censors. He promoted an understanding of public culture that was devoid of a single dominant moral code. Gilman's argument reflected a pluralistic culture brought to a new level. The point of Burstyn's case was to create an umbrella under which all kinds of content in films could flourish, even that which might be offensive to some. Obscenity in the form of pornography was the final frontier, so to speak, of such pluralism. And so, when *Curious* became part of the mainstream, the bounds of the post-*Miracle* culture expanded a bit more.

The courts had ruled, the critics had spoken, the audiences had voted with their ticket buying, and then the federal government weighed in. President Lyndon Johnson authorized a federal study of the U.S. sex scene; the result was a report published by the Federal Commission on Obscenity and Pornography in September 1970. Courting considerable controversy, the commission's majority said it favored elimination of all restrictions on adults who wanted to possess pornographic material, either by reading it, watching it, or owning it. The report stated flatly: "Federal, state, and local legislation prohibiting the sale, exhibition, or distribution of sexual materials to consenting adults should be repealed." Of the commission's eighteen members, twelve agreed that "pornography did not cause crime, delinquency, sexual deviancy, or emotional disturbances." Five dissented from this opinion and one abstained. The dissenters fired back that they believed porn had "an eroding effect on society, on public morality, on respect for human worth, on attitudes toward family love, on culture." To counter such concerns, the majority advocated a massive sex education program to provide "a powerful positive approach to the problems of obscenity and pornography."

William B. Lockhart, dean of the University of Minnesota Law School, chaired the commission and defended the majority's position against attacks from the dissenters led by Charles H. Keating Jr. The report ran 622 pages, the dissent 318 pages, and the force of this massive report provoked a popular reaction similar to the response to Alfred Kinsey's studies on sexual behavior in 1948 and 1953. The commission's majority urged the nation's lawmakers to treat adults with respect, and to consider that because U.S. society was pluralistic rather than monolithic in terms of values and morals, the best way to tell the difference between art and legal obscenity was to voice concerns through public debate rather than through the use of police action. The commissioners encouraged "continued open discussion based on factual information." Thus, they recommended the repeal of laws restricting what adults could see because "there is no warrant for continued government interference with the full freedom of adults to read, obtain, or view whatever material they wish."

Furthermore, the commission reasoned that because it could not find any serious effects on society stemming from the use of pornography, the time had come to dismantle many of the laws restricting obscene and pornographic material. "Public opinion in America does not support the imposition of legal prohibitions upon the right of adults to read or see explicit sexual materials," the commissioners in the majority explained. "Americans deeply value the right of each individual to determine for himself what books he wishes to read and what pictures or films he wishes to see. . . . The spirit and letter of our Constitution tells us that government should not interfere with these rights unless a clear threat of harm makes that course imperative."

Here was a major sea change from the assumptions that had guided censors through Burstyn's era. The majority of commissioners not only believed that most obscenity laws wasted the time of police and judges and opened the system up to "the possibility of misuse of general obscenity statutes," but they found it "wholly inappropriate to adjust the level of adult communication to that considered suitable for children." Thus what only a few committed civil libertarians had dared to express forty years earlier had been endorsed in a federal government study.

The Supreme Court had said something similar in the book censorship case of *Butler v. Michigan* back in 1957. Frankfurter, writing for the Court, had found that the effect of book censorship to protect children reduced the artistic inventory, and since that infringed the individual's liberty to read, "an indispensable condition for the maintenance and progress of a free society" had been curtailed. The major underpinning of the progressive rationale for censorship, protection of children, had started coming unglued in the 1950s. By the beginning of the 1970s, it had been completely undone in the minds of some. The commission did not suggest, however, that all offensive material be allowed everywhere. Although the commission still wanted to restrict offensive content intended for or targeted toward children, it advocated that access should be opened for adults.

The disagreement between the majority and the dissenters could not have been more stark. The dissenters called pornography an "epidemic" and the report "the Magna Carta for the pornographer." Keating had expected the report to "provide to our legislators a blueprint for coping with a problem." He had hoped that the report would bolster law enforcement tactics, but he saw instead a report that further eroded what he considered necessary restrictions: "Our law enforcement in the area of obscenity has been emasculated by courts seemingly divorced from the realities of our communities, determining from afar the standards of those communities. The law is capable of coping with the problem of pornography and obscenity, but it must be the law, coupled with the logic that an American is innately capable of determining for himself his standards of public decency and . . . that he has a right to make that determination."

Keating's argument reflected a persistent fear in U.S. culture — that the views of "sophisticates" such as Anthony Lewis would ultimately overwhelm the ability of communities to control their local culture.

A film that seemed to confirm Keating's dire warnings was *Deep Throat*, which premiered at Manhattan's World Theatre in the summer of 1972 and enjoyed a spectacular commercial run all over the country. Talk of the movie entered the public square through a disparate array of outlets, from *Harper's Bazaar* and *Women's Wear Daily* to *Playboy* and *Screw*. Such exposure seemed to imply that watching porn was an activity embraced by both the smart set — *New York Times* reporter Ralph Blumenthal called the phenomenon "porno chic" — as well as the masses. Moral watchdogs found all of this particularly troubling because they believed they had almost no way of controlling their civic culture. To them, the appearance of *Deep Throat* at the local theater was akin to barbarians at the gate. No other kind of cultural expression tested the viability of a public, pluralistic culture quite like hard-core pornographic films. Until the late 1960s, such films had been almost completely outside the public realm, existing in little theaters in the less savory parts of towns and cities. The notion that theaters on main streets across the country would be showing films with real sex was utterly unthinkable. But *Deep Throat* changed all that.

Made for a little more than $24,000 by former hairdresser Gerald Damiano, *Deep Throat* became the eleventh highest grossing film in 1972, pulling in more than $20 million. Obviously, the audience that made it so financially successful went well beyond the "raincoat" brigade, and included middle-class moviegoers. The film launched many imitators with similar box office returns. David Cook relates that four years after the introduction of the CARA system, "graphic depiction of sex" had become one of the most popular attractions for U.S. moviegoers, with three of the top fifteen most profitable films of 1972–1973 carrying the self-rating of XXX.

Not surprisingly, mainstream cinema tried to cash in on the sexual revolution, releasing features like *Last Tango in Paris* (1972) and *Emmanuelle* (1974). *New Yorker* critic Pauline Kael declared that the premiere of *Last Tango in Paris* at the New York Film Festival "should become a landmark in movie history comparable to . . . the night *Le Sacre du Printemps* was first performed." Kael reported that the audience for the closing of the festival gave *Last Tango*'s director Bernardo Bertolucci a standing ovation. Kael also observed that later, in the lobby, the moviegoers were quiet, perhaps because they were in a state of shock—they had just witnessed the "most powerfully erotic movie ever made," a film that "altered the face of the art form." Charles Champlin wrote in the *Los Angles Times*, "If *Deep Throat* is the cost of the new freedom, *Last Tango in Paris* is the reward."

But although some critics applauded the new film freedom, the nation's highest court failed to appreciate the new cultural pluralism. After years of liberalizing permissible content, the U.S. Supreme Court reversed direction and attempted to curtail the proliferation of porn in 1973. In two cases handed down on the same day, *Miller v. California* and *Paris Adult Theatre I v. Slaton*, the Court rejected the reigning test for obscenity, ruling that because there could be no national standard for defining pornography (as had been required by the Court in the *Jacobellis* decision nine years earlier), local communities should be able to regulate and prosecute pornography according to their own standards. *Miller* also revised the definition of obscenity from the rather loose "utterly without redeeming social importance" to more restrictive language. After *Miller*, questionable works could be pronounced legally obscene if they were "without serious literary, artistic, political, or scientific value," a phrase that came to be known as its acronym, the SLAPS test. The earlier test, in place since 1964, which allowed all works unless they were totally obscene, was revised nine years later to allow restrictions of works that were not serious in some artistic, political, or scientific way. This new test made it easier to find films like *Deep Throat* obscene.

Stephen Vaughn writes that "one might assume that these cases should have made it easier for prosecutors to suppress hard-core pornography." But the Court's decisions did not do much to kill porn's popularity—theatrical porn declined, but a technological advance made the distribution of film pornography easier: the introduction of the VCR in the mid-1970s. The pornography market exploded.

The *Miller* decision and the VCR pornography market offer an apt snapshot of a major paradox: Americans condemn even as they consume; judge but don't want to be judged; want both the courts and the market to influence public culture; and ultimately want a culture that is both public and fiercely individualistic. Perhaps these paradoxes exist because Americans remain both pluralists and moralists.

CHAPTER 8

The Era of Ratings and Violence

Today there is no absolute or final arbiter in the movie world. The closest thing to one is the market. Because most movies are made to turn a profit, there are few things filmmakers will fail to do to ensure financial viability, from cutting scenes to make a film more palatable to cranking out hard-core pornography because sex sells. The Supreme Court was at least half right in 1915 when it defined motion pictures as a business. However, *Burstyn* complicated that simple understanding by adding a qualification: movies are also legitimate cultural expression, and as such deserve protection from prior censorship. And so, movies—the public art that is also a corporate product—have become the ultimate legal conundrum for our mass-mediated age.

We all know that films have some effect on us, but there is no way to determine definitively if that requires us to constrain them. Since the decline of governmental censorship, the most persistent form of control in the movie world has been Hollywood's rating system. And even though CARA sees a minority of films released theatrically each year and is completely irrelevant in the movie world that exists outside of theaters, a rating still holds profound economic power. Beyond CARA, there is obscenity prosecution—an option that has consistently proven inadequate to judge art.

In the postcensor world, the rating system has been at the center of battles over movies. By the mid-1970s, Jack Valenti's rating board became the new gatekeeper. As a consequence, most studios established policies requiring filmmakers to bring in movies at nothing "worse" than an R rating. An X was simply not acceptable because it had become associated with pornography. Most theaters in the National Association of Theater Owners (NATO) refused to show films rated X, and many newspapers refused to run ads for them (as many today still refuse to show or carry ads for NC-17 movies). The logic behind such policies was simple and consistent with Hollywood's history: studios invest in a movie to make as much money as possible, and thus they enforce an industrial code either by contract or assumed agreement. Whether called economic coercion or outright censorship, this tactic has dominated mainstream filmmaking from the early days of the industry.

What does such a system do to movies Americans see? That question has plagued the rating board and its decision-making process since Valenti introduced CARA in 1968. As coercive as CARA is, it is not the PCA; it does not command authority over scripts, and it certainly does not rule Hollywood like Joe Breen and his staff did. The power CARA possesses comes from its relationship to major Hollywood studios. As head of the MPAA, Valenti appointed the first director of CARA, who in turn appointed members of the rating board. Only MPAA film companies are required to get their movies rated by CARA; all other films rated by CARA are submitted voluntarily. However, most theatrically released films go through the rating process because they are either an MPAA company production or an independent production that needs a rating to be distributed by theaters under NATO. Yet an enormous number of films released by foreign distributors and cable television and the home movie market are made well outside the purview of the MPAA and CARA, and therefore avoid the rating system altogether. Nevertheless, CARA gets a say in what is included or must be left out of the vast majority of films with wide theatrical distribution.

Throughout the relatively brief history of the rating system, one characteristic has irked both filmmakers and the moviegoing public alike – the secrecy that shrouds the rating board's decisions. The board began with five members in 1968, and expanded to its present size of ten in 1989. The members consistently have been of similar backgrounds – middle-class, educated, married with children. The way in which this group designates particular ratings for movies has always been contentious, because it has always appeared arbitrary and unjustly cautious, especially in regard to sex. CARA claims to base its ratings on the sensibilities of what it calls the AAP: the "average American parent." Although any rating can be appealed, CARA has made it a policy not to reveal any specific information regarding the process that leads to a rating. According to Vaughn, that is how Valenti wanted it.

When the MPAA boss hired Richard Heffner to direct CARA, he told him that the rating board was not a public platform: "It is important that the rating system speak with one voice. . . . The rating system is fragile because it is subjective. . . . If the press can drive a wedge between the Rating Board and Jack Valenti, they will exploit that seeming difference of opinion to the detriment of the system and its objectives." The bottom line for Valenti was protection of Hollywood's image (and product) from those who would censor movies to protect the public. In other words, Valenti could handle filmmakers who accused the board of violating their free speech. What he worried about most were calls for federal censorship after the demise of the Production Code.

For many filmmakers, the rating board often has appeared capricious. The inclusion of a sex scene or a film with extensive nudity will earn a tougher rating than scenes of death, dismemberment, and destruction. The effect of such decisions suggests that there is almost no way to make sex an integral part of a plot without jeopardizing the film's commercial marketability, though violence is no problem. In short, the "Terminator" could gun down dozens, but Stanley Kubrick could not portray social decadence through an orgy scene in *Eyes Wide Shut*.

One of the most biting condemnations of this process appeared in a documentary made by Kirby Dick titled *This Film Is Not Yet Rated* (2006). The film played as a witty polemic against the "Kafkaesque" nature of the rating process. Dick divided his film into two parts: he interviewed filmmakers who believed they had been wronged by CARA, and he attempted to track down and identify a few of CARA's anonymous raters. In an interview with *Cineaste* he called the rating process "a black hole" because "there is no information, no written standards. No information gets out at all." By avoiding the kind of scrutiny other "judges" in society must contend with, the rating board, according to Dick, has been able to craft an image of impartiality and genuine, objective public service. To most members of the public, the ratings materialize organically rather than as the product of a constant struggle that often pits the mainstream movie industry against independent films.

The same argument was made unsuccessfully by the Miramax Films Corporation in 1990 when it sued the MPAA over its X rating of Pedro Almodovar's *Tie Me Up! Tie Me Down!* The supreme court of the State of New York ruled that Miramax had failed to prove discrimination against foreign films and let the voluntary system stand. But the court had no trouble pronouncing the voluntary rating system outright censorship.

Does such obvious coercion, though, rise to the level of a violation of constitutional rights? Stephen Vaughn relates a discussion between Heffner, who ran CARA from 1974 to 1994, and ACLU Executive Director Ira Glasser regarding the censoring power of the rating system. Heffner acknowledged that the requirement of some studios that a film be delivered with a certain rating did create a climate similar to censorship. "But who was doing the censoring?" he asked. "It's the damn filmmaker, who subjects himself . . . for dollars, not for First Amendment reasons, to this kind of garbage." CARA, Heffner bluntly stated, does not outlaw anything. "We don't give two hoots in hell what segments they include or don't include in their films. We simply try, if they want a rating, to give them the one we believe most closely reflects parental attitudes." Heffner understates the power of the rating board, for it still exercises coercive economic power over filmmakers, though filmmakers can and do make handsome profits under this arrangement. But the supreme court of New York had no difficulty seeing this regime as censorship: "Censorship is an anathema to our Constitution and to this court," Justice Charles Ramos wrote in the Miramax case. "The present system of rating motion pictures 'G,' 'PG,' 'PG-13,' 'R,' and 'X' is an effective form of censorship. It is censorship from within the industry rather than imposed from without, but censorship nevertheless."

Industry leaders have never viewed themselves as defenders of the First Amendment—they make money, not abstract constitutional stands. Burstyn learned this lesson back in 1951. However, that does not mean Hollywood has not tried to use free speech as a tool to protect a film from potential financial ruin. An example of this was Valenti's defense of Martin Scorsese's *Last Temptation of Christ* (1988). Scorsese's film portrayed a delirious Christ on the cross hallucinating about marriage and children with Mary Magdalene, thus angering outspoken members of Christian organizations who saw it as the latest example of Hollywood's ill treatment of religion. The studio releasing the film, Universal, had not sunk a great deal into the production, but understood what a little controversy could do for ticket sales. The marketing campaign for the film emphasized the "free speech" battle between the filmmaker who wanted his vision seen and Christians who wanted the movie stopped. Many of Scorsese's fellow directors publicly supported him, but it was Jack Valenti who struck the most heroic pose. "No one, no matter how passionate their opposition, no matter how strenuously they disagree, can or should prevent the entry of point of view, whether it is political or creative or philosophical. . . . No prior censorship, ever!" This sounds eerily like the pronouncements of Eric Johnston, who forty years earlier had claimed to oppose "political censorship" wherever it was practiced, but would not lend his organization's support to fight Catholic interference with *The Miracle*. Ultimately, everybody won in the contest of wills over *Last Temptation of Christ*: the film opened to sell-out crowds, but public protests probably limited potential profits.

Every dispute over an individual rating exposes the fundamental problem with CARA: how can any group successfully assess the relative harm a movie might do? The rating system serves, so CARA contends, as a way to inform parents so they can protect their children. Most filmmakers who clash with CARA's decisions believe the board misunderstands their work. After all, what director makes a film with the intent to harm children? And yet, it also remains possible that both CARA and filmmakers can fail to appreciate the effect a movie might have on the audience. Since movies are speech and protected as such, does it also follow that when a movie acts as harmful speech, inciting dangerous action, that a movie and its maker should be held accountable? In other words, if it is illegal to incite violent action through speech, is it equally illegal for a violent film to provoke moviegoers?

Natural Born Killers

In 1997, controversial director Oliver Stone found himself in such a situation. The movie charged with inciting dangerous behavior was Stone's 1994 juiced-up version of the *Bonnie and Clyde* story, *Natural*

Born Killers. Stone had actually attempted to make the film safe for commercial consumption by cutting five minutes from it to secure an R rather than an NC-17 (the rating CARA adopted after 1990 when it discarded the X rating). Even though Stone had satisfied Hollywood's "parental" oversight and got the R rating he wanted, he still found himself embroiled in perhaps the most profound legal case to ensnare a film since *The Miracle*. At issue was whether Oliver Stone and his movie could be held culpable for murder.

The details of this case began on the afternoon of March 7, 1995, when Ben Darrus and Sarah Edmondson, two teenagers from Oklahoma, drove into Hernando, Mississippi. The couple pulled into a parking lot next to a modern cotton gin. Both got out of the Nissan Maxima Edmondson was driving and found a man working in a glass-walled cubicle. Darrus asked the man for directions to I-55, a highway that runs through that part of Mississippi. The man, William Savage, a resident of Hernando, gave the teens directions. Darrus took a step toward Savage, pulled out a pistol, and fired a shot. The two struggled in Savage's office briefly until Darrus was able to get off another shot. Darrus took the man's wallet and headed for the car. Once back on the highway, Darrus mocked the sounds of the wounded Savage; he laughed and told his girlfriend that killing made him feel powerful.

A day later, Edmondson walked into a supermarket in Louisiana. She shot and paralyzed Patsy Ann Byers, the lone clerk working that evening at the Winn-Dixie. The two killers continued to race across the country, eventually ending up at a beach on the California coast. Once they could go no further, they decided to return home. On a tip from one of Edmondson's old boyfriends, police easily and peaceably apprehended the young murderers. Both stood trial for the two violent crimes. Darrus ultimately received life in prison; Edmondson, thirty-five years.

Besides the apparent randomness and tragedy of both shootings, one other detail caused a considerable stir: Ben Darrus reportedly had watched Oliver Stone's *Natural Born Killers* over and over again while under the influence of copious amounts of hallucinogenic drugs.

John Grisham, the Mississippi lawyer turned best-selling novelist and a friend of the murdered William Savage, charged that Oliver Stone and his "product" must take some blame for the crimes. In a literary journal he co-owned at the time named the *Oxford American*, Grisham argued that Stone had to be held partly responsible for the influence he exercised through his movie. "The film was not made with the intent of stimulating morally depraved young people to commit similar crimes," Grisham wrote, "but such a result can hardly be a surprise." Grisham contended that when a movie operated like a defective product "and injury ensues, . . . its makers should be held responsible" in the way manufacturers were subject to product liability laws.

Stone's movie portrays an outlaw couple that kills and has sex in a kind of redemption narrative—society has brutalized them, and in turn, these monsters take revenge on society. Stone's indictment of contemporary U.S. culture was all-encompassing; he turned every traditional authority figure on its head. Parents were either rapists or accomplices, the police were corrupt and deranged, and the news media were parasitic and guilty of turning two sociopaths into heroes.

Of course this was not the first time Stone had played havoc with tradition. Many historians found his demonization of the entire U.S. government in *JFK* a dangerous abuse of history. He used a pseudo-documentary style in both movies to create a didactic argument that was almost seamless; it was as if the totality of events surrounding the assassination of President Kennedy and the lives of two young killers had been captured on videotape and only rewound by Stone for the U.S. public to watch. In neither movie did the director attempt to introduce a trace of ambiguity; instead many people believed that what they saw in *JFK* was the truth, and that the murderers in *Natural Born Killers* were cool.

Stone's response to accusations thrown at him from Grisham and others was predictable. He said that holding him and other filmmakers responsible for copycat crimes was "a disaster for our ability to speak. If an idea is conceded to be a product in a courtroom, they will be hauling in people like me for years, and there'll be no freedom of speech—there'll be fear, and a lawyer's paradise for Mr. Grisham."

Stone reminded his accuser, "An elementary principle of our civilization is that people are responsible for their own actions." Stone's attorney, Floyd Abrams, famous for his defense of the *New York Times* during the *Pentagon Papers* case, argued, "The notion that because one crazed person reacts to a book or a movie by doing something illegal the moviemaker or writer should be liable is at war with the First Amendment." Moreover, Abrams later added, the notion that a film is no different from other products that can harm, like breast implants or cigarettes, was preposterous.

The question in this case was stark: whether filmmakers have a responsibility to the public. In an interview, Stone explained that he used movies as provocations but felt little responsibility to censor himself lest he upset some sector of the public. He made films for adults, and believed that his obligation to the audience stopped with the distribution of his film. "Why must there be a contract?" he asked. "Why must there be a definition of a film?" To Stone, movies are a visual treat rather than a blueprint for action. Moviewatching is, Stone said, "a wholly subjective experience. . . . It is the subjective chasing the subjective." At a basic level, though, this situation begs the question: should movies be freed from control? Did Cardinal Spellman have a point when he insisted that *The Miracle* insulted all women and that Christian beliefs were endangered if New Yorkers could see the film?

Asked to account for the obvious moral depravity his film depicted, Stone explained: "*Natural Born Killers* is an in-your-face satire of a moral order turned upside down. . . . It's a wakeup call to a schizophrenic country and culture which decries violence but just can't get enough of it." Stone thought he had given Americans a strong dose of hypocrisy. Unfortunately for Stone, somebody answered back.

Stone and the studio that produced *Natural Born Killers*, Time Warner, were named in a civil suit that sought compensatory damages from the parties responsible for inciting Darrus and Edmondson. On January 23, 1997, *Byers v. Edmondson* went before State District Judge Robert H. Morrison of Tangipahoa Parish in Louisiana. The judge dismissed the case, noting that "similar contentions have been almost universally rejected . . . in courts of this country" because they run afoul of the First Amendment's free speech protection. That decision was appealed by Byers's attorneys to the Court of Appeals of Louisiana for the First Circuit, which reversed the lower court's ruling. The case was sent back to the trial court for discovery based on the notion that the plaintiff did not have an adequate chance to find out whether Stone intended to incite violence.

On March 9, 1999, the U.S. Supreme Court denied a request by

Stone and the producers of *Natural Born Killers* to review the decision handed down in the appeals court. That step allowed Byers's attorneys to begin deposing witnesses, including Stone. On July 20, 2000, Stone began giving his deposition in Los Angeles.

Six months later, Stone and Time Warner again sought to end the case by requesting a summary judgment. In an affidavit filed by attorneys for both the filmmaker and the studio, Stone explained (once again) that the movie was a satire intended to "encourage the audience to think critically about society's contradictory relationship to violence." He compared it to Jonathan Swift's infamous short story about eating babies to solve food shortages, "A Modest Proposal." "We rightfully condemn and moralize about [violence]," Stone said, "yet at the same time are fascinated by it."

Besides the intellectual argument raised by Stone, his lawyers also contended that the plaintiffs had failed to satisfy the test for determining why this particular type of speech did not deserve protection under the First Amendment—in other words, they had failed to prove that the movie incited unlawful behavior. As evidence, they could point to CARA, which had given the film a relatively harmless rating.

In March 2001 Judge Morrison, the same man who had thrown this case out of his court earlier, once again had a chance to rule. After an hour of oral argument, Morrison determined that after two years of discovery the plaintiffs still had not uncovered evidence that Stone and Time Warner intended to incite anyone to violence (much less imminent violence). The defendants and their legal team called this judgment both a reaffirmation of the First Amendment and a glimpse into a terribly litigious future. Stone remarked: "We've created a new legal hell where everyone is entitled and no one is responsible."

Stone was right about the litigious future. The case of Oliver Stone and the First Amendment was not over yet. Byers had died in 2000, but her husband appealed Morrison's decision, and the case returned to the Court of Appeals of Louisiana for the First Circuit. Citing *Burstyn* that motion pictures were a significant medium of expression protected by the First Amendment, and *New York Times v. Sullivan* that the threat of civil suit can have an equally chilling effect on speech as that of any government censor, the court found that there was no incitement to imminent lawless action in *Natural Born*

Killers, and it was not obscene. Therefore it was, indeed, protected speech. Citing *Hess v. Indiana*, the court further ruled that although Darrus and Edmondson's crime spree was of the "copycat" variety, the First Amendment still protected Stone and Time Warner's right to free speech. "Speech does not lose its First Amendment protection merely because it has 'a tendency to lead to violence.' Edmondson and Darrus may very well have been inspired to imitate the actions . . . but the film does not direct or encourage them to take such actions. Accordingly, as a matter of law, we find *Natural Born Killers* cannot be considered inciteful speech that would remove it from First Amendment protection."

Of course, the claims made against movies in this case were not unique. In 1958, nineteen-year-old Charlie Starkweather and his fourteen-year-old girlfriend went on a killing rampage that became, unbeknownst to them, the inspiration for four Hollywood movies: *Badlands*, *Wild at Heart*, *True Romance*, and *Natural Born Killers*. The movie *Child's Play 3* (1991) supposedly led two ten-year-olds to kill a two-year-old. Producers of *The Basketball Diaries* (1995) were sued by the family of one of three girls gunned down by a fourteen-year-old boy during a student prayer session in Paducah, Kentucky. The vulgar television show *Beavis and Butthead* was blamed for inspiring a five-year-old Ohio boy to set fire to his house, killing his younger sister. Nathaniel White admitted to going on a killing spree after watching Sylvester Stallone's *First Blood* (1982) twenty times. But *Natural Born Killers* has the distinction of being the only movie involved in multiple murder cases—one in the United States and another in France.

Contending with Controversial Culture

From the time of *Burstyn*, there has been no clear idea of how society should deal with movies it finds problematic. The courts, reacting to cases brought before them, can only rule on what can or cannot be done. They cannot create policy. Neither Congress nor state legislatures have been much interested in dealing with the issue—at least in part because of the Supreme Court's rulings on the First Amendment. Individual lawsuits might bring some satisfaction to the families of victims. Yet, such legal action is unlikely, as we have seen in the *Natural Born Killers* case, to stand the test of the First Amendment. Such cases stand atop a slippery slope as they threaten the sanctity of free speech as currently interpreted by the courts. Thus it is legally sound that Stone was not found culpable in the Byers case. Moreover, statistics do not reveal any causal link between on-screen violence and actual crimes: violence among young people has actually fallen in the last few years though levels of movie violence seem to remain high.

But clearly, the courtroom is not the best venue for dealing with violent movies — law and art rarely form a profitable partnership. And yet in the past when artists fought for their freedom, their cases seemed to have more at stake.

A partial explanation might be the changing role of artists in society. In his comprehensive survey of U.S. intellectuals and their relationship to society, historian Lewis Perry writes that since the 1920s "alienation and marginality became badges of creativity and independence — an ironic reversal of older conceptions of the public responsibilities of the cultivated classes." In the *Natural Born Killers* debacle, Stone clearly played the misunderstood artist, embracing the protection of free speech and the trappings of celebrity without much of a notion of public responsibility.

We know that, for better and for worse, such graphically violent movies would never have made it to theaters during the censors' regime. Then, after the end of most governmental censorship, First Amendment jurisprudence became even more protective of speech. In the landmark case of *Brandenburg v. Ohio* in 1969, the Supreme Court developed a fairly clear two-part test to determine when states can restrict dangerous speech. Although ostensibly in reference to political speech, the Court determined that in order to justify censorship, the words in question must be "directed to inciting or producing imminent lawless action" and that such speech must be "likely to incite or produce such action." Under such stringent requirements, it is not surprising that Stone and Time Warner ultimately won their case. After all, millions of people saw *Natural Born Killers*, but only a few actually committed copycat crimes after that experience, and copycat crimes do not meet the stringent standards set down by *Brandenburg*.

But there is a third trend that appears especially evident in Stone's case. Recently at least a few of the most respected public intellectuals in the United States have written on that murkiest of concepts, morality. Jeffrey Rosen, legal affairs editor for the *New Republic* and author of several books on the Supreme Court, and Alan Wolfe, a preeminent liberal thinker and professor at Boston College, both writing in the *New York Times Magazine*, approached the changing perception of morality in ways relevant to Stone's case. Rosen argued that "as trust in traditional authorities declines, we are increasingly turning to law to regulate the kinds of behavior that used to be governed by manners and mores." The rise of legalism — rather than law — corresponds to the revolution in rights that began in the mid-twentieth century as a drive to broaden protection of forgotten groups but has evolved into a cultist embrace of individual liberty at the expense of the idea of community.

Wolfe identified a similar trend, claiming that the United States is living in the age of "moral freedom." It is a time, he said, "in which individuals are expected to determine for themselves what it means to lead a good and virtuous life. . . . The ultimate implication of the idea of moral freedom is not that people are created in the image of a higher authority. It is that any form of authority has to tailor its commandments to the needs of real people." Vanished is the older idea, so prevalent during the Progressive Era, that in order to ensure freedom for all, individuals must exhibit self-restraint based on generally accepted social norms. What those norms were and what they did have varied over the years. Yet, no longer abiding by the idea that such rules exist is a profound break from the past.

Stone was, in a sense, caught between legalism and moral freedom: he played the victim of the first and the champion of the second. Michael Shnayerson, an editor at *Vanity Fair*, found Stone's position less than honorable. He noted not only that Stone was a Hollywood movie director rather than an unknown artist struggling against oppressive mores, but he seemed "oblivious to any sense of responsibility his role confers. Worse, shown the ways in which confused youths interpret his sophisticated message, he does not seem inclined to reflection concerning his artistic methods."

Indeed, it was also distressing that Stone's defense on free speech grounds failed to include any obligation to his audience. There was a case in the not-too-distant past, however, that involved a public figure with whom Stone might have identified personally, but who would not have identified with him intellectually. In 1931, when Theodore Dreiser took Paramount Pictures to court over *An American Tragedy*, Dreiser contended that Paramount had so distorted the message of the book that his artistic reputation had been seriously compromised. Dreiser sued Hollywood for dumbing down his art — for undercutting the power the movie would have on its audience.

Dreiser lost his case, and the studio released its film to lukewarm reviews and mediocre ticket sales. Yet both parties had agreed on a basic point: movies could influence people. Paramount simply refused to allow Dreiser's message to trump the mundane crime story it wanted to make using the title of his best-selling novel.

A comparison between Dreiser and Stone is instructive. Dreiser wanted his work to move people. He took Paramount to court not simply to reclaim his vanity (which was certainly a consideration), but with the belief that his artistic integrity deserved protection. After all, he hoped that the indictment of capitalism he had written would incite an audience living during the Great Depression. Stone attempted to indict mass media. In *Natural Born Killers*, he shows the media turning the two sociopathic killers into heroes. Yet when his work seemed to incite exactly what he was trying to condemn, he avoided responsibility for his influence by hiding behind the idea of free expression.

A significant difference separates these men: Dreiser was of a generation that believed intellectuals had a moral obligation to the public — giving people not necessarily what they wanted, but what they needed. But Stone came from a different era. Reflecting the tenor of his time, he rejected such an approach as antiquated and detrimental to artistic freedom.

Dreiser fought hard to gain popular recognition for the notion that forces stronger than the individual will move society. Stone identified those forces without considering that he was a part of them. And in the end, when things went wrong, he blamed someone else. He had made a movie that glamorized violence but then hid behind the First Amendment (what Burstyn had worked so hard for) when a few moviegoers emulated his "heroes." Dreiser wanted the public to take action. But it is hard to see what Stone wanted his public to do.

Perhaps, then, Stone should not have been surprised when a few of his fellow citizens asked the courts to remind him of the obligation he has to the public. It is impossible, of course, to determine with the precision of law what that obligation is, and the courts are not well equipped to deal with such questions. Yet it is the courts that have been left to try to decide whether free speech is an end in itself.

In an essay provocatively titled "There's No Such Thing as Free Speech, and It's a Good Thing, Too," scholar Stanley Fish explains that speech is never "free of consequences and free from state pressure" because "everything we say impinges on the world in ways indistinguishable from the effects of physical action." For that reason, "we must take responsibility for our verbal performances — *all* of them — and not assume that they are being taken care of by a clause in the Constitution." Applying this position to movies is daunting because we must consider not merely that they are a form of expression but that they might have an effect on those who watch them. Such discourse is discomfiting because it depends on our ability to deal in ambiguities rather than absolutes. For purists who defend either a moral code or a concept of free speech in absolute terms, the default position is righteous indignation. For those who reject such absolutes, there is no default position — there is debate and the responsibility to address intent, content, and consequences.

Such sentiments are not only the province of law professors like Fish, though. Stephen Prince, the former president of the Society for Cinema Studies, wrote a prescient essay for the *Chronicle of Higher Education* in August 2001 titled "Why Do Film Scholars Ignore Movie Violence?" That question might seem sensible, but to many in the academic study of film, it is fraught with ideological danger. To suggest that movies might act like a mere commercial product is to betray the legal progress made since *Burstyn*. Movies have become an art and a legal abstraction as well as something created by a massive, lucrative, and influential industry. But, Prince contends, "The issue central to debates over movie violence is not one of the filmmaker's ideological intent, or the viewers' ideological reception, but of the viewers' behavior, the attitudes that behavior may manifest, and the role that a film may play in fostering the behavior. Flesh-and-blood moviegoers don't have much of a place in our discipline's theoretical realm."

We know that Hollywood certainly cares enough about moviego-ers to give them what they want. But, as filmmaker Mike White sug-gests in an op-ed piece for the *New York Times*, perhaps the industry should consider that its relationship with the audience extends beyond the movie theater. Writing in the wake of the mass murders by Seung-Hui Cho of thirty-two classmates and teachers at Virginia Tech, White bluntly states: "The notion that 'movies don't kill peo-ple, lunatics kill people' is liberating to us screenwriters because it permits us to give life to our most demented fantasies and put them up on the big screen without any anxious hand-wringing. We all know that there's a lot of money to be made trafficking in blood and guts. . . . What a relief to be told that how we earn that money may be in poor taste, but it's not irresponsible." His sarcasm of course belies a message that must have been somewhat dangerous for him even to address. The fear always lurking under such discussions is that the kind of responsibility expressed by White can quickly turn into cultural repression — the slippery slope toward censorship.

That oft-used metaphor of the slippery slope is problematic, for it presumes that we start from a position of some height (moral, intel-lectual?) and that any movement from this position is "downward" and therefore wrong. Free speech absolutists might see it that way. But postmodern free speech theorists like Richard Delgado and Catharine MacKinnon see such a slope not as headed in the "wrong" direction but in a more positive one for the health of society. They maintain that unfettered speech can be harmful to society, and therefore must be controlled for the greater good.

But the key achievement of *Burstyn* was to establish protection from any slide toward the days of repression and prior censorship. The case was a legal landmark not merely because it reversed a poor-ly construed definition of movies but because it opened up discussion over culture to a new and more constructive kind of scrutiny. As Fish, Prince, and White all intimate, it is the process by which we determine limits within our culture that matters most, rather than simply standing behind the notion that all culture, even if viewed as legal abstraction, deserves the full protection of the First Amend-ment. After all, *Burstyn* signaled the beginning of a great and active debate over controversial culture, not its final resolution.

RELEVANT CASES

Regina v. Hicklin, L.R. 3 Q.B. 360 (1868)

Jake Block v. City of Chicago, 239 Ill. 251; 87 N.E. 1011 (1909)

Mutual Film Corporation v. Industrial Commission of Ohio, 236 U.S. 230 (1915)

Pathé Exchange v. Cobb, 202 A.D. 450 (1922) and *Pathé v. Cobb*, 236 N.Y. 539
  (1923)

Gitlow v. People of New York, 268 U.S. 652 (1925)

United States v. One Book Called "Ulysses," 5 F. Supp. 182 (S.D.N.Y. 1933)

United States v. One Book Entitled "Ulysses," 72 F.2d 705 (2d Cir., 1934)

Eureka Productions v. Lehman, 17 F. Supp. 259 (1936)

In re "Spain in Flames" 36 Pa. D. & C. 285 (1937)

Palko v. Connecticut, 302 U.S. 319 (1937)

Foy Productions v. Graves, 253 A.D. 475 (1938); *Foy Productions, Ltd. v. Graves*,
  278 N.Y. 498 (1938)

United States v. Carolene Products Co., 304 U.S. 144 (1938)

Mayer v. Byrne, 256 A.D. 431 (1939)

American Committee on Maternal Welfare v. Mangan, 257 A.D. 570; 14 N.Y.S.2d
  39 (1939); *American Committee on Maternal Welfare v. Mangan*, 283 N.Y.
  551; 27 N.E.2d 278 (1940)

Hannegan, Postmaster General v. Esquire, Inc., 327 U.S. 146 (1943)

Monroe Amusements, Inc., v. City of Rochester, 190 Misc. 304; 75 N.Y.S.2d 807
  (1947)

United States v. Paramount Pictures, Inc. et al., 334 U.S. 131 (1948)

Burstyn v. Wilson, 278 A.D. 253 (1951), *Burstyn v. Wilson*, 303 N.Y. 242 (1951),
  Joseph Burstyn, Inc. v. Wilson, Commissioner of Education of New York, 343
  U.S. 495 (1952)

Gelling v. Texas, 343 U.S. 960 (1952)

Commercial Pictures Corp. v. Regents of the University of the State of New York,
  280 A.D. 260 (1952) and *Commercial Pictures Corp. v. Regents of the University
  of the State of New York*, 305 N.Y. 336 (1953)

Superior Films, Inc. v. Department of Education of Ohio, 346 U.S. 587 (1954)

Brattle Films, Inc. v. Commissioner of Public Safety, 333 Mass. 58, 127 N.E.2d 891
  (1955)

Holmby Productions v. Vaughn, 350 U.S. 870; 76 S. Ct. 117; 100 L. Ed. 770 (1955)

Hallmark Productions, Inc. v. Carroll, 384 Pa. 348; 121 A.2d 584 (1956)

Butler v. Michigan, 352 U.S. 380 (1957)

Roth v. United States, 354 U.S. 476 (1957)

Times Film Corp. v. City of Chicago, 355 U.S. 35 (1957)

Times Film Corp. v. City of Chicago, 365 U.S. 43 (1961)

Bantam Books, Inc. v. Sullivan, 372 U.S. 58 (1963)

Jacobellis v. Ohio, 378 U.S. 184 (1964)

Freedman v. Maryland, 380 U.S. 51 (1965)

Interstate Circuit, Inc. v. City of Dallas, 390 U.S. 676 (1968)

Brandenburg v. Ohio, 395 U.S. 444 (1969)

Grove Press v. Maryland State Board of Censors, 401 U.S. 480 (1971)

Miller v. California, 413 U.S. 15 (1973)

Paris Adult Theatre I v. Slaton, 413 U.S. 49 (1973)

Miramax Films Corp. v. Motion Picture Association of America, Inc., 148 Misc. 2d 1; 560 N.Y.S.2d 730 (1990)

Byers v. Edmondson, 712 So. 2d 681 (1998), 95-02213 (La.App. 2001); No. 2001 CA 1184 (2002)

1907	Chicago, Illinois, becomes the first city to create and enact motion picture censorship laws.
1909	The National Board of Review (NBR) of Motion Pictures is founded in New York City.
1909	In the first movie censorship case to receive a hearing in court, the Illinois Supreme Court declares in *Block v. Chicago* that an ordinance restricting an exhibitor from showing movies deemed harmful by the chief of police falls within the state's police power to protect children, is not overly vague, and is therefore constitutional.
1911	Pennsylvania becomes the first state to enact a movie censorship law. The censors begin work in Pennsylvania in 1914.
1914	Ohio and Kansas enact statewide movie censorship laws.
1915	*The Birth of a Nation* premieres in the United States and sparks the first movie censorship controversy.
1915	The U.S. Supreme Court rules in favor of movie censorship in *Mutual Film Corporation v. Ohio Industrial Commission*.
1916	Maryland enacts statewide censorship law.
1916	Hugo Münsterberg's *The Photoplay: A Psychological Study* is published.
1919–1920	Chicago's Motion Picture Commission Hearings convene to discuss how better to contain the power of movies.
1921	Hollywood suffers a series of scandals prompting movie moguls to "clean up" the industry's image.
1921	New York enacts a statewide censorship law.
1921	Joseph Burstyn emigrates to New York City from Poland.
1922	Virginia enacts a statewide censorship law, the last state to do so.
1922	Will H. Hays becomes president of the Motion Picture Producers and Distributors of America (MPPDA).

1922	A statewide referendum on movie censorship law fails in Massachusetts.
1923	In *Pathé v. Cobb*, the New York Court of Appeals rejects a challenge from the Pathé newsreel company that New York's recently created movie censorship law amounted to unconstitutional prior restraint. The decision reinforces the precedent established eight years earlier in *Mutual*.
1924	Gilbert Seldes's *The Seven Lively Arts* is published.
1925	In *Gitlow v. New York*, the U.S. Supreme Court strengthens free speech protection by incorporating the Free Speech Clause within the "privileges and immunities" protected against state infringement by the Fourteenth Amendment.
1927	Hays publishes his "Don'ts and Be Carefuls" as a guideline for film production.
1930	Martin Quigley and Father Daniel Lord write a new production code to replace the "Don'ts and Be Carefuls." The Motion Picture Association of America adopts the code.
1931	In *Near v. Minnesota*, the U.S. Supreme Court strikes down prior restraint against newspapers, and incorporates freedom of the press within the protections guaranteed by the Fourteenth Amendment.
1931	Theodore Dreiser sues Paramount Publix Corporation over the studio's script for his novel *An American Tragedy*.
1929–1935	The Payne Fund studies (*Motion Pictures and Youth*) are conducted and published.
1933	Henry James Forman's *Our Movie-Made Children* is published.
November 1933	The American Catholic Church hierarchy, incensed at Hollywood's failure to follow its Production Code, creates the Episcopal Committee on Motion Pictures to study the situation.
December 1933	In response to pressure from American Catholics, MPAA creates the Production Code Administration (PCA) to ensure compliance, and names Joseph Breen its head.
April 11, 1934	The American Catholic Church creates the Legion of

{ *Chronology* }

Decency, a lay organization, to monitor motion pictures and organize mass actions against them.

1934   Millions of Catholics begin to take an annual pledge to patronize only those movies that do not offend Christian morality, and to follow the guidance of the church through its newly formed Legion of Decency.

1935   New York City's Museum of Modern Art opens the nation's first film library.

1936   *Eureka Productions v. Lehmann* affirms the right of state authorities to restrict or ban a film from public viewing even if a federal authority allows the importation of the film. In this case, federal customs agents had allowed the importation of a Czech film, *Ecstasy*, but the New York State movie censors had prevented its exhibition unless certain scenes were cut.

Mid-1930s   *Commonweal* takes an editorial stand critical of the Catholic Church's tacit support of Spanish dictator Francisco Franco.

1938   In *Foy Productions v. Graves* and *Matter of Foy Productions, Ltd. v. Graves*, attorneys for the distributors of *Tomorrow's Children* (1934) illustrate that it is possible to convince some judges (though a minority in this case) that movies deserved consideration as protected speech.

1936–1939   Joseph Burstyn and his partner, Arthur Mayer, bring suit against the New York censors over the French film *Remous*. In *Mayer v. Byrne*, the New York courts uphold the censors' determination that the film is obscene. Cuts to get a license make the film choppy, and movie critics begin to realize when they finally see the movie in 1940 the effect of state censorship on movie quality.

1939   In *American Committee on Maternal Welfare v. Mangan*, courts uphold the censoring of a film intended to lower the infant mortality rate through education of mothers-to-be.

1940   Bosley Crowther becomes the first-string film critic at the *New York Times*.

1945   Roberto Rossellini's *Open City* premieres in New York City and sets new box office records for a foreign film.

1946   In *Hannagan v. Esquire*, the U.S. Supreme Court decides that censorship of magazines by the postmaster general,

originally authorized by the Comstock Law, is
unconstitutional.

1946	Eric Johnston succeeds Will Hays as head of the renamed Motion Picture Association of America (MPAA).
1947	*Hughes Tool Co. v. Fielding*, the case brought by Howard Hughes over *The Outlaw*, raises First Amendment issues but fails to make headway against governmental censorship or the authority of the New York City commissioner of licenses.
1948	*Il Miracolo* (*The Miracle*) is released in Italy.
1948	The U.S. Supreme Court orders Hollywood production companies to begin the process of divesting their theater holdings in *United States v. Paramount Pictures, Inc. et al.*
1949	Vittorio de Sica's *The Bicycle Thief* premieres in New York City, breaking box office records for a foreign film.
December 12, 1950	*The Miracle* premieres in New York City.
December 23, 1950	New York City Commissioner of Licenses Edward T. McCaffrey demands removal of *The Miracle* from the Paris Theatre on threat of the theater's license.
January 5, 1951	*Burstyn v. McCaffrey* restricts the authority of the license commissioner to keep movies from New York City theater screens.
January 7, 1951	Cardinal Spellman condemns *The Miracle* through a letter read in all churches of the New York City archdiocese.
February 1951	The New York Board of Regents revokes the license it had previously granted to exhibit *The Miracle*.
May 1951	The New York Court of Appeals upholds both the appellate division and the *Mutual* precedent in *Burstyn v. Wilson*.
May 26, 1952	In *Burstyn v. Wilson*, the U.S. Supreme Court overturns *Mutual v. Ohio* and extends First Amendment protection to movies but allows movie censorship under narrowly drawn statutes to continue.
June 2, 1952	In *Gelling v. Texas*, the U.S. Supreme Court affirms

opposition to prior restraint of motion pictures, citing *Burstyn* as precedent.

1953 *Commercial Pictures Corp. v. Regents*, the case brought by the distributors of *La Ronde*, fails to convince the New York appellate courts to overturn movie censorship.

1954 In *Superior Films, Inc. v. Department of Education of Ohio*, the U.S. Supreme Court combines the *Commercial Pictures* case with a similar case from Ohio, striking down that state's use of "harmful" and New York State's use of "immoral" as censoring terms.

1954 Otto Preminger and United Artists release *The Moon Is Blue* without a code seal, and the movie becomes a box office success.

1955 Ohio becomes the first state in which courts invalidate movie censorship. *R.K.O. Radio Pictures, Inc. v. Board of Education* declares the Ohio censorship statute repugnant to "the sacred Bill of Rights."

1955 The Massachusetts Supreme Court overturns the censorship apparatus in that state in *Brattle Films v. Commissioner of Public Safety.*

1955 In *Holmby Productions v. Vaughn*, the U.S. Supreme Court overturns Kansas' censorship statute. Through a legislative mistake, however, the Kansas board of censors continues to work until 1966.

1956 Hollywood revises the Production Code for the first time since 1934.

1956 *Hallmark Productions v. Carroll* overturns the censorship statute of Pennsylvania. The state drafts a new censorship law in 1959, which is then overturned by the state supreme court in 1961.

December 1956 Elia Kazan's *Baby Doll* premieres in New York City.

1957 American Catholic bishops decide to add new categories to the Legion of Decency's rating system.

1957 The U.S. Supreme Court in *Butler v. Michigan* overturns a state statute that allowed censoring of books based on their effect on children.

1957 *Times Film Corporation v. Chicago* becomes the fifth per curiam movie censorship decision, and the fifth to find against government censors.

1957	*Roth v. United States* creates a five-part test for determining a work legally obscene.
1959	In *Kingsley Pictures v. New York*, the Supreme Court unanimously finds that New York's statutory definition of "immoral" is in violation of the First Amendment.
1961	*William Goldman Theatres v. Dana* overturns Pennsylvania's 1959 censorship statute, and Pennsylvania's censors cease operations.
1961	In *Times Film Corporation v. Chicago*, a split Supreme Court upholds a censor determination for the first time since it began reversing movie censors in 1952 with *Burstyn*.
1964	*Jacobellis v. Ohio* extends the *Roth* test of obscenity to movies.
1965	In *Freedman v. Maryland*, the Supreme Court declines to declare movie censorship unconstitutional, but does require that states cease their reverse-burden-of-proof system of prior restraint. The case sets out procedural requirements that place the burden of proof on the censor rather than on the movie owner.
1965	*Trans-Lux Distributing Corporation v. Regents* overturns New York's censoring of a single movie, citing *Freedman* as precedent. New York tries to rewrite its censoring rules to conform to the *Freedman* requirements after *Trans-Lux*.
1965	New York State ceases censorship after its Court of Appeals finds the new censoring rules unconstitutional in *Matter of Trans-Lux Distributing v. Board of Regents*.
1965	The Catholic Legion of Decency changes its name to the National Catholic Office for Motion Pictures (NCOMP).
1966	Kansas and Virginia cease censorship.
1966	Michaelangelo Antonioni's film *Blow-Up* wins critical acclaim and a popular following despite being denied a PCA seal and receiving a condemned (C) rating from the Catholic Church.
1966	The MPAA scraps the Production Code and substitutes a new, far more lenient code.
1968	*Interstate Theatre Circuit v. Dallas* overturns an

{ *Chronology* }

age-classification ordinance but hints that the Court would accept age classification under a more carefully worded statute.

1968	Hollywood unveils a new rating system under the control of the Code and Ratings Administration (CARA).
1968	U.S. customs officials seize the Swedish film *I Am Curious, Yellow*.
1969	*I Am Curious, Yellow* premieres in New York City.
1969	*Midnight Cowboy* wins the Academy Award for best picture despite being distributed with a rating of X.
1969	In *Brandenburg v. Ohio*, the Supreme Court declares that in order to justify censorship, words must be "directed to inciting or producing imminent lawless action," and that such speech must be likely to have its intended effect.
1970	*Grove Press v. Maryland State Board of Censors* frees *I Am Curious, Yellow* to be shown, but the Supreme Court splits four to four, leaving no clear direction to be taken from the case.
September 1970	President Lyndon Johnson releases a report completed by the Federal Commission on Obscenity and Pornography that strongly suggests the elimination of all restrictions on adults who want to possess pornographic material.
1972	*Deep Throat* sets box office records in New York City.
1972	Bernardo Bertolucci's *Last Tango in Paris* has its U.S. premiere at the New York Film Festival.
1973	In *Miller v. California* and *Paris Adult Theatre I v. Slaton*, the Supreme Court determines that localities may define obscenity based on community standards rather than abide by a national standard. It also replaces the Court's restrictive definition of obscenity with the far looser test that a work is "without serious literary, artistic, political, or scientific value."
1981	Maryland, the last state censor board, ends operations.
1990	CARA excises the rating of X and replaces it with NC-17.
1994	Oliver Stone's *Natural Born Killers* is released.

March 7 and 8, 1995	Ben Darrus and Sarah Edmondson fatally attack two people in Mississippi and Louisiana.
2002	*Byers v. Edmondson*, a series of cases in the Louisiana courts related to a copycat killing inspired by *Natural Born Killers*, exonerates Oliver Stone for culpability because his movie was not a direct incitement to violence and was therefore protected speech under the First Amendment.

BIBLIOGRAPHICAL ESSAY

Note from the Series Editors: The following bibliographical essay contains the primary and secondary sources the authors consulted for this volume. We have asked all authors in the series to omit formal citations in order to make our volumes more readable, inexpensive, and appealing for students and general readers.

All the cases presented in this volume are available online from Lexis-Nexis (available at most large libraries). For a list of the cases and their citations, see the Relevant Cases section of this book. Most of the research on the state and municipal censors and their legal challengers came from the records of the Motion Picture Division at the New York State Archives, the Maryland State Board of Censors at the Maryland State Archives, the Ohio Division of Film Censorship at the Ohio Historical Society, the Pennsylvania State Board of Censors at the Pennsylvania State Archives, the Virginia Division of Motion Picture Censorship at the Virginia State Library, and the Chicago Motion Picture Commission, 1918–1920, at the Chicago Historical Society. We also used records from the Production Code Administration at the Margaret Herrick Library in Beverly Hills, California, the American Civil Liberties Union Archives at the Seeley G. Mudd Manuscript Library at Princeton University, the Billy Rose collection at the New York Public Library, the Maryland Room of the Enoch Pratt Free Library in Baltimore, the Tom C. Clark papers at the Tarlton Law Library at the University of Texas, the Felix Frankfurter papers (on microfilm) at the Harvard Law School Library, the Robert Jackson papers at the Library of Congress, the Fred Vinson papers at the University of Kentucky Special Collections Library, the Harold Burton papers at the Library of Congress, the Bosley Crowther papers at the L. Tom Perry Special Collections Library housed in Brigham Young University's Harold B. Lee Library, and the Eric Johnston papers (available on microfilm). Unfortunately, Joseph Bursytn left little written record behind. His corporate papers are in private hands.

As far as scholarly inquiry into motion picture censorship, the record is uneven. There has been little historical or political science research into the issue of governmental motion picture censorship. The best sources are Richard Randall, *Censorship of the Movies: The Social and Political Control of a Mass Medium* (Madison: University of Wisconsin Press, 1968) and Ira Carmen, *Movies, Censorship, and the Law* (Madison: University of Wisconsin Press, 1966). Unfortunately, these are both dated. The only book-length study of any of the state censor boards is Gerald R. Butters Jr., *Banned in Kansas: Motion Picture Censorship, 1915–1966* (Columbia: University of Missouri Press, 2007). The most recent treatment, which looks at the seven states with censorship, their practices, and their legal challenges, is Laura Wittern-Keller, *Freedom of the Screen: Legal Challenges to State Film Censorship, 1915–1981* (Lexington: University Press of Kentucky, 2008). On the Pennsylvania censors, there is a fine article by a state archivist, Richard Saylor, "Banned in Pennsylvania," *Pennsylvania Heritage*, vol. 25, no. 3 (Summer 1999).

Although government censors have not attracted much attention, Hollywood's so-called self-censorship has. Some of the best of those studies include Murray Schumach, *The Face on the Cutting Room Floor: The Story of Movie and Television Censorship* (New York: Morrow, 1964); Lee Grievson, *Policing Cinema: Movie Censorship and Early Twentieth-Century America* (Berkeley: University of California Press, 2004); Thomas Doherty, *Hollywood's Censor: Joseph I. Breen and the Production Code Administration* (New York: Columbia University Press, 2007) and *Pre-Code Hollywood: Sex, Immorality, and Insurrection in American Cinema, 1930–1934* (New York: Columbia University Press, 1999); Gregory Black, *Hollywood Censored: Morality Codes, Catholics, and the Movies* (New York: Cambridge University Press, 1994) and *The Catholic Crusade against the Movies, 1940–1975* (New York: Cambridge University Press, 1997); Frank Walsh, *Sin and Censorship: The Catholic Church and Motion Picture Censorship* (New Haven, Conn.: Yale University Press, 1996); Frank Miller, *Censored Hollywood: Sex, Sin, and Violence in Hollywood* (Kansas City, Mo.: Turner Publications, 1994); Leonard Leff and Jerold Simmons, *The Dame in the Kimono: Hollywood, Censorship, and the Production Code from the 1920s to the 1960s* (Lexington: University Press of Kentucky, 2001), and Francis Couvares, *Movie Censorship and American Culture* (Washington, D.C.: Smithsonian Institution Press, 1996).

Two books are marvelous reference sources for anyone interested in censored films: Edward de Grazia and Roger Newman, *Banned Films: Movies, Censors, and the First Amendment* (New York: Bowker, 1982); and Dawn Sova, *Forbidden Films: Censorship Histories of 125 Motion Pictures* (New York: Facts on File, 2001). Other useful sources include *Variety, Box Office, Motion Picture Herald*, and *Moving Picture World*.

Chapter 1. Movie Censorship: Origins and Early Challengers

On the Protestants' loss of cultural hegemony, see Garth Jowett, *Film: The Democratic Art* (Boston: Little, Brown, 1976) and Allison Parker, *Purifying America: Women, Cultural Reform, and Pro-Censorship Activism* (Urbana: University of Illinois Press, 1997). Paul Starr discusses the early reception of movies as lowbrow entertainment and how this made them particularly susceptible to outside threats of control in *The Creation of the Media: Political Origins of Modern Communications* (New York: Basic Books, 2004). Good sources for context on Jane Addams and other progressive movie reformers are Grievson, *Policing Cinema* (2004) and Jowett, *Film* (1976).

To learn more about the intellectual origins of censorship, see Andrea Friedman, *Prurient Interests: Gender, Democracy, and Obscenity in New York City* (New York: Columbia University Press, 2000); and Nancy Rosenbloom, "Between Reform and Regulation: The Struggle over Film Censorship in Progressive America," *Film History* 1, no. 4 (1987): 307–325, and "From Regulation to Censorship: Film and Political Culture in the Early Twentieth Century," *Journal of the Gilded Age and the Progressive Era* 3, no. 4 (October 2004): 369–406. Both Allison Parker, *Purifying America*, and Leigh Ann Wheeler, *Against Obscenity* (Baltimore: Johns Hopkins University Press, 2004), explain the role of women in the push for censorship. The best history of the origins of the Production Code Administration are Gregory Black, *Hollywood Censored* (New York: Cambridge University Press, 1998), and Stephen Vaughn, "Morality and Entertainment: Origins of the Motion Picture Code," *Journal of American History* 71 (June 1990): 39. On the Jewish studio moguls, see Neal Gabler, *An Empire of Their Own: How the Jews Invented Hollywood* (New York: Crown, 1988), and Steven Alan Carr, *Hollywood and Anti-Semitism: A Cultural History up to World War II* (New York: Cambridge University Press, 2001).

The controversy surrounding *The Birth of a Nation* has been examined often. Among the most complete accounts are Arthur Lennig, "Myth and Fact: The Reception of *The Birth of a Nation*," *Film History* 16, no. 2 (2004): 117–141; Lary May, *Screening Out the Past: The Birth of Mass Culture and Motion Picture Industry* (New York: Oxford University Press, 1982); Grievson, *Policing Cinema*; and Robert Lang's valuable edited collection of primary sources and original essays, The Birth of a Nation: *D.W. Griffith, Director* (New Brunswick, N.J.: Rutgers University Press, 1994).

On the intent of the Fourteenth Amendment, historians and legal scholars do not agree. For opposing viewpoints on whether the framers intended it to protect citizens from infringement of the basic liberties of the Bill of Rights, see Michael Kent Curtis, *No State Shall Abridge: The Fourteenth Amendment and the Bill of Rights* (Durham, N.C.: Duke University Press, 1986) and Raoul Berger, *The Fourteenth Amendment and the Bill of Rights* (Norman: University of Oklahoma Press, 1989). See also William Nelson, *The Fourteenth Amendment: From Political Principle to Judicial Doctrine* (Cambridge, Mass.: Harvard University Press, 1988). On incorporation of the Bill of Rights, see Henry Abraham and Barbara Perry, *Freedom and the Court* (New York: Oxford University Press, 1994). On Johnston, the MPAA, and the Catholics, see Greg Black, *Catholic Crusade*. Some fine scholarship on *Mutual Film v. Ohio* can be found in John Wertheimer, "The Mutual Film Reviewed: The Movies, Censorship, and Free Speech in Progressive America," *American Journal of Legal History* 37, no. 2 (April 1993): 158–189; and Garth Jowett, "A Capacity for Evil: The 1915 Supreme Court Mutual Decision," *Historical Journal of Film, Radio, and Television* 9, no. 1 (1989): 59–78.

For a fascinating discussion of free speech activity before World War I, see David M. Rabban, *Free Speech in Its Forgotten Years* (New York: Cambridge University Press, 1997). On the Payne Fund studies, consult Arthur Jarvis, "The Payne Fund Reports: A Discussion of Their Content, Public Reaction, and Affect on the Motion Picture Industry," *Journal of Popular Culture* 25, no. 2 (Fall 1991): 127–140, as well as Garth Jowett, Ian Jarvie, and Kathryn Fuller, *Children and the Movies: Media Influence and the Payne Fund Controversy* (New York: Cambridge University Press, 1996). There has been little scholarly research on Joseph Breen of the Production Code Administration, who was so powerful and influential in Hollywood. Thomas Doherty, who has written widely on both movie and television censorship, published a much-needed study of Breen called *Hollywood's Censor: Joseph I. Breen and the Production Code Administration* (New York: Columbia University Press, 2007). A good overview of the career of Zechariah Chafee can be found in Jonathan Prude, "Portrait of a Civil Libertarian: The Faith and Fear of Zechariah Chafee, Jr.," *Journal of American History* 60, no. 3 (December 1973): 633–656. Although agreeing on Chafee's extraordinary influence, John Wertheimer correctly criticizes his scholarship in "Freedom of Speech: Zechariah Chafee and Free Speech History," *Reviews in American History* 22, no. 2 (June 1994): 365–377. Alexander Meikeljohn, *Free Speech and Its Relation to Self-Government* (New York: Harper, 1948), is a marvelously readable collection of his lectures.

Chapter 2. Origins of Movies as Art

There is no better academic resource on film history than the *History of the American Cinema*, published in multiple volumes by the University of California Press. Of particular relevance to this chapter are two volumes: Tino Balio, *Grand Design: Hollywood as a Modern Business Enterprise, 1930–1939* (Berkeley: University of California Press, 1995); and Thomas Schatz, *Boom and Bust: American Cinema in the 1940s* (Berkeley: University of California Press, 1999). Gerald Mast's edited volume, *The Movies in Our Midst* (Chicago: University of Chicago Press, 1982), remains the best single collection of documents pertaining to the history of U.S. motion pictures, including excerpts from influential essays by Jane Addams and Hortense Powdermaker. Among the first and best works on the development of movies as an art, see Lewis Jacobs, *The Emergence of Film Art: The Evolution and Development of the Motion Picture as an Art, from 1900 to the Present* (New York: Hopkinson and Blake, 1979) and Jowett, *Film*. For a more recent attempt to look at the way movies and movie critics changed the definition of art over time, see Raymond J. Haberski Jr., *It's Only a Movie: Film and Criticism in American Culture* (Lexington: University Press of Kentucky, 2001).

For a good survey of film and criticism in the Progressive Era, see Myron O. Lounsbury, *The Origins of Film Criticism, 1909–1939* (Cambridge, Mass.: Harvard University Press, 1973). For one of the first attempts to create a serious literary critique of film criticism, see Edward Murray, *Nine American Film Critics* (New York: Ungar, 1975). See also edited volumes, especially Phillip Lopate's indispensable volume from the Library of America, *American Movie Critics: From the Silents until Now* (New York: 2006), and David Denby, *Awake in the Dark: Film Criticism, 1915–Present* (New York: Vintage, 1977). On the significance of Gilbert Seldes, see Michael Kammen's biography, *The Lively Arts: Gilbert Seldes and the Transformation of Cultural Criticism in the United States* (New York: Oxford University Press, 1996). Iris Barry's transformative role as the curator of the Museum of Modern Art's Film Library is detailed in Hadee Wasson, *Museum Movies: The Museum of Modern Art and the Birth of Art Cinema* (Berkeley: University of California Press, 2005).

On the "carnivalization of culture," see James B. Twitchell's acerbic *Carnival Culture: The Trashing of Taste in America* (New York: Columbia University Press, 1992). Other works that deal with mass culture and movies include May, *Screening Out the Past;* Grievson, *Policing Movies;* Paul Gorman, *Left Intellectuals and Popular Culture in Twentieth-Century America* (Chapel Hill: University of North Carolina Press, 1996); and Robert Sklar, *Movie-Made America: A Cultural History of American Movies,* 2nd ed. (New York: Vintage, 1994).

To learn more about book censorship before World War II, see Paul Boyer, *Purity in Print* (Madison: University of Wisconsin Press, 1968). On theater censorship, particularly of the New York stage, see John H. Houchin, *Censorship of the American Theatre in the Twentieth Century* (Madison: University of Wisconsin Press, 2003); and Andrea Friedman, *Prurient Interests: Gender, Democracy, and Obscenity in New York City, 1909–1945* (New York: Columbia University Press, 2000). On censorship of newspapers, check Paul L. Murphy, *"Near v. Minnesota* in the Context of Historical Developments," *Minnesota Law Review,* vol. 66, no. 1 (1981); and Fred Friendly, *Minnesota Rag* (New York: Random House, 1981), which details the *Near v. Minnesota* case.

The creation of a U.S. audience for foreign films is well discussed by Barbara Wilinsky in *Sure Seaters: The Emergence of Art House Cinema* (Minneapolis: University of Minnesota Press, 2001). On the controversy over *The Bicycle Thief* and the rise of critic Bosley Crowther in the context of early post–World War II U.S. movie culture, see Leff and Simmons, *The Dame in the Kimono,* and Raymond J. Haberski Jr., *Freedom to Offend: How New York Remade Movie Culture* (Lexington: University Press of Kentucky, 2007).

Chapter 3. *The Miracle* on West 58th Street

For information on the free speech activists of the 1930s, good sources are Mark Graber, *Transforming Free Speech* (Berkeley: University of California Press, 1999); Paul L. Murphy, *The Meaning of Freedom of Speech: First Amendment Freedoms from Wilson to FDR* (Westport, Conn.: Greenwood, 1972); and Richard Steele, *Free Speech in the Good War* (New York: St. Martin's, 1997). The transformation of Supreme Court jurisprudence during the twenty years after 1937 is well detailed in Reuel E. Schiller, "Free Speech and Expertise: Administrative Censorship and the Birth of the Modern First Amendment," *Virginia Law Review* 86, no. 1 (February 2000): 1–102.

On Joseph Burstyn, little has been written. Unfortunately, Burstyn's corporate papers are not available to researchers. They remain in private hands, so what we know of him comes largely from what others had written about him. Burstyn's partner, Arthur Mayer, wrote a wonderful memoir of his years in the film business — with and without Burstyn — called *Simply Colossal* (New York: Simon and Schuster, 1953), which gives valuable (and colorful) insight into Burstyn's character. Mayer also gave an oral history interview that can be found at the Columbia University Oral History Collection. Several critics wrote articles about Burstyn. There is a collection of these clippings in the Billy Rose collection at the New York Public Library.

For the background story of *The Miracle*'s reception, the best starting places remain Alan F. Westin, *The* Miracle *Case: The Supreme Court and the Movies* (Tuscaloosa: University of Alabama Press, 1961); and the two installments of Lillian Gerard, "*Ways of Love*, or a History of the Ways of Censorship," published in consecutive issues of *American Film* (1977). See also William Bruce Johnson, *Miracles and Sacrilege: Roberto Rossellini, the Church, and Film Censorship in Hollywood* (Toronto: University of Toronto Press, 2008) as a resource that covers the story of Burstyn and *The Miracle* with different legal and cultural emphases from the focus of this book. A particularly good source on the ruckus in New York City over *The Miracle* for those who want to read primary sources is, of course, the *New York Times*. The New York State Archives has an extensive collection of clippings and court documents related to *Burstyn v. Wilson* in its Film Scripts Archive (see the Motion Picture Scripts Collection at http://www.archives.nysed.gov/a/research/res_topics film.shtml).

John Cooney's biography of Francis Cardinal Spellman, *The American Pope: The Life and Times of Francis Cardinal Spellman* (New York: Times Books, 1984), reveals just how powerful the high-profile cardinal was. For background on midcentury American Catholicism, a good choice is John T. McGreevy, *Catholicism and American Freedom* (New York: W. W. Norton, 2003).

On the American Civil Liberties Union, the best source remains Samuel Walker, *In Defense of American Liberties: A History of the ACLU* (New York: Oxford University Press, 1990). Because oral arguments in *Burstyn* occurred in 1952, before the Supreme Court began taping, the best source on the oral arguments remains *United States Law Week*, vol. 20, no. 42 (April 29, 1952).

To learn more about the 1951–1952 Supreme Court, see John P. Frank's thorough and lively summation in *Chicago Law Review*, vol. 20, no. 1 (August 1952). For a more in-depth discussion, see William M. Wiecek, *The Birth of the Modern Constitution: The United States Supreme Court, 1941–1953*, vol. 12 of the magisterial series *The Oliver Wendell Holmes Devise History of the Supreme Court of the United States* (New York: Cambridge University Press, 2006).

Chapter 4. The Supreme Court and *The Miracle*

Most of the information in this chapter came from the records of the Motion Picture Division at the New York State Archives. The files on the *Burstyn* case include a huge collection of newspaper clippings, letters both denouncing and supporting the showing of *The Miracle*, and many of the original court document files. Other information came from Gerard's article and a longer, unpublished manuscript version of the same article in the authors' possession. For details on the case's progress, Alan Westin's small case study, *The* Miracle *Case: The Supreme Court and the Movies* (University, Ala.: University of Alabama Press, Inter-University Case Program, 1961), remains invaluable, although its lack of footnotes leaves the reader guessing about sources. Background information on the Vinson Court can be found in Melvin Urofsky, *Division and Discord: The Supreme Court under Stone and Vinson* (Columbia: University of South Carolina Press, 1997); and in Wiecek, *Birth of the Modern Constitution* (2006), as well as in the long standard work, C. Herman Pritchett, *Civil Liberties and the Vinson Court* (Chicago: University of Chicago Press, 1954).

Chapter 5. *Burstyn*'s Progeny

Carmen, *Movies, Censorship, and the Law* along with Randall, *Censorship of the Movies* were for many years the only published sources related to this chapter. Ernest David Giglio's 1964 doctoral dissertation (unfortunately never published), "The Decade of *The Miracle*," contains much useful information. Wittern-Keller, *Freedom of the Screen*, details the cases following *The Miracle* and the effects each had on governmental censorship and Hollywood's Production Code. On the overturning of the Kansas censor board in *The Moon*

Is Blue controversy, see Gerald R. Butters Jr., *Banned in Kansas* (Columbia: University of Missouri Press, 2007). Charles Rembar, *The End of Obscenity* (New York: Random House, 1968) details the obscenity trials against the novels *Lady Chatterley's Lover, Fanny Hill*, and *Tropic of Cancer*. The other resources for this chapter are various law review articles from the 1950s.

Chapter 6. The Legion of Decency after *Burstyn*

The decline of the Legion of Decency, first noted by Richard Corliss in *Film Comment* (Summer 1968), is well documented in Gregory Black's two books, *Hollywood Censored* and *Catholic Crusade*, as well as in Frank Walsh's comprehensive *Sin and Censorship*; James M. Skinner, *The Cross and the Cinema: The Legion of Decency and the National Office of Motion Pictures, 1933–1970* (Westport, Conn.: Praeger, 1993); and Mary McLaughlin's dissertation, "A Study of the National Catholic Office for Motion Pictures" (University of Wisconsin, 1974). On Catholic culture in the mid-twentieth century, see Una Cadegan, "Guardians of Democracy or Cultural Stormtroopers? American Catholics and the Control of Popular Media, 1934–1966," *Catholic Historical Review* 87, no. 2 (April 2001): 252–282; and John T. McGreevy, *Catholicism and American Freedom*. To see how virulent some anti-Catholic writings could be, see Paul Blanshard, *American Freedom and Catholic Power* (Boston: Beacon, 1949). The opposite side can be seen in William Clancy, "The Catholic as Philistine," *Commonweal* (March 16, 1951): 567–569. Haberski looks at the exchange between critics and the public over *The Miracle* and *Baby Doll* in *Freedom to Offend*. And Leff and Simmons recount the effects the *Burstyn* decision had on Hollywood in *The Dame and the Kimono*.

Chapter 7. Film Freedom and Sexual Content

For an interesting and thorough discussion of book and magazine censorship, see John E. Semonche, *Censoring Sex: A Historical Journey through American Media* (Lanham, Md.: Rowman and Littlefield, 2007). There is little to consult regarding the *Freedman v. Maryland* case. It has generated no books or articles other than law reviews. We have pulled all of the information on this case from research at the Maryland State Archives and from the excellent newspaper clippings collection in the Maryland Room of the Enoch Pratt Free Library in Baltimore. Ronald Freedman's generous interview before his death rounded out our research. Wittern-Keller, *Freedom of the Screen*, contains a full chapter on the *Freedman* case as well as the Maryland state censor board's continuing censoring activity through 1981.

For a critical overview of U.S. culture from the 1960s to the 1970s, see David Steigerwald, *The Sixties and the End of Modern America* (New York: St. Martin's, 1995); and Rochelle Gurstein, *The Repeal of Reticence: America's Cultural and Legal Struggles over Free Speech, Obscenity, Sexual Liberation, and Modern Art* (New York: Hill and Wang, 1996). For a more sympathetic take on similar topics, see David Allyn, *Make Love, Not War: The Sexual Revolution—An Unfettered History* (Boston: Little, Brown, 2000).

The places to start for an overview of the dynamism of 1960s and 1970s movie culture are Paul Monaco, *The Sixties: 1960–1969* (New York: Scribner's, 2000) and David A. Cook, *Lost Illusions: American Cinema in the Shadow of Watergate and Vietnam, 1970–1979* (New York: Scribner's, 2000). J. Hoberman, a longtime film critic for the *Village Voice*, wrote an insightful study of the exchange between film and culture titled *Dream Life: Movies, Media, and the Mythology of the Sixties* (New York: New Press, 2003). Film historian Jon Lewis blends histories of film censorship and sexual cinema in his *Hollywood v. Hard Core: How the Struggle over Censorship Saved the Modern Film Industry* (New York: New York University Press, 2000). The cinematic avant-garde has been well represented in studies such as Greg Taylor, *Artists in the Audience: Cults, Camp, and Film Criticism* (Princeton, N.J.: Princeton University Press, 1999); Juan Suarez, *Biker Boys, Drag Queens, and Superstars: Avant-Garde, Mass Culture, and Gay Identities in 1960s Underground Cinema* (Bloomington: Indiana University Press, 1996); P. Adams Sitney, *Visionary Film: The American Avant-Garde, 1943–2000* (New York: Oxford University Press, 2002); and Stephen Koch, *Stargazer: Andy Warhol's World and His Films* (New York: M. Boyars, 1985).

For the transition from the PCA to CARA, Stephen Vaughn, *Freedom and Entertainment: Rating the Movies in the Age of New Media* (New York: Cambridge University Press, 2006) is the most comprehensive account to date. An unpublished doctoral dissertation by Dorothy Hamilton reveals the continuity between the old PCA and the new rating system: "Hollywood's Silent Partner: A History of the Motion Picture Association Movie Rating System" (University of Kansas, 1999). Two indispensable firsthand accounts, though biased, are Jack Vizzard, *See No Evil: Life inside a Hollywood Censor* (New York: Simon and Schuster, 1970); and Jack Valenti, *This Time, This Place: My Life in War, the White House, and Hollywood* (New York: Harmony, 2007).

Chapter 8. The Era of Ratings and Violence

Along with Stephen Vaughn, *Freedom and Entertainment*, and Dorothy Hamilton, "Hollywood's Silent Partner," Stephen Farber, *The Movie Rating Game* (Washington, D.C.: Public Affairs, 1972), provides insight into the machinations behind Hollywood's rating system. Another interesting source on the current rating system is Kirby Dick, *This Film Is Not Yet Rated* (Genius Entertainment, 2006). Charles Lyons, *The New Censors: Movies and the Culture Wars* (Philadelphia: Temple University Press, 1997), recounts debacles over ratings given to specific films, including *Last Temptation of Christ*, and the public controversies that ensued after the films were released. The book has some factual errors about the *Miracle* case but remains a useful and highly readable source on pressure group activity. On the controversy involving Oliver Stone and his film *Natural Born Killers*, see Gavin Smith, "Oliver Stone: Why Do I Have to Provoke?" *Sight and Sound* 4, no. 12 (December 1994): 9–12; and John Gibeaut, "Deadly Inspiration," *American Bar Association Journal* 83 (June 1997): 62–67. On the subject of violence and movies, Stephen Prince has written and edited a number of fine works, including *Screening Violence* (New Brunswick, N.J.: Rutgers University Press, 2000); *Savage Cinema: Sam Peckinpah and the Rise of Ultraviolent Movies* (Austin: University of Texas Press, 1998); and *Classical Film Violence: Designing and Regulating Brutality in Hollywood Cinema, 1930–1968* (New Brunswick, N.J.: Rutgers University Press, 2003). For arguments dealing with law and mass media, see Christopher E. Campbell, "Murder Media – Does Media Incite Violence and Lose First Amendment Protection?" *Chicago–Kent Law Review* 76 (2000): 637–669; and Martin Garbus, "Law and the Media: Striking a Balance for the Future," *Annual Survey of American Law*, vol. 169 (2000).

Legal and cultural interpretations of free speech have, of course, fostered hot debates and extensive literature. Among the works relevant to this study are Stanley Fish, *There's No Such Thing as Free Speech, and It's a Good Thing, Too* (New York: Oxford University Press, 1994); Richard Delgado and Jean Stefancic, *Must We Defend Nazis? Hate Speech, Pornography, and the New First Amendment* (New York: New York University Press, 1997); Catharine MacKinnon, *Only Words* (Cambridge, Mass.: Harvard University Press, 1993); and Marjorie Heins, *Not in Front of the Children: "Indecency," Censorship, and the Innocence of Youth* (New York: Hill and Wang, 2001).

INDEX

law, 24, 26, 125, 157–159, 167, 169,
    173, 176, 177, 180, 181
  reviewers as experts on, 31, 32
  tariff law and, 31
  See also Federal Commission on
    Obscenity and Pornography;
    Jacobellis v. Ohio; *Roth* case
Office of War Information, Film
  Reviewing and Analysis
  Section, 50
O'Hara, Archbishop John Francis,
  150
Ohio censor board (Ohio Division
  of Film Censorship), 11, 16, 17,
  129
  challenges to, 126–127, 128–129,
    130–131 (see also *Mutual Film
    Company v. Ohio*)
  end of, 130–131, 163
  standards and definitions, 16
  See also *Jacobellis v. Ohio*
Oliver Twist (1950), 139, 140
O'Neill, C. William, 129
Open City (1945), 4, 52, 55
Ophuls, Max, 127
Our Movie Made Children. See
  Forman, Henry James
Outlaw, The (1943), 67, 82

Paisan (1946), 4, 55
Palko v. Connecticut, 34
Paramount Pictures, 4, 39, 194
Paramount Pictures case. *See United
  States v. Paramount Pictures*
Paris Adult Theatre I v. Slaton, 180
Paris Theatre (New York City), 5,
  62, 63, 64, 65, 66, 69–70, 72,
  82–83, 113, 119
Parke, Richard, 64
Pathé Company, 29, 64
Patterson, Joseph Medill, 40
Pawnbroker, The (1965), 165
Payne Foundation, 30
Payne Fund studies (*Motion Pictures
  and Youth*), 30
Peck, Seymour, 62

Pennsylvania censor board
  (Pennsylvania State Board of
  Censors), 11, 16, 17, 29, 36
  end of, 131, 163, 173
  political message censorship in,
    35
Pentagon Papers case, 17, 188
Perry, Lewis, 192
Photoplay: A Psychological Study, The,
  41
Pinky (1949), 80, 89, 124. See also
  Gelling v. Texas
Polier, Shad, 101
pornography, 176, 177, 181, 182
  Catholic concerns over, 166
  definition of, 157, 176–177, 180
    (see also *Miller v. California*)
  See also Federal Commission on
    Obscenity and Pornography; *I
    Am Curious, Yellow*
postwar America, 5, 7, 121, 142
  movie industry and, 49–51, 53, 54,
    57, 78, 121
Powdermaker, Hortense, 47
Preminger, Otto, 147–148
Price, Vincent, 66
Prince Stephen, 195, 196
Princeton Theological Seminary, 73
prior censorship. *See* prior restraint
prior restraint, 8, 9, 11, 18, 86, 37, 151
  artistic considerations and, 6, 15,
    39, 48–49
  burden of proof and, 73–74, 117,
    125, 161–162
  Burstyn v. Wilson and, 81, 82, 84,
    101, 104, 105, 106, 112–114, 117,
    134, 182, 196
  censorship statutes and, 11, 17, 37,
    173
  challenges to, 29, 33, 60, 75, 126,
    160–162 (see also *Burstyn v.
    Wilson*)
  on expression, 2, 7, 18, 75, 77, 98,
    134
  delay caused by, 130, 133–134,
    160–162

{ *Index* }